Plant Hardiness Zones of North America

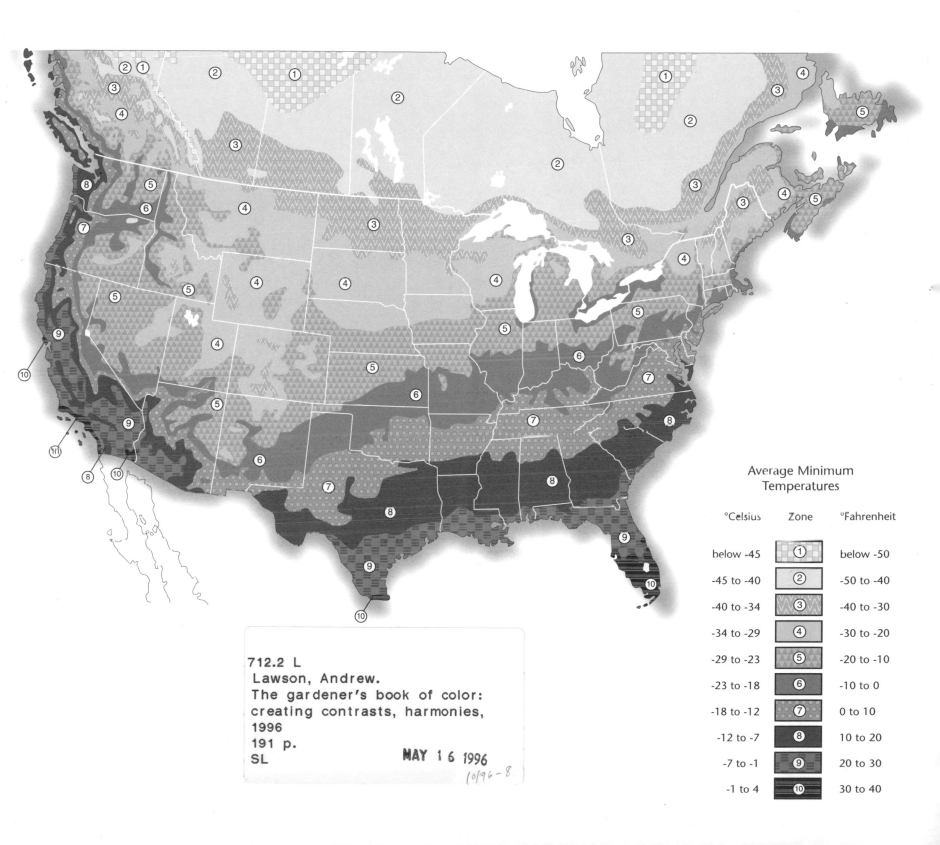

Average Minimum Temperatures

°Celsius	Zone	°Fahrenheit
below -45	1	below -50
-45 to -40	2	-50 to -40
-40 to -34	3	-40 to -30
-34 to -29	4	-30 to -20
-29 to -23	5	-20 to -10
-23 to -18	6	-10 to 0
-18 to -12	7	0 to 10
-12 to -7	8	10 to 20
-7 to -1	9	20 to 30
-1 to 4	10	30 to 40

The Gardener's Book of
COLOR

The Gardener's Book of
COLOR

Creating contrasts,
harmonies,
and multicolor themes
in your garden

WRITTEN AND PHOTOGRAPHED BY

ANDREW LAWSON

Reader's Digest

THE READER'S DIGEST ASSOCIATION, INC.
Pleasantville, New York/Montreal

NOTES ON PLANT LISTS AND USEFULNESS ZONES

The plant lists that appear within the chapter on *Single Colors* comprise brief descriptions of the most prominent plants illustrated in the book, together with a selection of plants that are highly recommended for gardening with color. Plants have been placed within broad color categories, but it should be emphasized that related colors merge together imperceptibly, and the delineation between them cannot be precise. Also plant color can be variable. The distinction between blues and violets is especially difficult and depends on factors such as the maturity of the flowers and on light conditions. Color photography brings different hazards. The human eye is sensitive to certain wavelengths of light, and color film has slightly different sensitivity. Film, for instance, will pick up bands of infrared light that the eye cannot see. Some "blue" flowers reflect infrared, and so they appear pinker on film than they do in reality.

The heights and spreads of plants, indicated as H and S on the lists, represent the average dimensions of a mature plant. The spread is a measure of the diameter of a single plant, which is the recommended minimum planting distance between two plants. Soil, climate and plant husbandry will have a bearing on these dimensions and they may diverge from those indicated.

The Usefulness Zones quoted in each plant entry represent the range of zones, according to the USDA system, in which the plant may be successfully grown in North America. The lower figure gives the coldest zone in which the plant will be hardy without winter protection, the higher shows the limit of its tolerance of hot summer weather. The map on the endpapers at the beginning and end of this book shows the average annual minimum temperature of each zone. It must be remembered that zoning data can only be a rough guide. Plant hardiness depends on a great many factors, such as the depth of a plant's roots, the speed at which the temperature falls, and wind force. Within any one zone particular regions may be endowed with more or less favorable conditions, just as on a smaller scale in any one garden, plants can be positioned in individual situations that will suit their needs to a greater to lesser extent.

A READER'S DIGEST BOOK

Conceived, edited, and designed by Frances Lincoln Ltd., London

Copyright © 1996 Frances Lincoln Ltd.
Text copyright © 1996 Andrew Lawson
Photographs copyright © 1996 Andrew Lawson
Artwork copyright © 1996 Frances Lincoln Ltd.

Library of Congress Cataloging in Publication Data
Lawson, Andrew
    The gardener's book of color : creating contrasts, harmonies, and multi-colored themes in your garden / written and photographed by Andrew Lawson.
    p. cm.
    Includes bibliographical (p.) references and index.
    ISBN 0-89577-858-0
    1.Color in gardening. 2.Plants, Ornamental. 3.Gardens —
Design. 4.Color in gardening — Pictorial works. 5.Plants,
Ornamental — Pictorial works.   I. Title.
    SB454.3.C64L38 1996
    712'.6—dc20
                                    95-39686

Printed in Hong Kong

PAGE ONE Color demarcation. This garden is divided into areas devoted to different color combinations. Here the "cool" colors of a violet-blue clematis (*C.* 'Perle d'Azur') and a pale pink rose (*Rosa* 'New Dawn') give way to "hot" colored daylilies and bee balm beyond.

PREVIOUS PAGES Color echoes. A bi-colored pink and white lupine (*Lupinus* 'The Chatelaine') has been cleverly partnered with a rose (*Rosa* 'Wife of Bath') in which the bud and the fully open flower echo the same two colors.

OPPOSITE Primary contrast. Red tulips (*Tulipa praestans*) with blue Armenian grape hyacinths (*Muscari armeniacum*) and blue glory of the snow (*Chionodoxa lucilae*) make a bright combination for spring.

Contents

THE POWER OF COLOR

Color is the gardener's most potent weapon. Nothing in a garden makes more impact. It can stop you in your tracks or beckon you onwards. It can suggest coolness or warmth, evoking different moods. You can even use color to manipulate the sense of space. Understanding the power of color will help you to orchestrate color's impact upon the emotions, so that some parts of your garden will become areas of repose while others will be exhilarating or – if you wish – even shocking.

Yet despite the infinite variety of colors, the sensory cells in our eyes can only distinguish between them on the basis of five choices.

How red? How yellow? How blue? How dark? How light? The brain organizes these relatively crude signals and creates from them the images of extraordinary subtlety and beauty that we experience. Although physicists can explain different colors in terms of wavelength of light and physiologists can describe the cells in the eye that respond to color, we are still very much in the dark when it comes to explaining how the brain responds to the messages it receives from the eye. Memory and symbolic associations, without doubt, play a very strong part in our experience of color. Certain colors trigger associations and create atmosphere in a garden. The

LEFT Red and yellow flowers seem to give out heat and draw the eye like flames in a garden room. Hot colors are bold, aggressive, and showy. In mixed company, they can overpower their neighbors, which is why it is a good idea to grow them all together, in isolation from cooler colors in one glorious, fiery display. Here, in early summer, red and yellow columbines (*Aquilegia* hybrids) fill the foreground, with yellow lupines (*Lupinus arboreus*) and red roses (*Rosa* 'Dusky Maiden') behind them, while another red rose (*Rosa* 'Parkdirektor Riggers') is just visible on the wall beyond. Used in an enclosed space like this within a much larger garden, a planting of hot colors creates an area of excitement that is a stimulating part of a garden stroll. However, if this were a complete garden in itself, you might find the effect of the hot colors disquieting and might not be inclined to sit out among them for too long.

idea that we "see red" when we are angry, "feel blue" when we are sad, and "are green" when we care for the environment, are blunt metaphors but they derive from fundamental distinctions among these colors. You may find that red has an agitating effect wherever it appears in the garden, and that blue is calming and dreamy. Green, perhaps because it makes us think of the countryside, tends to make us feel comfortable. Yellow can cheer us up because it reminds us of the sun. The chapter on *Single Colors* looks at the qualities that are associated with particular colors, and the dramatic effect that these colors can make in the garden.

We also often associate colors with familiar things. For instance, reds, oranges, and yellows remind us of fire and heat. For this reason we think of them as "hot" colors, and the warmth of these colors can even affect us in a physical way. Indoors, we can paint our rooms red or deep yellow to make them seem warmer. In our gardens, a planting of hot colored flowers can have a similar result. In contrast, we tend to associate blues and violet-blues with the colors of the sky, the sea, and distant hills, and we think of them as "cool" colors. In our gardens, the effect of cool colors tends to be calming and relaxing.

The "temperature" of color is important to gardeners because the hottest colors tend to jump forward in space and to dominate their cooler neighbors. Hot colors may even give the illusion that they are in front of their neighbors, when in fact they are side-by-side. The opposite is true of cool colors. Cool colored flowers can seem to contract in size and withdraw in space. You can exploit the spatial distinctions between hot and cold colors. You can deceive the eye and make the garden appear to be longer than it really is by

RIGHT When a color scheme is dominated by blues, we are subliminally reminded of images of cool water and distant hills. Compared with the hot colors seen in the garden *opposite*, this planting appears calm, subdued, and peaceful. This is a garden of repose. True blues appear in the delphinium and in the meadow cranesbill (*Geranium pratense* 'Mrs Kendall Clark') beside it. Tufts of violet-blue catmint (*Nepeta* 'Six Hills Giant') visually bind together the pink roses ('Magenta' in the foreground, with 'Reine Victoria', 'Commandant Beaurepaire' is on the right, and 'William Lobb' grows up the obelisks at the back). Pink cranesbill (*Geranium endressii*) and old-fashioned Cheddar pinks (*Dianthus gratianopolitanus*) clothe the terrace walls. All the pink flowers have been selected for the blue bias of their color. The greens of the foliage, too, look bluish in the cool, shaded light of a summer afternoon. The colors meld together to produce an effect that is subtle and comforting.

planting hot colored flowers in reds and oranges at the near end, and blues and violets at the far end.

It is not so much individual colors that are important, but how they are put together. Each color has an influence on how you perceive its neighboring colors, so it is the relationship between them that catches your attention. The most successful schemes involving more than one color fall broadly into two categories: if the colors of the plants are similar in some way, they make a harmony, and if the colors are quite different, they make a contrast. These two approaches create widely differing effects – harmonies tend to be soothing, while contrasts are usually stimulating. The bases of these color combinations is explained in the chapters called *Harmonies* and *Contrasts*.

The way that you use color in your garden is as personal as the way you decorate your home. We all interpret color differently. We all have different tastes, and there are no rules about right and wrong. What seems subtle to one person may seem dull to another. You might consider a color scheme bright and cheerful, whereas your neighbor may regard it as garish. Your taste will be influenced by many factors, but what matters most is that you use color in your own way, in the way that you like best.

You can pick up useful ideas about color from visits to garden centers and from garden pictures in books and magazines, but be receptive also to ideas from outside the sphere of gardening. Paintings, textiles, and fashion design can point to new ways to use color in the garden. Within garden design itself there are changing trends in approaches to color. The Victorians liked the combination of rich color and strong pattern. A more restrained approach passed down from Gertrude Jekyll in the early years of this century and reached its apogee with Vita Sackville-West's white garden at Sissinghurst Castle in the 1930s. Today the "state of the art" may be in the use of bold, rich color, and natural looking plantings with grasses whose color effects are judged successful to the extent to which they reflect nature. With all these conflicting influences you will be most successful with color by being true to your own preferences.

Whether you make color associations by instinct or by following examples you have seen, it helps to have an understanding of how color works. Then you can refine your color sensibilities and take new directions by experimentation. While there are no strict rules governing the use of color, there are underlying principles you might like to draw upon for guidance. These are outlined in the sections on *Understanding Color*. However, if you reject them altogether you will be in good company, because some highly original gardeners have found that to be adventurous with color involves flouting all preconceptions. The chapter on *Mixed Colors* looks at some daring

RIGHT It is surprising how far you can extend an illusion of space with color alone. The scarlet oriental poppies (*Papaver orientale*) in the foreground catch the eye and their color makes their position plain at the very front of the border. Beyond, clumps of delphiniums with catmint behind them make a shimmering haze of blue, suggesting a distance far greater than it is. By exploiting the illusion that hot colors seem to come forward in space and cool ones tend to recede, you can make your garden appear bigger than it really is. And if you have a long, narrow garden, and want it to appear wider, try planting blue flowers along the sides, while avoiding alignments that emphasize perspective.

examples of this type of planting and analyzes why they work despite going beyond the usual color conventions.

Before you make any final decisions concerning color schemes, you need to assess both the opportunities and the limitations of your particular garden. Your success with color will depend upon good plant care. Before you choose any plant, make sure you can satisfy its special needs for full sun or shade, or for soil that is acid or alkaline, well drained or boggy. The temperature extremes in your district will have the most influence upon your choice of plants. Use the hardiness zone map to check whether the trees, shrubs, and perennials that you want to grow are likely to survive over winter in your area. Above all, be sensitive to your climate and quality of light. You might find that brighter colors are needed in tropical climates where the sun is stronger, the light is very clear and the prevailing vegetation colorful. Muted colors can look insipid in these harsh conditions but reveal their subtlety in the softer light of temperate regions.

When making color choices for your garden, it is also wise to take account of your immediate surroundings. Begin by taking a look at the building materials of your house, and at the hard landcaping of your garden – the walls, fences, and paths. These permanent structures impose their own demands upon the plant colors that you introduce. Make sure that your garden complements your house, using, for example, a scheme of white and green with white weather boarding, *right top*. It is worth remembering that many of your garden fixtures – from pergolas and fences, gazebos and garden sheds, down to the last garden chair or bench – can be tied in to your plant colors with a coat of stain or paint. White is an obvious color candidate, but it is stark and bright and can eclipse surrounding colors. Blue-green, green or gray are proven choices for garden furniture, but you might be more daring and try a color that makes a complete contrast, such as bright blue or rusty red.

The colors of surrounding buildings, especially in the city, and even the trees in neighboring gardens will influence your color selection. In the country, too, bring the colors of the borrowed landscape into your schemes to ease the transition from the garden into the surrounding countryside. Gardens look best in partnership with their environment and not in conflict.

The most challenging goal for gardeners is to keep the color interest alive in every season of the year. Broadly speaking, you can choose between two planting approaches, and your choice will depend partly on the size of your garden. If you have plenty of space you can devote separate areas of the garden to distinct seasonal effects. By grouping together plants that peak at the same time, you can be sure of an intense focus of color. Each one might be short-

ABOVE AND TOP These two plantings have been carefully planned to complement the colors of the architecture in the background. A good solution for a white building is an all-white planting that uses flowers such as Himalayan balsam (*Impatiens glandulifera*), tobacco plants (*Nicotiana x sanderae*), and white hydrangeas (*Hydrangea paniculata* 'Tardiva'), as well as a Japanese angelica tree with white-variegated foliage (*Aralia elata* 'Variegata'). A perfect choice of plants to surround a brick-built pavilion is a copse of azaleas (*Rhododendron kaempferi*) with flowers of a dark salmon pink that makes a near-match with the color of the brick. The underplanting of ferns (*Matteuccia struthiopteris*) is clever, too, because their fresh green matches the color of the emerging foliage of the azaleas.

lived, but if you have enough space to spread them through the year, there can be at least one colorful corner in the garden for every season. This way you would have separate "gardens" for winter and spring, and beds or borders that come to a peak at different moments through the summer and fall.

If you have a small garden, you cannot afford to leave parts of the garden inactive for very long; you need to keep the whole garden working for you through the seasons. The way to do this is to select plants that will grow up through each other and perform in sequence in the same area, as seen in the three photographs shown *right*. Use shrubs, bulbs, herbaceous perennials, and annuals together in mixed borders, with the widest seasonal spread among them. In any one border the year might begin with early bulbs – aconites, snowdrops, and crocuses under winter-bare shrubs, with daffodils and tulips following. By the time the spring bulbs have passed, herbaceous plants have pushed through to take their place. As the summer progresses, fill any gaps with annuals or place a container to hide an empty space. To keep control over your colors, decide on a particular scheme for each section of the garden – it might be an all white scheme, for instance, or a more complex mix of colors as seen here – and use only plants within this restricted color range in each season. This is labor-intensive gardening because you need to constantly cut back plants as they fade to make room for the newcomers in the cycle. However, it is a regime that ensures you will be able to enjoy your chosen colors on the same patch of ground for the longest possible time. You do not have to rely on flowers alone for all-year color. Foliage provides color over a longer period and changes interestingly with the seasons. For winter color, capitalize on evergreen foliage and colored bark and stems, fruit and berries, seedheads, and even the mosses that grow on garden surfaces.

Gardening is always a partnership with nature – even when you are experienced, nature can sometimes have the last laugh. A combination of plants that flower together in one region may have staggered flowerings in another. Even in the same garden the succession of flowering can be inconsistent from one season to the next. The lesson is to leave room for the happy accident and welcome the unplanned effect that may even turn out better than the one you originally had in mind.

ABOVE Successional color is orchestrated here in a small space with foliage contributing to the effect in every season. This border is loosely restricted to blues and violets contrasted with yellows and lime-greens. In spring, deep purple 'Queen of the Night' tulips, soft lilac onion (*Allium rosenbachianum*), and forget-me-nots are set the against the foliage of bridal wreath (*Spiraea japonica* 'Goldflame') and mock orange (*Philadelphus coronarius* 'Aureus').

ABOVE A few weeks later, perennial cranesbills (*Geranium* x *magnificum* and *G.* 'Johnson's Blue'), Italian bugloss, later-flowering ornamental onion (*Allium aflatunense* 'Purple Sensation'), and iris (*I. sibirica*) reinforce the violet and blue theme. More yellow foliage comes into play now, with Bowles' golden grass (*Milium effusum* 'Aureum') in the foreground, and the small golden-leaved black locust tree (*Robinia pseudoacacia* 'Frisia') at the back.

ABOVE By late summer, the scheme is dominated by the tall blue-pink annual cosmos (*C.* 'Imperial Pink'). Young plants are planted between the perennials in early summer. This results in a slight shift in the overall color balance of the border. But the blue/yellow bias is maintained by a blue beard tongue, a globe thistle and a clematis (*C.* 'Perle d'Azur'), with the yellow foliage of the black locust and golden hop (*Humulus lupulus* 'Aureus') against the back wall.

UNDERSTANDING COLOR

The color red makes an impact in any context, but it is especially powerful when it is seen in contrast with green, its complementary color. Red flowers, such as those of montbretia (*Crocosmia* 'Lucifer'), shown here arching over a clump of sneezeweed (*Helenium* 'Moerheim Beauty'), seem all the more intense when seen against a background of bright green foliage.

The Color Wheel

Nature conveniently arranges colors in an order – the spectrum – that establishes relationships between them. The sun's electromagnetic energy arrives at the earth in waves and the wavelengths are measured by their frequency. Each frequency relates to a different color, so the sequence in which the colors appear in the spectrum is immutable. When the spectrum is bent around to make a circle, it forms a color wheel, *opposite, large diagram,* which is a simple guide to the most fundamental color relationships in the garden.

The three primary colors, red, blue, and yellow, are the three essential colors from which, in theory, all other colors are constructed. This is because there are only three types of color-sensitive cells, known as cones, in the retina of the eye – one to respond to each of the primary colors. Each of the three secondary colors, green, orange, and violet, is a "mixture" of two primaries and lies between them on the color wheel. Green, for instance, is perceived as a mixture of yellow and blue, and is shown halfway between them. These six main colors of the rainbow are linked by infinite gradations of color, represented here by only six intermediate colors. Missing from this diagram are black and white and the more subtle "mixtures" of colors such as pinks and browns and grays that are so important in our gardens. There are two reasons for this. White is a combination of all wavelengths, and black is an absence of wavelengths, so they do not appear in the rainbow. Along with gray, they are inert colors that do not react with other colors. Pinks, browns, and an infinite range of muted colors could be plotted on a more complex diagram, but they would obscure the simple message of the color wheel. When using any of these colors, be guided by its dominant component: you might treat a pink, for instance, as a cool red, or lilac as a muted violet.

The two most important approaches to planning color themes for the garden – using harmonious colors or contrasting colors – are best explained by studying the color wheel. Harmonious colors are those that are adjacent or near-neighbors on the wheel. Red, orange and yellow, for instance, make a harmonious scheme. Colors from opposite sides of the wheel form contrasting schemes. The most intense contrasts are between colors that lie directly opposite one another: red with green, blue with orange, yellow with violet. These highly contrasting pairs are called complementary colors.

A complementary color makes up for everything that its opposite color lacks. There is a fundamental physiological relationship between the two. Stare at a bright red patch for half a minute without deflection. Then turn your eyes immediately onto a sheet of white paper in good light. You should see a phantom green patch on the white paper. There is a simple explanation for this. When the eye concentrates on the original red spot, the red-sensitive cones react and soon become fatigued, so they start to under-perform. The new white subject ought to stimulate all the cone cells equally, but the fatigued cones for red will transmit a false message to the brain. They now suggest to the brain that there is a shortage of red, in other words, that there is more of its complementary, which is green. Thus the brain perceives a green phantom on the white paper.

The principle of phantom images between complementaries has a bearing on our perception of color in the garden. The eye is constantly being affected by what it has just seen. Take the following sequence of events. First we look at a blue flower; the blue-sensitive cones are stimulated and become fatigued. Next we look at orange. The eye, tired of blue, is already perceiving its complementary – orange – so the orange appears enhanced. In other words, looking at the blue has made the orange all the more intense. The eye has been stimulated by one color to see its complementary in the next thing it looks at. In other words, the difference between the two colors is slightly exaggerated. When the two colors are adjacent and seen together, the effect is the same and is called "simultaneous contrast". Since any color stimulates the eye to see the complementary color in its neighbor, simultaneous contrast accounts for the intense "zing" of color that we sometimes experience when two complementary colors such as blue with orange are put together. The same process also helps us to distinguish between subtle colors, and explains why groupings of plants that are only slightly different from each other in color can be intensely pleasing. Place a blue-green hosta beside a green one, and the blue tinge pushes our perception of the green color very slightly towards yellow-orange. In the same way a yellow leaved hosta will make the neighboring greens seem slightly more violet-blue.

The color wheel also illustrates how colors fall into two distinct families. The wheel can be divided roughly into two halves, *opposite, small diagram,* with "hot" colors on one side, and "cold" colors on the other. When complementary colors such as blue and orange are put together, the two components come from opposite sides of the color wheel so one of them is bound to be hot and the other cold. This is broadly true of all color contrasts, so they always involve a hot-cold relationship. In color harmonies, on the other hand, the components are usually relatively close in color temperature. However, some seemingly similar colors, such as orange and pink, diverge in color temperature. This creates a contrast disguised as a harmony, and results in a color "shock".

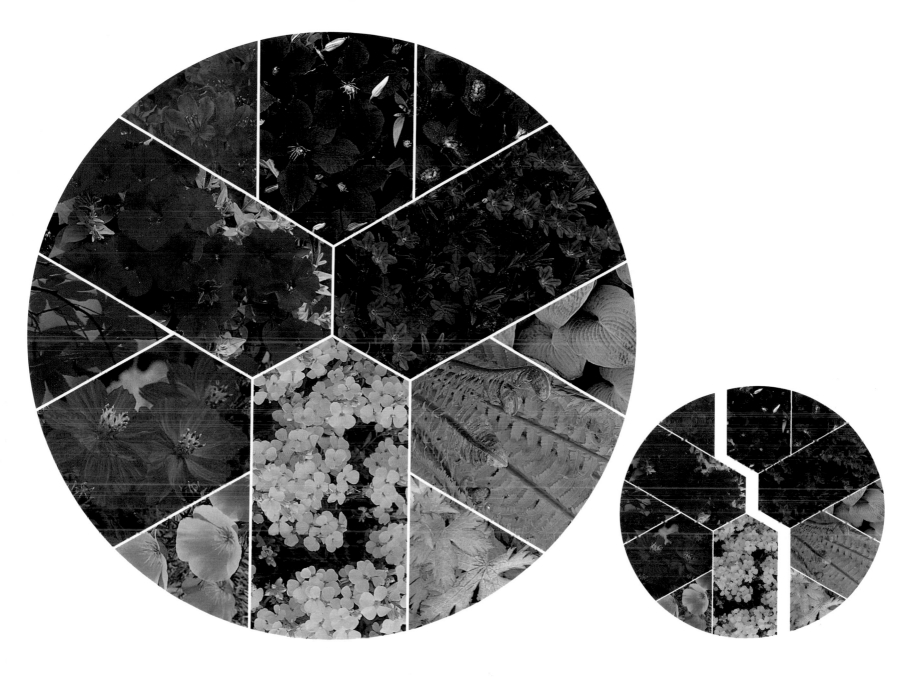

ABOVE The color wheel is formed by rolling up the colors of the spectrum to create a circle. The three largest spokes are the three primary colors, red, yellow, and blue. They are the main building blocks of color. The three shorter spokes are the secondary colors, green, orange, and violet. The six small wedge-shaped sections represent just a few of the intermediate colors that link the main colors. Each section on this diagram is illustrated by a plant and the result is a hodgepodge of colors that would be alarming if it were reproduced in a garden. The wheel is best used as a summary of color relationships – and, of course, it is not recommended to use them all at once.

ABOVE Divided in two, the wheel shows how colors fall roughly into two groups governed by color temperature. "Hot" or "warm" colors are based on red and orange, and "cold" or "cool" colors are based on blue. Magenta and green, the colors at the tips of the divisions, vary between warm and cool according to context.

Saturation

Saturation describes the intensity of a color: a saturated color is one in its purest form, at full strength. These nine photographs illustrate varying intensities of red. The lobelia, *center*, shows red at its purest, while those around it – some lighter, some darker, some tending to blue or yellow – are all less intense, less pure.

Artists produce lighter unsaturated versions of color by diluting it. The pink of the peony's petals, *center right*, may be thought of as red diluted by white. Similarly, adding muddy colors dulls the intensity of the saturated original. The dusky foliage of the maple, *top left*, leans toward blue and is often inaccurately described as purple, but it is really a muted, unsaturated red. The dull crimson of the clematis, *top center*, is a clearer color but still lacks intensity.

Light can also affect a color's saturation. Bright sun picks out the red undertones of the cosmos, *center left*, but in a softer light they can appear almost black. The dogwood stems, *bottom left*, appear to be an unsaturated red because the direct sunlight has leeched their color and cast dark shadows between the stems. Similarly, the smooth, reflective texture of the double poppies' petals, *bottom center*, reduces the intensity of their color.

Juxtaposition of color, or any variegation, within a flower or its foliage, also affects saturation. In the clematis, the dull crimson of the petals is further softened by the flower's paler center. The already pale crimson of the bellflower is diluted by the flower's near-white edges, which make the petals appear almost pink. Similarly, a flower's stamens, whether lighter or darker than the petals, can change the perceived intensity of the flower's color. In the peony, the already pale pink of the flower appears even more unsaturated because of its pale stamens. However, this effect varies according to the distance from which it is seen.

For the gardener, color saturation is a consideration when planning a scheme. Usually an intense, clear color will stand out from its unsaturated surroundings. This is especially true of saturated reds, yellows, and oranges which will always stand out from the garden's green foliage framework. Unsaturated colors, on the other hand, seem to sink into the background, especially if they have blue or violet in them.

The gardener can achieve a harmonious effect by combining plants that are from the same color family but vary in level of intensity. Flowers ranging from palest pinky white to deepest crimson, for example, are all different saturations of blue-red. Choose a narrow range of pale, pastel colors to create a tranquil scene, or a limited range of deep colors for a rich, more somber effect, or juxtapose hues from each end of the scale for more stimulating results.

Maple (*Acer palmatum* 'Ornatum')

Chocolate cosmos (*C. atrosanguineus*)

Siberian dogwood (*Cornus alba* 'Sibirica')

Clematis (*C. viticella* 'Purpurea Plena Elegans')

Bellflower (*Campanula* 'Elizabeth')

TOP ROW These three reds, tinged with blue, are less saturated in varying degrees. Even though the maple is such a dark, muted color, and the bellflower is so pale, both are recognizable as versions of red.

Lobelia (*L. x speciosa*)

Tree peony (*Paeonia* x *lemoinei* 'Madame Louis Henri')

MIDDLE ROW Here red is seen in its purest, fully saturated form in the lobelia, *center*. On either side are unsaturated reds, the cosmos having some black in it, the tree peony some white.

Oriental poppy (*Papaver orientale* 'May Queen')

Poinsettia (*Euphorbia pulcherrima* 'Rosetta')

BOTTOM ROW These are unsaturated reds that lean toward yellow. The dogwood and poppies, both already somewhat unsaturated by the addition of some yellow, show the added effect that light can have in draining a color's saturation. The poinsettia demonstrates how, with the addition of even more yellow, the new color still retains an echo of the original red.

Light and Dark Tones

Tone is a measure of brightness – the lightness or darkness of a thing. Every color has its intrinsic tone. Violet, for instance, is dark in tone, and yellow is light. Tonal differences are what you see in a black and white photograph. They are perceived in the eye by separate light-sensitive cells called the rods, that only detect differences in light and dark. In dim light the rods function better than the color-sensitive cells, the cones. This is why you can still distinguish between light and dark in the failing light of dusk, even when you can no longer tell the difference between colors.

The tonal differences between colors are very important in garden planning. In some plant partnerships the contrast of tone affects us more than the contrast of color. For instance, if you grow deep violet and pale yellow flowers together, such as the verbena and achillea shown *opposite, above,* the strong tonal contrast between them tends to dominate the color contrast, even though violet and yellow are complementary colors.

Putting together colors that are close in tone usually makes the the strongest color contrasts. Complementary colors such as red

and green make a powerful color contrast. These colors are so close in tone that the difference does not show up in a black and white photograph, *opposite, below right.* On the other hand, putting together colors like yellow and green will usually make strong tonal contrasts, even though they are not far apart in color terms. These will show up well in a black and white photograph, *below.* You can use this test to guide your choice of plant combinations for use in dim light conditions, such as in dense shade, or in parts of the garden where you sit out in the late evening. It is a good idea to use variegated plants in shady areas, for example, because they provide interesting patterns of light and dark in a situation where the eye cannot easily distinguish colors.

White and black are tonal extremes, and although true black flowers and foliage do not exist, there are many near-black plants available to the gardener. Extreme tonal differences can be used to create dramatic effects in the garden. For instance, a deep green foliage background to a border of pale flowers, seen *opposite, above,* emphasizes the lightness of the flowers, while the pale flowers, in

ABOVE In this masterful planting, the diversity of shapes of flowers and foliage stand out as much for their tonal differences as for their color. This is demonstrated by the clarity of the black and white photograph, in which the topiary cone of golden privet (*Ligustrum ovalifolium* 'Aureum'), and the rim of the white edged leaves of a variegated hosta (*H. crispula*) stand out as light shapes against the darker foliage. The yellow spires of golden ray (*Ligularia* 'The Rocket') and the white flowers of wood cranesbill (*Geranium sylvaticum albiflorum*) and white horned violets (*Viola cornuta* Alba Group) growing with yarrow (*Achillea ageratum* 'W.B.Childs') also stand out clearly in black and white. But the occasional touches of blue in Jacob's ladder, bellflower, and delphinium are incidents of pure color that do not translate into monochrome.

turn, make the dark hedge seem even darker. The drama is heightened by strong sunlight, which further increases the tonal differences. The background seems to recede into the shadow, while the light flowers, seen in clear outline, are visually thrown forward.

Since it is the lightest color in the gardener's palette, white provides a tonal contrast with almost all foliage and all but the very lightest colors among flowers. You need to use whites with care, especially those with solid or heavy shapes, because they set up such strong tonal contrasts in the garden, and the eye is always drawn to the lightest tones.

RIGHT In this border, tonal contrasts are cleverly combined with color contrasts. Violet and yellow are the darkest and lightest colors on the color wheel, so they make a strong tonal contrast. They are also complementary colors, so the combination of violet verbenas (*V. rigida*) with yellow yarrow (*Achillea* 'Taygetea') and yellow torch lilies (*Kniphofia citrina*) makes a bold color contrast as well. White is the lightest color of all, and seen in bright sunlight against heavy shadow, the white fireweed (*Epilobium angustifolium album*) makes a striking silhouette of purely tonal impact.

LEFT The impact of this hot border is the result of pure color contrasts, with scarlet sage (*Salvia splendens* 'Blaze of Fire', and 'Lady in Red'), vermilion alonsoa, orange-red sneezeweed (*Helenium* 'Moerheim Beauty'), and montbretia (*Crocosmia* 'Lucifer') making a strident contrast with the complementary green of their foliage. In black and white, however, the contrast disappears almost entirely and the border's impact is lost. This is because red and green are very close in tone. There is a lesson to be learnt from this exercise. It is always worth introducing some strong shapes and tonal contrasts into a planting by using, for instance, light, dark and patterned foliage. This tonal interest adds another layer of subtlety, and usually lasts after the color contrasts of the flowers themselves have faded.

The Influence of Light

To get the greatest pleasure from your color schemes, it helps to understand the effect of light at different times of day, in different seasons and in different weathers. The French Impressionist painter Monet planted a "sunset" border along the western edge of his garden at Giverny and it is still maintained to this day. Here he used a preponderance of orange and yellow flowers, such as sunflowers, tithonias, and marigolds. His idea was to exploit the warm orange light of sunset, so that this border glows like the embers of a fire in evening light. If you observe the transition of the sun in the course of a full day in your own garden, you may be able to plan your colors to catch particular effects of the changing light.

At sunrise and sunset, the sun is at its lowest point in the sky. At these times, the light passes obliquely through the earth's atmosphere, receiving the most interference from dust and other particles in the air. The result is to diffuse the light and to warm it up in color, so that we often see red skies at sunrise and sunset, and our gardens are bathed in red or orange light. The hot flower colors, reds, oranges, and yellows, shine out in this light, while the blues, greens, and violets become muted and dark because there is so little blue light to reflect. You can exploit the low sun at the beginning and end of the day by placing sculptures, painted garden structures, and trees with colored bark or leaves where they will catch the first or last light, *below right*. You can also obtain dramatic effects with shadows which are long at these times in summer, and for most of the day in early spring and winter, *below left*.

At the middle of the day when the sun is high in the sky, light passes at right angles through the earth's atmosphere and is hardly affected by it. The sun itself has a yellowish cast but blue sky, acting as a reflector, compensates for this, so that the light at midday is close to white. The reflecting action of the blue sky is greatest in shadow, where it provides the only illumination so that, on a sunny day, the light in shadow has a blue tinge. In shaded areas at midday, then, the most effective colors to use are the blues and violets – like the catmint that lines a shadowy path, *opposite* – which show up especially well in blue light, and also white, which appears pale blue in this context.

ABOVE Autumn-tinted vine leaves (*Vitis vinifera* 'Purpurea') become translucent, like stained-glass windows, in the slanting, low, late season sun.

LEFT A circle of Kaufmanniana tulips reflects back the early spring sunshine. The sun is quite low in the sky in spring, giving a soft light and longish shadows. When the air is clear, the light is somewhat cool and has the effect of softening the intensity of yellows, which predominate in this season.

After the sun has gone down and the orange glow of sunset has faded, the natural light becomes distinctly blue again. The eye can still make out blues for some time after reds and oranges have begun to appear black. Whites are visible then, too, so it is a good idea to plant blue and white flowers in that part of the garden where you like to sit on long summer evenings.

Climate and the strength of the prevailing light also have a bearing on the colors in your garden. On overcast days when the light is diffused and shadows are softened, our eyes can pick out the most subtle color effects. This is why muted colors and restrained harmonies of pastel colors are most appropriate in countries farthest from the equator where the summer sun is relatively weak and the skies frequently gray. In hotter climates and tropical countries, fierce summer sun creates a harsh contrast between the sunlit colors and their sharp blue-black shadows. Understated color cannot compete with these powerful tonal contrasts. In such climates, bold color statements are needed, with saturated colors making vibrant contrasts.

Changing seasonal light affects garden color, too. In spring, the soft, cool quality of the light is kind to bright colors, preventing them from looking garish and making them look clean and fresh, like the circle of clear yellow tulips, *opposite, left.* In summer, the most benign light for color is found at the beginning and end of the day. At midday, sunlight is so strong and casts such dark shadows that color is fragmented and relationships obscured. By fall, the sun is getting low in the sky and the light is again soft and flattering, especially when it is diffused by mists. In winter the sun casts its longest shadow, and creates its greatest dramas. It lights up garden structures and the bare trunks and branches of trees and throws them into silhouette against bright snow or dark earth.

The places with the greatest seasonal changes in climate and light also have the most variation in the year's natural cycle of plant color. In early spring, fall, and especially in winter in these places, it is not easy to control color because relatively few plants are performing at their peak. Be flexible at these times, and go along with the characteristic colors of the season. Spring garden colors tend towards fresh yellows with clear blues and violets. Emerging leaves are more yellow than green. In fall, colors are again largely dictated by nature. Celebrate this season with glowing reds and golds of berries and falling leaves, even if these hot colors are not your choice for the rest of the year. Winter is dominated by the browns and khakis of dead perennials and the dark greens of evergreens. Any additional color will be welcome. It does not matter at all if it hardly adds up to a color scheme, since the function of winter color is to cheer up the dreary expanse of damp soil, and to give hope to the gardener of more colorful times to come.

ABOVE Late evening light catches an elegant stone vase and throws it into silhouette. At this time of day, ornaments, sculptures, and garden structures acquire a theatrical quality. Notice how the warm light casts a cool shadow, so that in shade the path becomes blue, and the pink of the rose 'Mevrouw Nathalie Nypels' becomes cooler, and the blue of the catmint (*Nepeta nervosa*) is rendered more intense.

Color Distribution

Once you have settled on your color schemes but before you have chosen all your plants, it is important to think about the shapes created by the overall habits of plants, and how you are going to place them together so that they react most effectively.

A flat sheet of a single color could lose its initial impact and become boring in a garden (although it can be an inspiring sight in the wild). A haphazard jumble of color, on the other hand, becomes confusing because the eye is never able to come to rest on any particular color or relationship. At the same time, a garden in which the plants are all the same mass and shape, but in carefully composed color schemes, would be a nightmare of monotony. So while deciding whether to plant in blocks, or in ribbons, or in dots and dashes of color, you also need to think about varying the shapes and sizes of your plants.

Your approach will depend upon the scale of your planting, the main point from which the planting will be seen, and on whether you opt for a single or a complex color theme. The larger your garden, the broader the effects can be; the closer your viewpoint, the more intricate they can be. If you plant in defined blocks, *below right*, individual colors will remain clearly distinguishable; if you scatter the colors, *below left*, the effect will be speckled at close range, but from farther away, the colors will merge and diffuse.

If you opt for clumps of perennial color, try planting elongated "drifts" of plants instead of round color blocks. Drifts of plants will interlock with their neighbors without precise lines of demarcation. One advantage of this is that when a plant has faded and been cut back, it will not leave too much of an unsightly scar since adjacent drifts will soon grow into its space.

ABOVE These two plantings by the same gardener demonstrate two distinct approaches to presenting color. In the "pointillist" approach, *above left,* plants with small dispersed flowers, such as cinquefoils and verbenas, are enmeshed with sweet Williams, white yarrow and scattered beard tongues. Seen close, the effect is jewel-like, the border spotted with color like a post-Impressionist painting. From a distance, the color will fuse into a haze. In the garden, *above right,* the same beard tongues are planted in generous-sized drifts, with dense clumps of pinks and white campion underplanting the old roses, which themselves form substantial blobs of pink and mauve.

RIGHT This blue and yellow scheme includes drifts of yarrow, catmints, lupines, bellflower, lady's mantle and veronica that spill over onto an informal path. Plants thrive and look best if they are grown in much the same way that they occur naturally in the wild. In nature perennials tend to form clumps that expand over the years as their roots spread out from the center. They may also spread by seeding, so that new clumps spring up some distance from the parent plant. This natural process takes years, but you do not have to wait so long. Instead, imitate nature by your method of planting. Be generous, if you can afford it, and use several plants of each variety to establish good-sized clumps at the outset.

It is often more effective to plant repeated drifts of the same plant, rather than to seek constant variety and change. Repetition of color, provided it is not too symmetrical and regular, can establish a rhythm in the planting that is the visual equivalent to music, as shown in the border, *above*. Also, repetition of the same plant in drifts of different sizes is reminiscent of the natural process of propagation, and will make your plantings look more convincing.

A totally different result can be achieved by distributing single plants of one color among clumps of other colors. In spring, for instance, individual yellow daffodils growing through mounds of blue lithodora intensify the blue and prevent any possible monotony. In summer, plants with small, dispersed and brightly colored flowers like cinquefoils and avens are invaluable for adding vitality to a planting that might otherwise appear bland.

The arrangement of shapes in a garden contributes to our appreciation of the color relationships between plants. Whether you are dealing with trees or shrubs on a large scale, or with smaller climbers and perennials, the basic habits and outlines of plants as well as their flower and leaf shapes, create outlines against which neighboring colors react. Sometimes a variation in shape can bring interest to a passage of color, even if the new shape is more or less the same color. Imagine a stand of purple foxgloves, for instance, next to a rounded clump of bee balm of the same color. The distinction in shape between the two plants is refreshing. In the border *above,* the variety of yellow shapes – the starbursts of broom, spikes of lupines, and disks of yarrow – animates the planting. Single color schemes depend even more on variety of shape as well as texture. This is explored in greater detail on pages 24–25.

ABOVE The dark and light patterning of these Californian hybrid irises makes the color appear to shimmer, and to look less dense that it would be if the flowers were a flat mid tone. The variegated foliage of the thistle and its outlines give the impression of dappled sunlight. The veins on the small flowers of the cranesbill animate their color, too, but in a more subtle way.

BELOW Rhododendrons have enormous flowerheads that are massed together on the shrub to make it into a mound of color. Seen close, especially in a small garden, they can seem ungainly. A fringe of campion with matching pink flowers softens the impact and helps them to blend into the landscape.

Density, Shape, and Texture

Every plant variety presents its color in a particular way, and one challenge for the garden artist is to create a balance between the varying shapes, densities of color, and textures of the flowers and plants that make up a scheme. For example, there is a world of difference between the haze of color that comes from a mass of tiny flowers like baby's breath, *opposite, above left*, and the solid "mounds" of color of some rhododendrons, or between the clear outlines and waxy surface of a tigrida, *opposite, above right,* and the intricate silhouette and brittle texture of an eryngium, *opposite, below left*.

Flowers like begonias, lilies, and the large-flowered roses and clematis may supply the strongest color accents in a bed or border. Large-flowered plants, however, can be ungainly, and a border devoted exclusively to them would be crude in the extreme. It would be far better to soften their effect by combining them with more delicate-looking neighbors, especially ones of the same or similar color. Partner a pink rhododendron with pink campion, *left below,* so that the rhododendron's globes of color appears to be dispersed through the tracery of the campion's delicate flowers. Similarly, airy sprays of gypsophila will counterbalance the dense white flowerheads of roses, *opposite, above left*.

When color is broken up into patterns in flowers or foliage, it appears less dense. The flowers of some irises, for example, are streaked with different colors, *left above*; pansies are often spattered with contrasting colors such as yellow and violet; and flowers like fuchsias may be bicolored. At close range these patterned flowers make a bold color scheme in themselves. From a greater distance, the colors seem to merge, but the effect is softer and more dispersed than that of a flat, single color.

You also need to think about the shapes and textures of flowers and foliage because it is surprising how much these influence our experience of color. Seen at close quarters, the star-shaped, shiny petaled flowerhead of a daisy has a brighter effect than the rounded matt flower of a verbena, *opposite, above left*, because of its shape. The star shape, like a sunburst, suggests energy and light, whereas a dense, double shape is relatively inert. Textural differences among leaves are even more marked. If you compare the velvety green leaf of Sargent's hydrangea with the shiny, brittle leaf of common holly, you will see that although they are not very far apart in color, their textures and the effect they have are fundamentally different. The closer the colors, the more obvious become the differences in texture and shape, as seen in the blue clematis and sea holly *opposite, below left*, the yellow lupines and buttercups, *opposite, below right,* and the pink tiger flower and verbena, *opposite, above right.*

RIGHT Three different flower shapes introduce variety to an all-white planting. The annual white freeway daisy (*Dimorphotheca* 'Glistening White') has been planted with perennial baby's breath (*Gypsophila paniculata*), which gives a veil of tiny white flowers that counters the solid double flowers of yarrow (*Achillea ptarmica* 'The Pearl').

FAR RIGHT The tiger flower bulb (*Tigridia pavonia*) comes in dark pink, scarlet, or yellow, and you need to select the right one to make a matching companion for tender perennial verbena (*V.* 'Sissinghurst'). The closeness of the color of this plant partnership enables you to enjoy their disparity of shape – triangles seen against circles.

RIGHT The flowers of the alpine sea holly (*Eryngium alpinum*) are close in color and in size to those of the herbaceous clematis (*C. integrifolia*), and so the eye tends to dwell on the difference in shape and texture between them. The frilled and spiny upward-facing flowers of the one are the perfect foil for the smooth, sinuous, and nodding flowers of the other.

FAR RIGHT Wild buttercups, growing at the foot of a tree lupine (*Lupinus arboreus*), provide dots of fully saturated yellow scattered among the larger but less saturated flowers of the lupine. The relationship between size and saturation is very pleasingly balanced, as you will see if you imagine the two yellows reversed.

GARDENING WITH COLOR

Gardening rarely gives instant results, and a gardener's artistry will sometimes reveal itself long after planting takes place. These early spring flowering Tommasini's crocus (*C. tommasinianus*) intermixed with cyclamen (*C. coum*) have taken years to self-seed and spread and make a glorious carpet of violet and pink.

SINGLE COLORS

Your favorite colors are always the best starting point, but before you embark on an ambitious planting, it is worth familiarizing yourself with the color palette available to the gardener and understanding the influence that color has, not only on neighboring colors, but on the overall mood of your garden.

We all perceive color differently, attaching to it our own memories and associations. Indeed, what might seem mauve to one person, might be termed lilac by another. However, there are a few recognized guidelines that will help you make the most of a color's qualities – whether you use it sparingly in a mixed color planting or concentrate it in a single color planting.

If you opt for a single color planting, make it more interesting by including varying tints and shades of that color, and as many different shapes and textures as possible. The yellow borders, *right,* make use of a wide range of yellow-green foliage plants as well as flowers that run the gamut from deepest yellow to palest cream. Spires of lupines contrast with the flatter yarrow heads, and dense spurges contrast with the lighter sprays of feverfew, while feathery fennel and bristly sea hollies add textural variety. Sparing use of neutral colors, such as gray and white, can also contribute an extra dimension to the planting, without adding any reactive color.

Even if you do not devote a whole part of the garden to a single color, use color to make matches between plants – for example, to link a yellow flowered marguerite and the yellow stamens of a nearby spiderwort, or the yellow-green foliage of a golden mock orange and a yellow clematis growing through it. One of the delights of gardening is that color can be used to bold effect, or subtly, creating an echo that reverberates throughout the garden.

RIGHT These yellow double borders, pictured at the height of summer, look cheerful and sunny even in overcast weather. The differing hues, shapes, and textures prevent the yellows from looking uniform; and the sprinkling of white flowers and mounds of silvery foliage add highlights, offset by the comparatively dark foliage of the surrounding hedges. (For a diagram of this planting, see page 172.)

Yellows

Think of yellow and the sun comes to mind. Even on a dull day, yellow flowers – especially those with daisy shapes such as golden marguerites – can look like a patch of sunlight, radiant and luminous. Yellow adds its cheerfulness to the garden, but can be overpowering, swamping more subtle colors and sometimes setting up violent contrasts with strong ones, so you need to be especially careful when using it in the garden.

The effect of yellow varies according to the season. In summer the sun is high in the sky, casting dense black shadows. The combination of bright yellow with dark shadows is especially fierce, so for gentler midsummer displays, take care not to use bright yellow plants on a large scale. In spring and fall, with the sun low in the sky, the light is softer, moderating the intensity of pure yellow. Swathes of brilliant yellow narcissi can look exhilarating in spring, whereas a

ABOVE This tunnel of yellow laburnum (*L.* x *watereri* 'Vossii') flowers in early summer. Laburnums are quick-growing and amenable to training. Here, they have been planted at intervals of 5ft/1.5m and trained over hooped metal arches. They are shaped by pruning in early winter. The wallflowers make a daring underplanting. Preferring full sun, they normally flower earlier than the laburnum, but have been held back by the trees' shade. A yellow leaved hosta such as *H.* 'Gold Standard' would be an alternative underplanting, but would need watering in summer since the laburnums take so much moisture.

ABOVE A spring bedding planting consists of 'Golden Melody' tulips teamed with the biennial wallflower 'Golden Bedder'. The wallflower is grown from seed sown in the summer; the young plants can be planted out in the fall at the same time as the bulbs. Tulips usually have a better chance of flowering again the following year if they are lifted and kept cool and dry during the summer. But if they do well in your ground for a second season, then leave them in and use a perennial wallflower such as 'Moonlight' for a repeat show of yellow the following year.

broad expanse of the same color in high summer can look garish. Similarly, in the fall, softer light makes large expanses of butter-yellow foliage acceptable.

To temper an all-yellow midsummer planting, use plenty of unsaturated yellows. Pale yellows are less boisterous than strong ones, and lemon yellows, with their touch of green, are cooler, making more comfortable companions for other colors. You could consider mixing bright yellow black-eyed susans with golden marguerites and creamy freeway daisies, as in the planting *below right*. The different colors and textures will shimmer in the late summer sun. Primrose-yellow and cream are the most companionable of all the family of yellows, and can associate with other colors with impunity – even with pink, which does not usually sit well with brighter yellows. Cream flowers especially have a calming influence in all color relationships, acting like green foliage to separate colors that might otherwise fight.

For an all-yellow display in spring, you might like to include some paler, primrose-yellows, such as winter hazel, some of the paler yellow brooms, and creamy-yellow narcissi. These all make particularly good companions for the delicate yellow-greens of spring's emerging foliage.

For a yellow border, do not limit your choice to flowers: take advantage of the wide range of yellow-green foliage plants, too (see the next page). If you include white flowers with either yellow centers or yellow stamens, such as daisies with yellow centers or white lilies with bright yellow stamens, you will add glittering highlights, and set up echoes with yellows elsewhere in the border.

The lightening effect of yellow can be exploited elsewhere in the garden. Just as yellow stamens can brighten a red flower, so yellow flowers, introduced sparingly as dots among flowers that are red and orange, will add sparkle to a planting that might otherwise appear dark and heavy.

ABOVE All-yellow plantings in windowboxes can light up a dark courtyard in spring. Wallflowers in two tones of yellow have been planted the previous fall with a cream-edged ivy that trails over the containers. To extend the effect over the summer, replace the spent wallflowers with annuals such as snapdragons in a range of yellows, or with a tender perennial like fern leaf beggar tick (*Bidens ferulifolia*). To maintain these densely planted containers, water daily and, unless you have mixed a slow-release fertilizer into the compost, remember to feed them once a week.

ABOVE Four perennials make up this densely planted late-summer planting. Two are hardy – orange coneflower (*Rudbeckia fulgida* var. 'Goldsturm'), and the pale yellow marguerite (*Anthemis tinctoria* 'E. C. Buxton') – and two are tender – the small flowered fern leaf beggar tick (*Bidens ferulifolia*), and the creamy freeway daisy (*Osteospermum* 'Buttermilk'). All these have daisylike flowers, and to introduce variety of shape, you could add golden rod (*Solidago*) with its plumes of tiny yellow flowers, spikes of creamy blue-eyed grass (*Sisyrynchium*), and torch lilies (*Kniphofia*).

Yellow Foliage Effects

Yellow leaved foliage or foliage with yellow variegation is another way to introduce yellow to your garden. Foliage is longer lasting than flowers, so yellow leaved trees and shrubs can provide the backbone for a yellow border. But the effect of yellow foliage can be very subtle. To ensure that you do not eclipse its subtlety, only use small quantities of bright yellow flowers with it. Yellow variegated foliage is attractive in its own right, and just as yellow flowers can be used to lighten a red and orange planting, so yellow variegated foliage can brighten up dark green foliage in a shady spot. Ponds can look very dark, particularly when they are overhung by trees. You can brighten them up by planting their boggy edges with yellow foliage plants or foliage variegated with a touch of yellow as in the plantings *below left* and *right*.

RIGHT Bowles' golden sedge dominates its subtle neighbors, gardener's garters, and the perennial variegated manna grass. In the foreground are Tibetan primrose, fronds of the royal fern, and a few small yellow monkey flowers. The stately flowers of the oriental iris echo the theme of yellow with creamy white, and thrive, like the other plants in this group, in the boggy conditions around a pond or stream. (For a diagram of this planting, see page 172.)

ABOVE In spring, the color in the foliage of a vigorous clump of yellow variegated flag iris (*I. pseudacorus* 'Variegata') is picked up by water buttercup (*Ranunculus lingua* 'Grandiflorus') and Candelabra primulas beyond. Golden club (*Orontium aquaticum*) with its yellow snakeshead flowers has crept to the edge of the pond, although it normally favors deeper water.

ABOVE The bold summer flowering yellow loosestrife (*Lysimachia punctata*) is cooled by the pale yellow foliage of the evergreen boxleaf honeysuckle (*Lonicera nitida* 'Baggesen's Gold'). The loosestrife makes dense clumps and can easily be propagated by division.

ABOVE In this original combination for a yellow border in shade, the spiky, pale yellow flowers of willow-leaved jessamine (*Cestrum parqui*) are enhanced by combining them with the brittle-looking foliage of a golden English yew, trained and pruned to edge the border.

Bright Yellows

SPRING

Aurinia saxatilis (syn. *Alyssum saxatile*) BASKET OF GOLD Evergreen perennial that forms a dense mat of small brilliant yellow flowers. Prefers sun. '**Citrina**' with paler flowers looks good trailing from a raised bed or rock garden. H 9in (23cm) S 12in (30cm) Z4-7

Corydalis lutea YELLOW CORYDALIS Evergreen perennial with racemes of tubular flowers with short spurs, and blue-green filigree foliage. Tolerates sun and partial shade. H and S 12in (30cm) Z5-8 [ill.p.136]

Doronicum LEOPARD'S BANE Perennial with large daisy-like flowers on long stems, and heart-shaped leaves. [ill.p.141] Tolerates sun or shade. Good varieties include *D. x excelsum* '**Harpur Crewe**' and *D. orientale* '**Magnificum**'. H 3ft (1m) S 2ft (60cm) Z4-8

Eranthis hyemalis WINTER ACONITE Tuberous perennial whose bright yellow flowers, borne close to the ground, are often the first sign of spring. Frilled foliage follows, and dies back in summer. Prefers partial shade and humus-rich soil. H and S 4in (10cm) Z5-9

Erysimum cheiri WALLFLOWER Short-lived perennial usually treated as a biennial. Single color selections, such as '**Golden Bedder**,' are available, or mixtures from deep cerise to pale primrose. Requires sun. H and S 12in (30cm) Z7-9 [ill.p.30]

Erythronium '**Pagoda**' TROUT LILY Tuberous perennial that produces pendant lily-like flowers, up to twelve on a stem, with broad, mottled leaves. Requires partial shade and humus-rich soil that is protected from drying out during summer. H 14in (35cm) S 8in (20cm) Z4-8 [ill.p.125]

Forsythia Shrub whose bare stems are covered with brilliant star-like flowers before the leaves open. Good varieties include *F. x intermedia* H 5ft (1.5m) S 8ft (2.4m) Z5-9; *F. suspensa* has paler flowers .H and S 6ft 6in (2m) but higher when trained against a wall. Best in sun Z6-8

Fritillaria imperialis '**Maxima Lutea**' CROWN IMPERIAL Bulb whose crown of hanging, bell-like flowers is held on a tall, erect stem. Tolerates sun or partial shade. H 5ft (1.5m) S 12in (30cm) Z5-8

Kerria japonica Reliable, arching shrub for mid to late spring. The single-flowered variety is preferable to the more familiar double. Tolerates sun or partial shade and any but waterlogged soil. H and S 6ft (1.8m) Z5-9

Lysichiton americanus SKUNK CABBAGE Perennial whose large flower spathes, which have an unattractive smell, appear before the foliage. Later, broad, paddle-shaped leaves are a feature. Needs boggy ground. Prefers full sun but will tolerate partial shade. H 3ft (1m) S 30in (75cm) Z7-9

Mahonia aquifolium OREGON GRAPE Evergreen shrub with tight-packed sweet-smelling flowerheads that precede bunches of blue berries. Tolerates shade or partial shade. H and S 5ft (1.5m) Z5-8

Narcissus DAFFODIL The yellow trumpets of this popular bulb are an essential herald of spring. Naturalizes best in ground that does not dry out. Prefers sun or partial shade. Good early flowering varieties include the Cyclamineus '**February Gold**' H 13in (32cm) and '**Peeping Tom**' H 18in (45cm) Z 3-9; and the shorter '**Tête-à-Tête**' H 10in (25cm) Z4. Good later flowering varieties include '**Yellow Cheerfulness**' JONQUIL with double, scented flowers. H 16in (40cm) Z5-8

Rhododendron luteum Deciduous shrub with sticky buds and broad heads of sweetly scented tubular flowers. Needs neutral to acid soil, and prefers light shade. H and S 8ft (2.4m) Z6-9

Ribes odoratum CLOVE CURRANT Shrub whose starry flowers, borne along arching stems, have the spicy scent of cloves. Does well against a sunny wall. H and S 6ft (1.8m) Z5-7

Trollius europaeus GLOBE FLOWER Perennial with rounded, curved flowers like giant buttercups, and graceful divided foliage. Tolerates sun or shade, but requires moist soil. H 24in (60cm) S 18in (45cm) Z3-7

Tulipa TULIP Bulb that appreciates summer baking. Good cultivars include early flowering '**Bellona**' H 12in (30cm) S 8in (20cm) Z3-8; '**Golden Melody**' H 12in (30cm) S 8in (20cm) Z3-8 [ill.p.30]; and elegant Lily-flowered '**West Point**' H 20in (50cm) S 10in (25cm) Z3-8 [ill.p.169]

Uvularia grandiflora MERRYBELLS Rhizomatous perennial with graceful pendant flowers on long stems that appear among the young foliage. Requires peaty soil in partial shade. H 24in (60cm) S 12in (30cm) Z4-9

SUMMER

Achillea YARROW Perennial with flat, plate-shaped flowerheads that make a welcome counterpoint to the predominantly vertical emphasis in borders, and there is the added bonus of fern-like foliage. Needs sun and is tolerant of dry conditions. Good varieties include '**Coronation Gold**' H 3ft (90cm) S 2ft (60cm) Z3-9; and *A. filipendulina* '**Gold Plate**' GOLD PLATE FERN LEAF YARROW H 4ft (1.2m) S 2ft (60cm) Z3-9 [ill.pp.157,180]

Allium moly LILY LEEK Bulb with good clear-yellow flowerheads, and grass-like leaves. Will spread into clumps in an open sunny position with well drained soil. H 14in (35cm) S 5in (12cm) Z3-9 [ill.p.183]

Anthemis tinctoria GOLDEN MARGUERITE Evergreen perennial with brilliant yellow daisy-like flowers, and feathered leaves. Will keep flowering if dead-headed regularly. Likes a sunny, open situation. H and S 3ft (90cm) Z4-8 [ill.p.181]

Bidens ferulifolia FERN LEAVED BEGGAR TICK A trailing yellow perennial daisy, with broad florets and narrow leaves. Tender, but ideal for container plantings. H 30in (75cm) S 3ft (90cm) Z7-9 [ill.pp.31,177]

Buphthalmum salicifolium WILLOW LEAF OXEYE Perennial giving masses of daisy-like flowers with narrow florets. Spreads into clumps that may need staking. Prefers sun. H 24in (60cm) S 3ft (90cm) Z6-9

Cassia artemisioïdes WORMWOOD SENNA\CASSIA Evergreen shrub with spikes of cup-shaped flowers and divided leaves, covered with white down. Frost tender, so suitable for a conservatory. Requires sun. H and S 6ft (1.8m) Z9-10

Eranthis hyemalis **(Spring)**

Fritillaria imperialis 'Maxima Lutea' **(Spring)**

Narcissus 'February Gold' **(Spring)**

Uvularia grandiflora **(Spring)**

Allium moly **(Summer)**

Clematis
Climbing or scrambling plants that tolerate sun or partial shade but need a cool root run. Good late-summer flowering varieties include climbing '**Bill Mackenzie**' which has nodding bell-shaped flowers with upturned tips to the sepals, followed by fluffy round seedheads. H and S 22ft (7m) Z3-9; and *C. tangutica*, which has smaller, daintier flowers and similar seedheads. H and S 15ft (4.6m) Z3-9

Coreopsis verticillata TICKSEED
Perennial with a mass of bright, star-shaped flowers and finely divided foliage. Requires sun. H 24in (60cm) S 12in (30cm) Z3-9

Crocosmia MONTBRETIA
Corm with sprays of trumpet-shaped flowers and sword-shaped leaves. Prefers sun. [ill.p.163] Good yellow varieties include '**Norwich**' H 30in (75cm) S 8in (20cm) Z5-9

Fremontodendron californicum
FLANNEL BUSH Evergreen or semi-evergreen shrub bearing large, bright, saucer-shaped flowers borne throughout the summer. Best grown against a sheltered, sunny wall in not over-rich soil. H 20ft (6m) S 12ft (3.7m) Z8-10

Genista aetnensis MOUNT ETNA BROOM Shrub with bright pea-like flowers on arching branches giving an explosion of color. Best in sun, in not over-rich soil. H 25ft (7.5m) S 30ft (9m) Z8-10

Glaucium flavum HORNED POPPY
Perennial with poppy flowers, opening like crinkled tissue paper, and light blue-green foliage. Prefers sun. H 2ft (60cm) S 18in (45cm) Z5-9

Helenium SNEEZEWEED
Perennial with robust sprays of flat, bright yellow flowers that cover the plant in late summer. [ill.pp.177,180] '**Butterpat**' is a good variety. Requires sun. H 3ft (90cm) S 2ft (60cm) Z3-8

Helianthus SUNFLOWER
Annual *H. annuus* is the arche-typal sunflower, with whorls of seeds at the center, rimmed with curling yellow florets. H 10ft (3m) S 18in (45cm); perennial *H. salicifolius* WILLOW LEAVED SUNFLOWER has relatively small daisy-like flowers on very tall stems. H 7ft (2.1m) S 2ft (60cm). Both require full sun. Z4-9

Hemerocallis DAYLILY
Grassy-leaved perennial whose exquisite lily-shaped flowers last only a day but appear in succession. Good varieties include graceful, early flowering *H. lilioasphodelus*; '**Golden Chimes**' [ill.p.177], and '**Stella de Oro**' [ill.p.157] Best in full sun. H and S 3ft (90cm) Z3-9

Hypericum
Shrub bearing flowers with prominent stamens. Tolerates sun or partial shade. Good varieties include *H. calycinum*, which is tolerant of drought and poor soil and makes a good spreading groundcover, H 2ft (60cm) S 4ft (1.2m) Z5-8; *H. x inodorum* '**Elstead**' has bright red fruit. H and S 3ft (90cm) Z5-8

Inula magnifica ELECAMPANE
Perennial with daisy-like flowers, the size of tea-plates, above broad, hairy leaves. Makes huge clumps in damp ground in sun. H 6ft (1.8m) S 3ft (90cm) Z5-8

Iris
Rhizomatous perennials [ill.p.40]. Good tall, bearded irises that do best in sun include '**Big Dipper**' H 3ft (90cm) S 18in (45cm) Z4-9. *I. pseudacorus* YELLOW FLAG IRIS is good for waterside planting and needs partial shade. H 4ft (1.2m) S 18in (45cm) Z5-9 [ill.p.32]

Isatis tinctoria WOAD
Biennial producing a haze of tiny flowers in a diffuse spray. Requires sun. H 4ft (1.2m) S 30in (45cm) Z7-9

Kniphofia citrina TORCH LILY
A yellow variety of the familiar perennial with poker-like flowers. Needs sun and moist soil. H 3ft (90cm) S 18in (45cm) Z5-9 [ill.p.19]

Laburnum x watereri '**Vossii**'
Tree with graceful hanging racemes of pea-like flowers. Amenable to training, it looks marvelous bent to form an arch. Does best in sun. H 30ft (9m) S 25ft (7.5m) Z5-7[ill.pp.30,139]

Ligularia przewalskii SHAWALSKI'S LIGULARIA Perennial with tall pointed spikes of small flowers that appear above elegant finely cut foliage [ill.p.178]. *L.* '**The Rocket**' GOLDEN RAY has larger flowers [ill.pp.18,177]. Tolerates sun or partial shade, and requires moist soil. H 5ft (1.5m) S 3ft (90cm) Z4-8

Lilium LILY
Good cultivars of this bulb, that does best in sun, include the **Citronella Group** with pendant spotted turkscap flowers. H 3ft (90cm) [ill.p.122]; '**Connecticut King**' with radiant upward-facing flowers. H 3ft (90cm); and the **Golden Splendour Group** with trumpet-shaped flowers. H 5ft (1.5m). All Z4-9

Limnanthes douglasii MEADOW FOAM Annual that becomes a cheerful mass of brilliant egg-yolk yellow flowers edged with white. Requires sun. H 12in (30cm) S 15in (40cm) [ill.pp.167,179]

Lysimachia punctata YELLOW LOOSESTRIFE Perennial with spikes of vivid yellow flowers. Forms clumps and may be invasive. Requires sun or partial shade and moist soil. H 30in (75cm) S 2ft (60cm) Z4-9 [ill.pp.32,180]

Meconopsis cambrica WELSH POPPY
Perennial poppy that seeds itself liberally, good for creating scattered spots of color. Prefers a cool situation in neutral to acid moist soil. H 18in (45cm) S 12in (30cm) Z6-8 [ill.pp.136,183]

Oenothera macrocarpa (syn. *O. missouriensis*) OZARK SUNDROP Perennial producing large funnel-shaped flowers that open in the evening followed by large seed-pods. Requires sun and prefers sandy soil. H 10in (25cm) S 16in (40cm) Z4-8

Orontium aquaticum GOLDEN CLUB
A perennial floating, deep-water plant that also grows at pond margins. Produces curious pointed flowers, yellow at their tip, that look like snakes' heads. S 24in (60cm) Z7-9 [ill.p.32]

Phlomis JERUSALEM SAGE
P. fruticosa is an evergreen shrub with sage-like gray-green foliage and whorls of rich yellow flowers that are followed by attractive pepperpot-shaped seedheads. Requires sun. H and S 4ft (1.2m) Z7-9 [ill.pp.162,169]. *P. russeliana* is an evergreen perennial with similar qualiaties. H 3ft (90cm) S 2ft (60cm) Z5-9

Piptanthus nepalensis (syn. *P. laburnifolius*) Semi-evergreen shrub that produces racemes of pea-like yellow flowers among attractive leaves. Requires sun. H 10ft (3m) S 6ft (1.8m) Z7-9 [ill.p.174 (foliage only)]

Potentilla fruticosa '**Elizabeth**'
SHRUBBY CINQUEFOIL A compact rounded shrub, with small saucer-shaped flowers among small, divided leaves. Requires full sun. H 3ft (90cm) S 5ft (1.5m) Z3-7 [ill.p.178]

Clematis 'Bill Mackenzie' (**Summer**)

Glaucium flavum (**Summer**)

Iris pseudacorus (**Summer**)

Lilium 'Connecticut King' (**Summer**)

Phlomis fruticosa (**Summer**)

Ranunculus lingua 'Grandiflora' WATER BUTTERCUP A tall perennial buttercup for pond margins or a bog-garden. H 3ft (1m) S 1ft (30cm) Z4-8 [ill.p.32]

Rosa ROSE
A good climbing variety is 'Golden Showers,' which has clusters of vivid yellow semi-double flowers in succession. H 7ft (2m) S 6ft6in (2.2m) Z5-9. Good shrub roses include 'Graham Thomas,'a fine yellow "English" rose. H 4ft (1.2m) S 5ft (1.5m) Z5-9 [ill.pp.141,172]

Rudbeckia CONEFLOWER
Perennial with yellow daisy-like flowers that appear in late summer and have dark, cone-shaped centers. Good varieties include *R. fulgida var. sullivantii* 'Goldsturm' H and S 3ft (90cm) Z3-9 [ill.pp.31,177]; and *R. nitida* 'Herbstonne,' a good back-of-border plant H 7ft (2.1m) S 30in (75cm) Z4-9. Need sun or partial shade.

Sedum acre GOLD MOSS STONECROP A mat-forming succulent that readily colonizes stone walls and screes, in full sun. H 2in (5cm) S indefinite Z3-9 [ill.p.172]

x *Solidaster luteus*
Perennial, the result of crossing an *Aster* with a *Solidago,* with sprays of small daisy-like flowers. x *S. l.* 'Lemore' has plumes of tiny yellow flowers late in summer, forms large clumps that may become invasive. Enjoys sun or shade.

H 2ft (60cm) S 30in (75cm) Z4-8 [ill.p.139]

Tagetes 'Disco Yellow' AMERICAN MARIGOLD A good single-flowered annual with narrow dark green leaves. Requires sun. H 15in (40cm) S12in (30cm)

Verbascum 'Cotswold Queen' MULLEIN Perennial that puts up spikes of deep yellow flowers from a rosette of broad mid-green leaves. Prefers sun but will tolerate shade. H 4ft (1.2m) S 2ft (60cm) Z6-9 [ill.p.125]

FALL FOLIAGE

Fall foliage can be yellow with no trace of green. For "yellow" foliage see yellow-greens on p. 86

Acer cappadocicum COLISEUM MAPLE A stately tree, whose lobed leaves turn butter-yellow in fall. Tolerates neutral to acid soil and sun or partial shade. H 70ft (20m) S 50ft (15m) Z6-7

Ginkgo biloba MAIDENHAIR TREE The fan-shaped leaves of this slow-growing tree turn yellow in fall. Requires sun or partial shade. H 100ft (30m) S 25ft (7.6m) Z4-8 [ill.(in spring) p.136]

WINTER

Hamamelis mollis CHINESE WITCH HAZEL Shrub with sweet-smelling flowers, curiously shaped like twisted wires, that appear on bare branches in mid-winter.

Requires sun or partial shade and peaty, acid soil. H and S 12ft (3.7m) Z5-8

Jasminum nudiflorum WINTER JASMINE Usually trained as a wall-shrub. In mild weather through the winter, waxy, yellow flowers open on bare arching stems. Requires full sun. H and S 10ft (3m) Z6-10

Mahonia x media 'Charity' Evergreen shrub with clusters of sweet-scented flowers above dark spiny foliage. Prefers shade. H 12ft (3.7m) S 10ft (3m) Z7-8

STEMS

Cornus stolonifera 'Flaviramea' REDOSIER DOGWOOD Shrub whose bare young stems are yellow; cut them back to near ground level in spring to stimulate new growth. Prefers sun. H 6ft (1.8m) S 12ft (4m) Z2-7

Pale Yellows

SPRING

Corylopsis pauciflora BUTTERCUP WITCH HAZEL Shrub with small, fragrant bell-shaped flowers that hang from spreading branches before the leaves appear. Prefers acid soil in partial shade. H 6ft (1.8m) S 8ft (2.4m) Z5-8

Cytisus x praecox 'Warminster' WARMINSTER BROOM Pale, lemon-yellow, pea-like flowers cover

the shrub in spring. Requires full sun and soil that is not over-rich. H and S 5ft (1.5m) Z6-8 [ill.p.179]

Erysimum cheiri WALLFLOWER Short-lived perennial usually treated as a biennial. A cheerful accompaniment for spring bulbs. Prefers sun. [ill.pp.30,31, 167,169] Good cultivars include 'Moonlight' H 18in (45cm) S 12in (30cm) Z7-9; and 'Primrose Bedder' H and S 15in (38cm)

Narcissus DAFFODIL
Good miniature varieties of this bulb that have clusters of delicate looking trumpets include 'Hawera' H 8in (20cm) Z3-9 [ill.p.141]; and 'Jack Snipe' H 9in (23cm) Z3-9

Primula
Perennial with flowers that rise from a rosette of oval leaves. Prefers sun or partial shade and moist, peaty soil. *P. florindae* TIBETAN PRIMROSE is sweet-scented. H 3ft (90cm) S 2ft (60cm) Z6-8 [ill.p.32]; *P. vera* COWSLIP has heads of tubular flowers. H and S 8in (20cm) Z5-9; *P. vulgaris* ENGLISH PRIMROSE has flat flowers, borne singly. H and S 8in (20cm) Z5-9 [ill.p.136]

Tellima grandiflora ALASKA FRINGECUPS Semi-evergreen perennial that produces spires of small cream bell-shaped flowers, above heart-shaped hairy leaves. Requires a cool

situation in partial shade. H and S 2ft (60cm) Z4-8 [ill.pp.71,139]

Tulipa TULIP
Bulb that appreciates summer baking. Good varieties include *T. acuminata* with twisted, pale yellow petals rimmed with red, H 18in (45cm) S 9in (23cm) Z3-8; early-flowering *T. kaufmanniana* WATERLILY TULIP H 14in (35cm) S 8in (20cm) Z3-8 [ill.p.20]; and *T. tarda*, which is very short stemmed, and opens out into a star shape in full sun. H and S 6in (15cm) Z3-8 [ill.p.149]

SUMMER

Achillea YARROW
Perennial with flowerheads like flat disks above feathery gray-green foliage. Prefers sun. Good varieties include 'Moonshine' [ill.p.179] and 'Taygetea' [ill.p.19]. H 24in (60cm) S 20in (50cm) Z3-9

Aconitum MONKSHOOD
Perennial with poisonous tuberous roots that prefers sun. 'Ivorine' has spikes of helmet-shaped, creamy yellow flowers, and elegantly divided leaves. H 4ft (1.2m) S 2ft (60cm) Z5-8 [ill.p.181]

Anthemis tinctoria 'E.C. Buxton' YELLOW MARGUERITE Perhaps the best choice for a primrose-yellow daisy-like flower. Fine, feathery foliage. Prefers sun. H and S 3ft (90cm) Z4-8 [ill.pp.31,157]

Rudbeckia nitida 'Herbstonne' **(Summer)**

Acer cappadocicum **(Fall)**

Cornus stolonifera 'Flaviramea' **(Winter)**

Narcissus 'Jack Snipe' **(Spring)**

Anthemis tinctoria 'E.C.Buxton' **(Summer)**

Antirrhinum SNAPDRAGON
Seed for this annual is available for single colors, such as pale yellow, in most of the series, such as **Coronette Hybrids** or **Monarch Hybrids**. Prefers sun. H 18in (40cm) S12in (30cm) [ill.p.139]

Asphodeline lutea JACOB'S ROD
Perennial rhizome with star-shaped flowers on tall spikes that grow from a fringe of spiky gray-green leaves. Prefers sun. H 4ft (1.2m) S 3ft (90cm) Z6-8

Cephalaria gigantea GIANT SCABIOUS Perennial with sprays of pin-cushion-shaped flowers held high above the jagged-edged leaves. Prefers sun. H 6ft (1.8m) S 4ft (1.2m) Z3-8 [ill.p.181]

Clematis rehderiana
Climber producing clusters of little bell-shaped flowers that give an exquisite late-season scent. H and S 15ft (4.6m) Z6-9

Dietes bicolor AFRICAN IRIS
Evergreen perennial. The flat, creamy yellow flowers have brown blotches at the base of the petals. Narrow grass-like leaves. Prefers sun. H 3ft (90cm) S 2ft (60cm) Z9-10

Digitalis grandiflora YELLOW FOXGLOVE Perennial with spikes of soft, tubular flowers that grow from a rosette of smooth oblong leaves. Best in partial shade and moist soil. H 3ft (1m) S 12in (30cm) Z3-8

Gentiana lutea GREAT YELLOW GENTIAN Perennial with starry

flowers arranged in whorls around tall, sturdy spikes above tufts of large oval leaves. Prefers sun or partial shade and moist, neutral to acid soil. H 4ft (1.2m) S 2ft (60cm) Z6-9

Helianthemum 'Wisley Primrose' SUNROSE Evergreen shrub whose little saucer-shaped flowers last only a day, but are produced in succession over several weeks to give a mound of color. Best in full sun. Suitable for rock gardens and dry banks. H 18in (45cm) S 24in (60cm) Z6-9

Helichrysum 'Sulphur Light'
Perennial that makes clumps of small, tufty flowers, which dry well when picked, and silvery foliage. Prefers sun. H 24in (60cm) S 12in (30cm) Z5-8

Hemerocallis citrina DAYLILY
Perennial with flowers that open in the evening. Prefers full sun and moist soil. Slug and snail control is essential. H and S 30in (75cm) Z3-9

Hypericum olympicum 'Citrinum'
Open, creamy-yellow flowers with darker yellow stamens cover the compact, rounded shrub through the summer. Prefers full sun. H and S 12in (30cm) Z6-8

Kniphofia 'Little Maid' TORCH LILY
Perennial with poker-shaped spikes of creamy-yellow tubular flowers that grow out of clumps of narrow, grass-like leaves. Prefers sun. H 24in (60cm) S 18in (45cm) Z5-9

Lilium monadelphum (syn. *L. szovitsianum*) CAUCASIAN LILY
Bulb with exquisite large pendant flowers, with crimson tips to the curving petals. Prefers sun. H 4ft (1.2m) S 12in (30cm) Z4-9

Lonicera japonica 'Halliana'
JAPANESE HONEYSUCKLE Evergreen climber with scented flowers that open cream but mature to pale straw-yellow. Needs sun or partial shade. H and S 30ft (10m) Z4-9

Lupinus LUPINE
L. arboreus TREE LUPINE is a quick growing but short lived shrub with spikes of fragrant flowers. H 8ft (2.4m) S 6ft (1.8m) Z4-8 [ill.pp.6,25,168]. 'Chandelier' is a perennial with spires of pea-like flowers above cut foliage. H 4ft (1.2m) S 2ft (60cm) Z4-8 [ill.pp.141,172]. Both prefer sun.

Nepeta govaniana CATMINT
Perennial producing sprays of small, hooded creamy-yellow flowers with a touch of brighter yellow on the lip. Useful for creating a haze of yellow. Prefers sun and moist soil. H 3ft (90cm) S 2ft (60cm) Z4-8 [ill.p.157]

Oenothera biennis EVENING PRIMROSE Annual or biennial with delicate, saucer-shaped flowers that open in succession in the evening, and fade to pale pink by the following day. Prefers full sun and sandy soil. H 5ft (1.5m) S 8in (20cm) Z4-9 [ill.p.180]

Osteospermum 'Buttermilk'
FREEWAY DAISY Tender in all but the most benign climates, this

evergreen perennial daisy is useful for summer bedding and container plantings. Best in sun. H 24in (60cm) S 12in (30cm) Z8-10 [ill.p.31]

Phygelius aequalis 'Yellow Trumpet' CAPE FUCHSIA Evergreen or semi-evergreen sub-shrub that produces clusters of hanging, tubular flowers in a sheltered situation. Prefers sun. H and S 4ft (1.2m) Z6-9 [ill.p.166]

Potentilla recta CINQUEFOIL
Perennial with cup-shaped flowers in loose clusters, and lobed leaves. Prefers sun. H to 18in (45cm) S 24in (60cm) Z3-7 [ill.p.172]

Rosa ROSE
Good climbing varieties include 'Albéric Barbier' which is semi-evergreen and tolerates a shady wall. H 15ft (5m) S 10ft (3m) Z6-9; *R. banksiae* 'Lutea' LADY BANKS' ROSE which has clusters of double flowers like frilly buttons and enjoys the shelter of a warm wall. H and S 30ft (10m) Z7-10; and 'Mermaid' which has broad, single flowers and a slightly stiff, awkward habit and so looks best trained against a wall. H and S 8ft (2.5m) Z5-9. Good shrub varieties include 'Golden Wings' which has exquisite pale yellow single flowers with bright yellow stamens, repeating through the summer. H 5ft (1.5m) S 3ft (90cm) Z5-9; and *R. xanthina*

f. *hugonis* H 8ft (2.4m) S 12ft (3.7m) Z5-9

Santolina pinnata subsp. **neapolitana** LAVENDER COTTON
Evergreen shrub with small, round primrose yellow flowers above feathery silvery-green foliage. May be shaped to make a low hedge. Prefers sun. H 30in (75cm) S 3ft (90cm) Z7-9[ill.pp.176,178]

Sisyrinchium striatum BLUE-EYED GRASS Semi-evergreen perennial with towers of small flowers that emerge from tufts of sword-shaped leaves. Prefers sun. H 24in (60cm) S 12in (30cm) Z6-8 [ill.p.167]

Verbascum 'Gainsborough' MULLEIN
Semi-evergreen perennial with branching spikes of cupped flowers that make a frothy mass of creamy yellow. Tolerates shade but prefers a sunny, open site. H 4ft (1.2m) S 2ft (60cm) Z6-9 [ill.pp.141,157]

WINTER

Clematis cirrhosa var. **balearica**
Evergreen climber whose nodding down-turned flowers have crimson spots toward their throats. H and S 10ft (3m) Z7-9

Hamamelis x intermedia 'Pallida'
WITCH HAZEL A lovely variety of this deliciously scented shrub with spiky flowers that open on bare branches. Tolerates sun or partial shade and is best in peaty, acid soil. H and S 12ft (4m) Z5-8

Clematis rehderiana (**Summer**)

Kniphofia 'Little Maid' (**Summer**)

Lilium monadelphum (**Summer**)

Rosa banksiae 'Lutea' (**Summer**)

Clematis cirrhosa var. *balearica* (**Winter**)

ABOVE Plant the paperbark maple (*Acer griseum*) so that it can be seen with the sun behind it, and the peeling bark will look like orange flames. The late summer sun will also add an orange cast to the scarlet flowers of montbretia (*Crocosmia* 'Lucifer'). Here, the edges of the rodgersia foliage at the foot of the tree offer an echo of brownish orange. *Acer griseum* is a fine tree in all seasons, but is especially useful in winter when its mahogany trunk and branches, with their peeling orange skins, bring color to the garden.

Oranges

Orange is a demanding, attention-grabbing color which can be difficult to place because it reacts so fiercely with other colors, harmonizing only with either orange-red and yellow, or with unsaturated versions of itself, such as bronze and ivory. Some gardeners banish it from their gardens altogether, but if you crave strong color, orange brings to the garden its richness and intensity.

Falling between red and yellow on the color wheel (see page 15), pure orange is at the core of the "hot" group of colors. The most obvious way to use it is with other hot colors. For a cheerful hot splash in spring, plant orange tulips with red and yellow ones. A bold, "hot" planting of oranges with reds and yellows more than holds its own in midsummer, especially in strong, bright sunlight. Try vivid orange sun roses with glowing orange Peruvian lilies and daisy-like yellow-orange St. John's chamomile, as in the fiery planting *opposite, below left*. In late summer, use orange montbretia with red and yellow torch lilies and dahlias. Later in the year, orange combines with red and yellow in the autumnal foliage of maples, fothergillas, and euonymus to make a glowing harmony.

A way to moderate the intensity of orange flowers is to partner them with bronze or cream. There are very few bronze flowers – 'Irish Molly' violet is an example – but there are several foliage plants, including alumroot, New Zealand flax, smokebush, grass palms, and fennels that make excellent bronze or bronze-red foliage companions. As seen in the planting, *left*, the interesting mahogany color and peeling texture of tree bark – here a paperbark maple, but you could also consider the strawberry tree (*Arbutus* x *andrachnoides*) or the cherry (*Prunus serrula*) – can make valuable contributions to color harmonies with orange.

Because orange is so dominant, it is easier, especially in a small garden, to use it as an isolated patch of color, rather than for a complete border, where it could quickly become overpowering. Or choose delicate orange flowerheads, like the spurge's, *opposite, below right,* whose color is diffused by the form of the flowers. Orange is also effective when seen among plentiful greenery. The orange tulips in the garden *opposite, top left*, make a bold statement against the boxwood. You could also limit orange to a container planting. Because of its harmonizing color, a simple terracotta pot would make a good base for a sequence of orange and bronze plantings.

A blue ceramic pot would make the orange all the more intense since orange and blue are complementary colors. You can appreciate this effect on a larger scale in the sunny midsummer planting *opposite, below left*, where the bluish stone urn and walls in the background enhance the orange flowers.

LEFT The color of the orange tulips here is so intense that, even planted 18in/45cm apart, they stand out vividly against the green of the boxwood parterre. The sparse planting style dates from the seventeenth century when tulip bulbs were rare and expensive.

BELOW LEFT The orange flowered sun rose (*Helianthemum*), the orange Peruvian lily (*Alstroemeria aurea*), and the daisy flowered St John's chamomile (*Anthemis sancti-johannis*) bask in the heat reflected from the stone. All these plants tolerate sun but be sure not to let the soil dry out completely.

BELOW The bushy perennial spurge (*Euphorbia griffithii*) and bronze fennel (*Foeniculum vulgare* 'Purpureum') provide support for a pale orange form of the oriental poppy (*Papaver orientale*) which would otherwise need staking. The sword-shaped foliage at the back is montbretia (*Crocosmia*), which will continue the orange theme later with its bright orange flowers.

Pale Orange and Apricot

Pale orange and apricot are unsaturated versions of their parent color, and share some of the same properties. Delicate and warm, they bridge the divide between pinks and yellows, and they translate into flowers of exquisite beauty, often naturally producing soft harmonies within the same plant, flower, or strain. In the planting *below*, the hybrid musk rose 'Penelope' has buds of pale orange which lighten to pale apricot as they open, then fade to cream. Certain strains of Candelabra primulas run

the whole gamut from pale orange to warm pink, making a natural harmony in the planting *opposite, below*.

However, although these warm colors look good with closely related tints of pale yellow and yellow-pink, and with muted russets and bronzes, they are difficult to place with other colors, especially with cool blue-pinks, because the warm and cool elements fight one another. Instead, limit them to plantings restricted almost to a single color. Choose one particular pale orange

plant, and build up a collection of flowers around it, perhaps based on color echoes. In the photograph *below center*, the orange stamens of a lily make a link with the whiskers on the fall of a bearded iris.

Alternatively, you can flatter and subdue apricot by surrounding it with creams, pale yellows, and the yellow-greens of foliage. As in the planting *opposite, above*, try soft orange irises with creamy yellow irises and the yellow-green of a golden-leaved hop, or of spurges.

ABOVE Partner the rose 'Penelope' with creamy hybrids of common foxgloves (*Digitalis purpurea*). The best variety for this context is 'Sutton's Apricot'. Foxgloves are biennials so they will not flower in the first year. It can be more convenient to grow them in pots so that you can plant them in the second year shortly before flowering.

ABOVE A clump of the yellow turkscap lily with bright orange stamens, is teamed with an apricot iris with an orange beard. Both plants flourish in sunny, well drained conditions.

ABOVE The wispy buff colored flowers of a grass, and the 'Bright Star' lily, with its pale, orange-throated cream trumpets, soften the contrast between the bright oranges and yellows of daylilies and the annual African daisy (*Lonas annua*). Lift and divide the daylilies every few years to ensure they do not overrun the true lilies.

RIGHT The muted ginger-orange flowers of the clump of irises in the foreground have yellow centers that make a link with the more distant pale yellow irises and the yellow-green flowerheads of the spurges and the foliage beyond. Tall bearded irises like these will nearly always dominate a scheme because they present large globes of rich color, but they have a short flowering period – two weeks at most – so do not rely on them as the backbone for a color scheme.

RIGHT In boggy ground beside a stream, Candelabra primula hybrids stretch as far as the eye can see. To achieve an effect like this, set young plants at intervals in the damp soil by a stream, and let nature do the rest. Provided that you keep the ground clear for them at the start, the primulas will seed themselves and colonize the whole waterside over the years. Plant the tall perennial St. Bruno's lily (*Paradisea liliastrum*), with its white lily-like flowers, higher up the bank as here, since it needs a well drained soil.

Oranges

SPRING

Aquilegia canadensis CANADIAN COLUMBINE Perennial with bicolored flowers, yellow at the center with vermilion spurs, that look orange at a distance. Prefers an open sunny site. H 24in (60cm) S 12in (30cm) Z3-9

Erysimum cheiri WALLFLOWER Evergreen perennial, best treated as a biennial. Requires an open sunny situation. H to 24in (60cm) S 14in (38cm) Z7-9 [ill.pp.132,178,179]

Fritillaria imperialis CROWN IMPERIAL Bulb with a ring of bell-like flowers, orange or yellow, topped by a fringe of green bracts suspended on a tall stem. Tolerates sun or partial shade. Grows best in soil that dries out slightly in summer. H 5ft (1.5m) S 12in (30cm) Z5-8

Rhododendron kaempferi Semi-evergreen shrub with funnel-shaped flowers that vary from orange through apricot to biscuit-color. Needs acid soil. Best in dappled shade. H and S 8ft (2.5m) Z6-8 [ill.p.9]

Trollius chinensis '**Golden Queen**' GLOBEFLOWER Perennial with buttercup-like flowers that are uniformly orange with prominent stamens. Lovely cut foliage. Requires moist soil. H 30in (75cm) S 15in (35cm) Z3-7

Tulipa TULIP Sun-loving bulbs that appreciate summer baking [ill.pp.39, 179]. Good varieties include *T. clusiana* var. *chrysantha* (syn. *T. aitchisonii*) LADY TULIP graceful for the rock garden. H 12in (30cm) S 8in (20cm); *T.* '**General de Wet**' is the best of the plain and simple orange tulips. H 18in (45cm) S 9in (23cm) All Z3-9

SUMMER

Alstroemeria aurea (syn. *A. aurantiaca*) PERUVIAN LILY Perennial with large flowerheads composed of small lily-like flowers that are bright orange, streaked with crimson. Prefers sun and a sheltered site. H and S 3ft (1m) Z7-10 [ill.p.39]

Asclepias tuberosa BUTTERFLY WEED Perennial with small, upright, crown-shaped flowers arranged in clusters, and narrow lance-shaped leaves. Requires sun and a humus-rich, peaty soil. H 30in (75cm) S 18in (45cm) Z4-9

Calendula officinalis POT MARIGOLD Annual producing a succession of daisy-like flowers through the summer, and thriving on poorest of soils. Double-flowered mixtures include **Art Shades Hybrids** and **Fiesta Gitana Hybrids**. Requires sun. H and S 12in (30cm)

Crocosmia MONTBRETIA Corm with flowers held on arching sprays above broad sword-shaped leaves. Thrives in a sunny, open situation. Good varieties include *C. masoniorum* H 5ft (1.5m) S 12-18in (30-45cm) Z5-9 [ill.pp.122,177]. *C.* '**Venus**' has larger, more open flowers on a smaller plant, giving more concentrated color.

Dahlia Countless varieties of this late flowering tuberous perennial are available, ranging from the small-flowered orange species *D. coccinea* to Cactus with double spiky flowers, Pompons with small spherical flowers, and singles. All require sun, and the tubers need storing in frost-free conditions for the winter. Good varieties include '**Prime Time**' H 3ft (90cm) S 2ft (60cm) Z8-10

Eschscholzia californica CALIFORNIAN POPPY Annual producing single, vivid orange four-petalled flowers that open in the sun and make a striking contrast with their own feathery blue-green foliage. Requires sun and tolerates poor soil. H 12in (30cm) S 6in (15cm)

Euphorbia griffithii '**Fireglow**' SPURGE Perennial with glowing orange flowerheads above short, narrow leaves with red midribs. Much used but can be invasive. Tolerates sun or partial shade and requires moist soil. H 3ft (90cm) S 20in (50cm) Z5-9 [ill.pp.39,125,178]

Geum AVENS Perennials that interweave well with others toward the front of a border. Good varieties include '**Borisii**' with single orange flowers with brilliant yellow stamens held on sprawling stems; and '**Fire Opal**' with double bronze-red flowers [ill.p.133]. Need sun and moist soil. H and S 12in (30cm) Z4-8

Helenium SNEEZEWEED The wild species of this perennial has sprays of yellow daisy-like flowers, but *H. autumnale* is a good garden variety [ill.p.144], and '**Wyndley**' has deep yellow flowers flecked with orange [ill.pp.171,180]. Require full sun. H to 5ft (1.5m) S 2ft (60cm) Z3-8

Helianthemum SUN ROSE Good orange varieties of this evergreen shrub, such as '**Ben Hope**' and '**Fire Dragon**,' make compact mounds of color from countless small flowers packed tight among small blue-green leaves. Requires full sun. H to 18in (50cm) S 24in (60cm) Z6-9 [ill.pp.39,178]

Hemerocallis DAYLILY Perennial with long arching leaves. Good varieties include *H. fulva* and *H. f.* '**Kwanso Variegata**'. Best in sun and moist soil. H and S 3ft (90cm) Z3-9

Ipomoea lobata (syn. *Mina lobata*) SPANISH FLAG Annual climber with tubular flowers that are bright red in bud, fading to orange as they open, and then to cream. Clusters have flowers at each stage, giving a jazzy multi-color effect.. Requires sun and moist soil. H and S 10ft (3m)

Iris Tall bearded irises flower best when their rhizomes are on the surface of the soil and bake in full sun. [ill.p.41] Muted orange and brown varieties include '**Olympic Torch**' and '**Autumn Leaves**' H 3ft (90cm) S 15in (40cm) Z4-9

Ligularia dentata '**Desdemona**' BIG LEAF LIGULARIA Perennial with clusters of vivid orange daisy-shaped flowers, and dark green leave that are purple-red beneath. Tolerates sun or partial shade. Requires moist soil. H 4ft (1.2m) S 2ft (60cm) Z4-8

Lilium LILY The following bulbs do best in sun: '**Enchantment**' has clusters of upward-facing flowers with black markings. H 3ft (90cm) Z4-9; *L. henryi* is late-summer flowering with pale orange turkscap flowers, and flourishes in limey soil. H 3ft (90cm) Z5-9 [ill.p.132]; *L. pardalinum* LEOPARD LILY has bears hanging turkscap flowers, vermilion above, orange below with red spots. H 6ft (1.8m) Z5-9

Lonicera x *tellmanniana* HONEYSUCKLE What this climber lacks in scent it makes up in its vivid yellow-orange color. Tolerates sun or partial shade H and S 15ft (5m) Z6-8

Trollius chinensis (**Spring**)

Tulipa 'General de Wet' (**Spring**)

Eschscholzia californica (**Summer**)

Hemerocallis fulva 'Kwanso Variegata' (**Summer**)

Lonicera x *tellmanniana* (**Summer**)

Mimulus aurantiacus MONKEY FLOWER
A useful shrub for a container. It produces a succession of trumpet-shaped flowers, which vary in color from peach to red-orange, through the summer. Requires sun and moist soil. H and S 5ft (1.5m) Z8-10

Rudbeckia hirta BLACK EYED SUSAN
Perennial, grown as an annual, with daisy-like flowers with cone-shaped black centers produced through the summer. The leaves and stems are hairy. *R. h.* 'Marmalade' is a good orange variety. Tolerates sun or shade and needs moist soil. H 18in (45cm) S 12in (30cm)

Solanum pyracanthum
Shrubby perennial grown for its blue-violet flowers, like those of a potato, and for the orange spines along its stems. Requires full sun. H and S 3ft (90cm) Z10-11 [ill.p.34]

Tagetes AMERICAN MARIGOLD
Stubby, low-growing annual for the front of a border or as a colorful edging to a path. Flowers right through the summer. Requires sun. Good varieties include 'Disco Orange' H and S 12in (30cm); 'Star Fire' H and S 12in (30cm); 'Tangerine Gem' with single flowers of an intense all-over orange. H 8in (20cm) S 12in (30cm) [ill.p.134]

Tithonia rotundifolia MEXICAN SUNFLOWER Annual with deep orange daisy-like flowers with paler orange centers, on tapering tubular flower-stalks. Requires sun. H 5ft (1.5m) S 2ft (60cm)

Tropaeolum majus NASTURTIUM
Annual with brilliant trumpet-shaped flowers with spurs borne among aromatic rounded leaves. Trailing varieties are available for hanging baskets, and more compact ones with upturned flowers, for borders. Requires sun. Trailing varieties: H and S 5ft (1.5m), others: H and S 2ft (60cm) [ill.pp.163,173]

FALL

Kniphofia TORCH LILY
Perennial producing dramatic spikes of flowers, like candle flames, on long stems. *K.* Royal Castle Hybrids have stout, tight-packed tapering flowerheads with orange buds, opening to yellow. H 5ft (1.5m) S 4ft (1.2m) Z7-9. *K. triangularis* has looser flowerheads, uniformly orange, and narrow, grass-like leaves. H 3ft 3in (1m) S 30in (75cm) Z5-9

Physalis alkekengi CHINESE LANTERN
The sepals that frame the tiny white flowers of this perennial in summer expand into bright orange bladders that enclose the fruits in fall. Tolerates sun or partial shade. H 18in (45cm) S 12in (30cm) Z6-9

BERRIES

Malus 'John Downie' CRAB APPLE
Tree that prefers full sun but tolerates shade and any except waterlogged soil. H 30ft (10m) S 20ft (7m) Z4-7

Pyracantha FIRETHORN
Shrub that tolerates sun or partial shade and needs a sheltered site and is effective trained against a wall. 'Orange Glow' has clusters of small berries that cover the plant in such profusion that the leaves become almost invisible. H 15ft (5m) S 10ft (3m) Z6-9

WINTER

STEMS

Salix alba var. *vitellina* 'Britzensis' (syn. *S.a.* 'Chermesina') RED STEMMED WHITE WILLOW Tree that prefers full sun and tolerates any soil but very dry. H 80ft (25m) S 30ft (10m), but H 8ft (2.4m) when coppiced annually. Z2-8

Apricots

SPRING

Acer pseudoplatanus 'Brilliantissimum' PLANE TREE MAPLE The young leaves of this tree are the color of boiled shrimps for a few weeks in spring, before they fade to dull yellow and then turn green. H and S 20ft (7m) Z5-7

Tulipa 'Apricot Beauty' TULIP
A reliable and early-flowering bulb, apricot at the base and cream around the edges of the petals. Tolerates full sun or light shade. H 20in (50cm) S 9in (23cm) Z3-9

SUMMER

Crocosmia 'Solfaterre' MONTBRETIA
Corm with spikes of apricot flowers that make a unity with the khaki-colored spear-shaped leaves. May need winter protection. Requires an open, sunny site. H 2ft (60cm) S 9in (23cm) Z5-9

Diascia 'Salmon Supreme' TWINSPUR Perennial with loose spikes of small pale apricot flowers, useful for edging beds containing roses of the same color. Requires sun and humus-rich soil. H 12in (30cm) S 18in (45cm) Z6-8

Digitalis purpurea 'Sutton's Apricot' FOXGLOVE Biennial with spires of tubular pale apricot flowers. Prefers partial shade and moist soil. H 5ft (1.5m) S 2ft (60cm) Z4-8 [ill.pp.57,175]

Lilium LILY
Bulb. 'Bright Star' has downward-facing flowers with swept back petals marked with central apricot-yellow streaks. H 5ft (1.5m) S 12in (30cm) Z4-9 [ill.p.40]. *L. x testaceum* NANKEEN LILY has creamy apricot waxy flowers with vivid orange stamens. H 5ft (1.5m) Z5-9

Potentilla fruticosa 'Daydawn' SHRUBBY CINQUEFOIL Shrub with small, open flowers of delicate apricot, merging into the yellow center. They appear in succession through the summer months. Requires shading from the hottest sun. H 3ft (90cm) S 4ft (1.2m) Z3-7

Rosa ROSE
Most roses require an open, sunny site and moist soil. Good climbing varieties include 'Gloire de Dijon' with large double "cabbage-shaped" flowers that are gingery-apricot in bud, and fade to cream with age. H and S 12ft (3.7m) Z5-9. Good shrub varieties include 'Buff Beauty' with flowers that are apricot in bud and when young, becoming creamy yellow as they fade. H and S 8ft (2.4m) Z5-9; 'Chicago Peace' with touches of pink and cream overlying a base color of apricot. H 4ft (1.2m) S 3ft (90cm) Z4-9; 'Penelope' with pale apricot-pink flowers, makes a good hedge. H and S 5ft (1.5m) Z5-9 [ill.p.40]; and *R. x odorata* 'Mutabilis' with floppy single flowers that open apricot and fade to pink and later crimson, all visible together on one plant. H and S 8ft (2.4m) Z7-9

Verbena 'Peaches and Cream'
Perennial, usually grown as an annual, with rounded flowerheads that have some orange flowers and some creamy yellow, giving an overall apricot effect. Requires sun. H 18in (45cm) S 12in (30cm) Z9-10

Tithonia rotundifolia (**Summer**)

Physalis alkekengi (**Fall**)

Pyracantha 'Orange Glow' (**Fall**)

Lilium x *testaceum* (**Summer**)

Rosa 'Buff Beauty' (**Summer**)

Reds

For most people, red stands for danger, excitement, and passion. Artists know how to play on the potency of red, perhaps using just a dab of this color to draw the eye into a picture. It has the same effect in a garden where a few vibrant red flowers – poppies, for instance – will attract attention like fireworks in a dark sky. Used in profusion, pure red flowers will dominate everything around them. Used as as an occasional touch of brilliant color, red flowers can give weight to a planting, spicing up neighboring colors that might otherwise appear insipid. For a multicolor planting, the most useful red flowers are those such as avens, alumroot, verbenas, and cinquefoil, that punctuate with small dots of red, brightening adjacent colors without swamping them. The same flowers also help to soften the edges of the all-red planting *opposite, right*.

Unlike most other colors, red is only truly red in its saturated form. Mixed with another color, it assumes a different character altogether. Red with yellow becomes orange; red with blue becomes purple; and mixtures of red with white make pink. You need to be careful when using these derivatives of red in the garden: they do not all sit happily together, and warm scarlet-red has an especially uneasy relationship with any pink. These combinations may be exploited in small doses, but are jarring on a large scale.

Red flowers and dark red foliage can look gloomy *en masse* and are best kept as dramatic incidents. Otherwise use some bright green foliage or flowers to alleviate the dark tones, or introduce either smaller, orangey-red flowers, or red flowers with bright yellow stamens to lighten the effect. The combination of scarlet pelargoniums with matching dahlias in the planting *left*, works without being overpowering not only because the flowers are evenly spaced among abundant foliage, but also because of the introduction of the lime-green flowering tobacco plants. Similarly, the green poppy foliage "lifts" and brightens the effect of the all-red planting of poppies, roses, snapdragons, and sweet Williams *opposite, left*, just as the cinquefoil foliage does among red dahlias and cardinal flowers in the planting *opposite, right*.

ABOVE This skillful summer combination is of the 'Bishop of Llandaff' dahlia, a bright red pelargonium, and a flowering tobacco (*Nicotiana* x *sanderae* 'Lime Green'). Either cut back the pelargoniums and overwinter them ina sun room or on a frost free windowsill, or take softwood cuttings during the summer for a fresh supply next year. The dahlia tubers need to be lifted and stored in a frost free place during the winter. The metal chair has been painted to match the dark dahlia foliage – a masterly touch that helps to enhance the planting.

ABOVE Silky red poppies accompany the 'Lilli Marlene' rose, the near black sweet William (*Dianthus barbatus* Nigrescens Group), and the dark red snapdragon with deepest red foliage (*Antirrhinum* 'Black Prince'). A budding stem of the evergreen pineapple sage (*Salvia elegans*) is slightly obscured by foliage toward the back. The poppies seed themselves every year, but the sweet Williams and snapdragons are best grown from seed, and the young plants placed where you want them to grow each spring.

ABOVE In this red border, clumps of cardinal flowers (*Lobelia cardinalis*) and a red dahlia grow through the perennial Himalayan cinquefoil (*Potentilla astrosanguinea* 'Gibson's Scarlet') which forms a carpet completely covering the soil. The smoky foliage of the dahlia is echoed in the backdrop of deciduous purple giant filbert (*Corylus maxima* 'Purpurea').

Red Borders

The best plants for a long lasting all-red border include those that flower nonstop from midsummer to fall, as well as some to provide foliage interest throughout this period. Many of these are tender perennials or annuals, which means that they need planting each year. Although this is labor intensive, it gives flexibility and opportunities to experiment with different combinations.

Let the background color of a border influence your choice of plants. In the late summer *tour de force* pictured *left,* the dark, purple leaved shrubs at the back of the border are echoed by the stonecrop, the castor oil plant, the near black foliage of one of the dahlias, and a fringe of red leaved beet. The pink variegated leaves of the bloodleaf, and the yellow stamens of the dahlias contribute a welcome light touch.

Lighter, vermilion red flowers make a link with the muted red brick wall, *right.* Note how much the foliage influences the effect – the pale green leaves of the red opium poppy lighten the mood and keep the inky foliage of the neighboring dahlia from casting a gloomy spell

LEFT Aside from the shrubs, only the bee balm and stonecrop can be left in the ground through the winter. Lift dahlia and begonia tubers, and overwinter cuttings of tender verbena and bloodleaf in a sun room or on a frost free windowsill. Flowering tobacco, castor oil plants, and beet should be sown under glass in spring and planted when danger of frost has passed. (For a diagram of this planting, see page 173.)

RIGHT Roses, daylilies, and Maltese cross form the backbone of this glowing summer border. They are infilled with the tender perennial African daisy, dahlias, opium poppies, and nasturtiums. (For a diagram of this planting, see page 173.)

Deep Plum Reds

Muted forms of red make subtler plantings than bright reds. Plum colored flowers contrast gently with the greens of the foliage *below left*. Red foliage, like copper beech or some of the barberries, contains green chlorophyll that overlies the red pigment to produce a near black color that in some lights can look purple. It harmonizes well with plum colored flowers, and has a cooling effect on "hot" reds.

Because it is so dense, red foliage can be gloomy on its own, but adds rich depths of color when it is interspersed with bright green foliage, *below right*, or with silver. Colored foliage needs to be used with discretion. In gardens where all the trees and shrubs are plum or yellow leaved, the eye yearns for the calming influence of green.

ABOVE The single flowered clematis (*C.* 'Ville de Lyon') and the double flowered Italian clematis (*C. viticella* 'Purpurea Plena Elegans') flower together in late summer, offering approximately the same plum red hue in quite different flower forms.

LEFT Well placed between two red leaved shrubs, the summer flowering perennial great masterwort (*Astrantia major* 'Hadspen Blood') stands out against the tall, dark barberry, and makes a close color match with the young leaves of the dwarf purple leaved Japanese barberry (*Berberis thunbergii* 'Atropurpurea Nana').

FAR LEFT A deep plum bearded iris has been perfectly color matched with a cultivar of an perennial oriental poppy. The dusky smokebush (*Cotinus coggygria* 'Royal Purple') that forms the backdrop picks up the darker shades of the iris falls, and the near black centers of the poppies. All three plants thrive in sunny, well drained conditions.

Scarlets and Vermilions

SPRING

Tulipa TULIP
Bulb that tolerates sun or partial shade and appreciates summer baking. Bold scarlet tulips look inviting in containers beside a front door. Good varieties include *'Plaisir'* H 8in (20cm) S 10in (25cm) Z5; *T. praestans* H 18in (45cm) S 9in (23cm) Z5 [ill.p.5]; and **'Red Shine'** which is Lily-flowered and blooms late and for a long period, H 24in (60cm) S 10in (25cm) Z3-9

SUMMER

Alonsoa warscewiczii MASK FLOWER
Annual that makes a soft haze of vermilion flowers. Requires sun. H 24in (60cm) S 12in (30cm)

Arctotis x hybrida (syn. x 'Venidio-arctotis') AFRICAN DAISY
A graceful annual daisy which only opens in full sun. Available in several colors; the vermilion one verges toward soft tangerine. Requires sun. H 20in (50cm) S 16in (40cm) [ill.p.173]

Canna indica INDIAN SHOT
Rhizome with huge translucent leaves and folded scarlet flowers that makes an exotic centerpiece for a container or summer planting. *C. 'Liberty Scarlet'* has deep red foliage. Requires sun and moist, rich, warm soil. H 6ft6in (2m) S 3ft (90cm) Z7-9

Crocosmia 'Lucifer' MONTBRETIA
Corm with arching sprays of vivid scarlet flowers and bright, spear-shaped foliage that make this a staple plant for the all-red border. Requires an open, sunny situation. H 3ft3in (1m) S 15in (40cm) Z5-9 [ill.pp.13,19,38, 122,173]

Dahlia 'Bishop of Llandaff'
Tuberous perennial whose single scarlet flowers have lightening yellow centers. Grown as much for its licorice-colored foliage. Requires sun. H and S 3ft (90cm) Z8-10 [ill.p.44,173,177]

Geum 'Mrs J. Bradshaw' AVENS
Perennial with small double flowers on longish stems that provide dots of strong color at the front of the border. Requires sun and moist soil. H 2ft8in (80cm) S 18in (45cm) Z5-8 [ill.p.173]

Helenium SNEEZEWEED
A good red variety of this late summer flowering perennial is **'Moerheim Beauty'** Requires full sun. H 5ft (1.5m) S 2ft (60cm) Z3-8 [ill.pp.13,19]

Hemerocallis 'Royal Mountie'
DAYLILY Perennial with flowers of a deep copper red, with arching leaves. Requires sun and moist soil. H and S 3ft (90cm) Z3-9

Lobelia cardinalis CARDINAL FLOWER
Perennial with tall spikes of vivid scarlet flowers that tolerates sun or partial shade in moist soil, even in boggy ground beside a pond. H 3ft 3in (1m) S 12in (30cm) Z2-9 [ill.pp.45,177].
'Queen Victoria' has near-black foliage. H 3ft3in (1m) S 12in (30cm) Z2-9 [ill.p.80]

Lychnis chalcedonica MALTESE CROSS Perennial with star-shaped flowers that are massed in compact flowerheads on tall stems, giving brilliant blobs of vermilion for the "hot" border. Requires sun. H 4ft (1.2m) S 18in (45cm) Z4-8 [ill.p.173]

Papaver POPPY
Annual *P. commutatum* **'Lady Bird'** has a black blotch at the base of scarlet petals. H and S 18in (45cm). The flowers of perennial *P. orientale* ORIENTAL POPPY open like crumpled tissue paper, their brilliance eclipsing all but the brightest companions. A good variety is *P. o.* **'Beauty of Livermere'** H and S 3ft3in (1m) Z3-8 [ill.p.167] All do best in full sun.

Pelargonium
Evergreen perennial, sometimes treated as an annual. A house, porch, or conservatory plant that will thrive outside in full sun in summer, in containers or borders that are not damp. Countless varieties available, with scarlet, crimson, pink, salmon or white flowers, some with patterned foliage [ill.pp.44, 128] Among the best with red flowers is **'Red Elite'** H and S 10in (23cm) Z9-10

Penstemon BEARD TONGUE
Semi-evergreen perennials that make clumps of flowers lasting over a long period. All do best in sun. Good varieties include: *P. barbatus* with spikes of slender tubular flowers Z3-8; *P. eatonii* EATON'S FIRECRACKER and **'Firebird'** have broader flowers giving a brighter splash of color. H up to 3ft (90cm) S 2ft (60cm) Z8-9

Potentilla atrosanguinea **'Gibson's Scarlet'** CINQUEFOIL Perennial with clusters of flowers of the most vivid red, contrasting with the intense green of the strawberry-like leaves. Tolerates sun, but partial shade gives the best color. H and S 18in (45cm) Z5-8 [ill.p.45]

Rosa ROSE
Good climbing roses include **'Dublin Bay'** H and S 7ft (2.2m) Z5-9; and **'Parkdirektor Riggers'** H and S 12ft (3.5m) Z5-9 [ill.pp.6,173]. Good shrub roses include *R. moyesii* which has single scarlet flowers and then brilliant yellow hips. H 13ft (4m) S 10ft (3m) Z5-9

Salvia SAGE
The sub-shrub *S. fulgens* has racemes of scarlet flowers on crimson-red stems borne above slightly hairy leaves. H and S 2ft8in (80cm) Z9-10. The evergreen shrub *S. microphylla* BABY SAGE has rounded and lipped scarlet flowers. H and S 4ft (1.2m) Z9-10 [ill.p.183]; *S. splendens* SCARLET SAGE, a perennial sub-shrub grown as an annual, is sometimes mocked as the archetypal summer plant, but undeservedly, as it can provide a useful flash of scarlet at the front of a border if sensitively used. Good cultivars include 'Blaze' and 'Lady in Red'. H and S 12in (30cm) [ill.p.19]

Tropaeolum speciosum FLAME NASTURTIUM Rhizomatous climber with clusters of spurred, scarlet flowers that hang like curtains from supporting plants or structures. Requires sun, but roots must be shaded. H and S 10ft (3m) Z7-9 [ill.pp.128,173]

Verbena
Useful for the front of a red border, or as a cascade of color from the edge of a container. [ill.p.144,173] Good varieties with clusters of tiny flowers include annual 'Blaze' and perennial 'Taylor Town Red' and *V. peruviana* [ill.p.128]. Requires sun. H 12in (30cm) S 2ft (60cm) Z7-10

Zauschneria californica (syns. *Epilobium californicum, E. canum*) CALIFORNIA FUCHSIA Perennial sub-shrub with dainty tubular vermilion flowers. Requires sun. H 18in (45cm) S 30in (75cm) Z8-10

Zinnia
Annual with generously sized daisy flowers to add zest to a summer borders. Requires sun. H 2ft (60cm) S 12in (30cm)

Tulipa 'Red Shine' **(Spring)**

Hemerocallis 'Royal Mountie' **(Summer)**

Papaver commutatum 'Lady Bird' **(Summer)**

Salvia fulgens **(Summer)**

Zauschneria californica **(Summer)**

FALL

Schizostylis coccinea KAFFIR LILY
Rhizome with graceful vase-shaped flowers and narrow leaves. Requires sun and moist soil. H 24in (60cm) S 12in (30cm) Z6-9

FOLIAGE

Acer MAPLE
A. palmatum JAPANESE MAPLE has seven-lobed leaves that turn crimson and scarlet for a week or two before falling. H and S 20ft (6m) Z5-9 [ill.p.129].
A. palmatum 'Osakazuki' has leaves that turn bright scarlet. H and S 15ft (4.5m) Z5-8.
A. japonicum 'Aconitifolium' FULL MOON MAPLE has delicately cut leaves that turn vivid red and yellow. H and S 22ft (7m) Z5-8.
A. rubrum RED MAPLE H 60ft (18m) S 36ft (11m) Z4-9. All tolerate sun and partial shade in neutral to acid soil.
Liquidambar styraciflua SWEETGUM Tree with brilliant red and yellow fall colors. Requires sun and moist soil. H 75ft (22.5m) S 40ft (12m) Z5-9
Parthenocissus quinquefolia VIRGINIA CREEPER Climber that can cover complete buildings, making them glow crimson for a short season. Requires sun or partial shade. H and S 50ft (15m) Z4-9 [ill.p.129]
Vitis coignetiae CRIMSON GLORY VINE Climber with large heart-shaped

leaves, up to 1ft (30cm) wide that take on crimson to orange tints. Tolerates sun or partial shade. Prefers chalky soil. H and S 50ft (15m) Z5-9 [ill.p.129]

WINTER

BARK

Cornus alba 'Sibirica' SIBERIAN DOGWOOD Shrub needing pruning to within 1ft (30cm) of ground level in spring, to encourage young shoots; these have brilliant scarlet bark, though less colorful on older growth. Tolerates sun and partial shade. H and S 6ft6in (2m) Z4-7 [ill.pp.16,170]

Crimsons and Deep Reds

SPRING

Paeonia officinalis 'Rubra Plena' PEONY Perennial cottage garden favorite that survives in the same garden for generations. Prefers sun but will tolerate light shade in rich soil. H and S 30in (75cm) Z4-7 [ill.p.183]

SUMMER

Centranthus ruber RED VALERIAN Perennial that remains in flower for much of the summer, and will regenerate if you cut it back.

Self-seeding, and a survivor in the most unlikely places. There are pink and white varieties too. Requires sun and thrives in an exposed situation and poor alkaline soil. H 30in (75cm) S 24in (60cm) Z4-9 [ill.p.131]
Clematis
Good crimson climbing varieties include 'Ville de Lyon' which has crimson flowers, with cream-colored anthers [ill.p.48]; and *C. viticella* 'Purpurea Plena Elegans' ITALIAN CLEMATIS which has muted crimson flowers like stuffed velvet buttons [ill.pp 17,48] Both tolerate shade or full sun but with roots shaded, and prefer rich soil. H and S 10ft (3m) Z5-8
Dianthus barbatus SWEET WILLIAM Perennial, treated as an annual. Flowerheads are like bouquets, each flower throbbing with rings of color. Needs an open, sunny situation in slightly alkaline soil. H 30in (75cm) S 12in (30cm) [ill.p.113]
Monarda BEE BALM/BERGAMOT Perennial whose rounded whorls of hooded crimson-red flowers have an overall jagged appearance that makes them useful as a softening influence in breaking up the hard edges of adjacent plants. Requires sun and moist soil. Good varieties include 'Cambridge Scarlet' [ill.p.177] H 3ft3in (1m) S 18in (45cm) Z4-9; *M. didyma* H 3ft (90cm) S 18in (45cm) Z4-9; and

'Mrs Perry' H 20in (50cm) S18in (45cm) Z4-9 [ill.p.173]
Penstemon BEARD TONGUE Semi-evergreen perennials that make clumps of flowers lasting over a long period. 'Garnet' is one of the most popular varieties. Requires full sun. H 30in (75cm) S 2ft (60cm) Z7-9 [ill.p.175]
Rosa ROSE
Most need an open, sunny site with moist soil. Good climbing roses include the dusky crimson and deeply scented 'Guinée' H 15ft (5m) Z5-9. Good shrub roses include 'Dusky Maiden' with semi-double flowers of deeply shaded scarlet, H 4ft (1.2m) S 5ft (1.m) Z5-9 [ill.p.6]; 'Frensham' which is cluster-flowered and deep red, H 4ft (1.2m) S 30in (75cm) Z5-9 [ill.pp.45,166]; and 'Tuscany Superb' a Gallica rose, double in form and velvety crimson in color, H and S 3ft6in (1.1m) Z5-9

Deep Plum and Smoky Reds

SPRING

Helleborus orientalis LENTEN ROSE Evergreen perennial with many flower colors available, from yellow-green to spotted pink, the most desirable are the dusky reds, and near-blacks. Requires

partial shade and moisture-retentive soil. H and S 18in (45cm) Z5-8
Tulipa 'Queen of the Night' TULIP Late flowering bulb with flowers of a deep velvety purple. H 24in (60cm) S 9in (23cm) Z3-9. Needs sun.[ill.pp.10,149,169]

SUMMER

Antirrhinum 'Black Prince' SNAPDRAGON Annual whose flowers are so dark that there is only a glint of red in good light. Requires sun. H 18in (45cm) S 12in (30cm) [ill.pp.45,131]
Astrantia major 'Hadspen Blood' MASTERWORT Perennial with deep muddied red crown-shaped flowers.Tolerates sun or partial shade. H 24in (60cm) S 18in (45cm) Z5-7 [ill.p.48]
Cosmos atrosanquineus CHOCOLATE COSMOS Tuberous perennial whose near-black flowers are coppery red in good light, and smell of chocolate. Requires sun and moist soil. H 24in (60cm) S 18in (45cm) Z6-8 [ill.p.16]
Dianthus barbatus Nigrescens Group SWEET WILLIAM Biennial whose flowers and foliage seem to create a black shadow. Requires an open, sunny situation in slightly alkaline soil. H 2ft4in (70cm) S 12in (30cm) [ill.pp.45,119,131,173]
Geranium phaeum MOURNING WIDOW'S CRANESBILL Perennial

Acer palmatum 'Osakazuki' (**Fall**)

Centranthus ruber (**Summer**)

Monarda 'Cambridge Scarlet' (**Summer**)

Rosa 'Tuscany Superb' (**Summer**)

Geranium phaeum (**Summer**)

with exquisite translucent small black flowers that glow deep purple with the light behind them. Requires shade and any but waterlogged soil. H 30in (75cm) S 18in (45cm) Z4-9 [ill.pp.183,184].

Knautia macedonica
Star performing perennial that produces a succession of small dark-shaded crimson flowers throughout the summer. Needs sun. H 30in (75cm) S 2ft (60cm) Z6-9 [ill.pp.164.184]

Rosa ROSE
Requires an open, sunny site and moist soil.Good shrub roses include the dusky crimson **'Cardinal de Richelieu'** H 4ft (1.2m) S 3ft (1m) Z5-9; and **'Nuits de Young'** H 4ft (1.2m) S 3ft (1m) Z5-9

Viola **'Molly Sanderson'** PANSY
The deepest black viola, but **'Bowles' Black'** is a good second choice. Tolerates sun or shade. H and S 10in (25cm) Z4-8

FOLIAGE

Acer MAPLE
Shrubs and trees that require sun or partial shade in neutral to acid soil. *A. palmatum* Dissectum Atropurpureum Group JAPANESE MAPLE Very slow-growing. Produces a mound of finely cut leaves that reach to the ground. H 5ft (1.5m) S 8ft (2.4m) Z5-8 [ill.p.16]. *A. platanoides* **'Crimson King'** NORWAY MAPLE is a good specimen tree with dark

purple-red foliage. H 50ft (15m) S 33ft (10m) Z4-7 [ill.p.177].

Anthriscus sylvestris COW PARSLEY
The deep red-black leaved variety that would be regarded as at best a wildflower, at worst a weed, if it were not for its lovely foliage, which makes a strong tonal contrast with its own diaphanous white flowers. H 3ft (1m) S2ft (60cm) Z6-8

Atriplex hortensis var.*rubra* RED MOUNTAIN SPINACH Annual with useful plum-red foliage. Requires full sun. Grows well in coastal situations. H 4ft (1.2m) S 1ft (30cm) [ill.pp.131,184]

Berberis thunbergii f. *atropurpurea* PURPLE LEAVED JAPANESE BARBERRY A useful, very easy but unostentatious shrub. Small-leaved and amenable to pruning, it canbe used as a hedge. Tolerates sun or partial shade. H 8ft (2.5m) S 10ft (3m) Z5-8 [ill.pp.48, 131]. *B. t.* **'A. Nana'** is a dwarf variety. H and S 2ft (60cm) Z5-8 [ill.pp.148,178].

Beta vulgaris BEETROOT
Dark-leaved varieties of annual make useful foliage plants for the front of an all-red border. H 10in (25cm) S 6in (15cm) [ill.pp.131,173]

Cercis canadensis **'Forest Pansy'** EASTERN REDBUD One of the loveliest small trees, with plum-colored heart-shaped leaves. Requires full sun. H and S 12ft (3.7m) Z5-9 [Ill.p.130]

Cimicifuga simplex Atropurpurea Group PURPLE LEAVED BUGBANE Perennial with lovely dark red cut-leaf foliage followed by plumes of white flowers. Requires light shade and moist soil. H 4ft (120cm) S 2ft (60cm) Z3-8 [ill.p.81]

Cordyline australis **'Purpurea'** PURPLE LEAVED GRASS PALM Evergreen shrub or tree that produces a sheaf of leathery purple foliage. Useful as a centerpiece for a container. Size when confined to a container: H and S 3ft3in (1m) Z9-11 [ill.p.80]

Corylus maxima **'Purpurea'** PURPLE GIANT FILBERT Vigorous shrub, good as a dark background, but needs pruning to keep it within bounds. Tolerates sun or partial shade. H 20ft (6m) S 15ft (5m) Z5-8 [ill.pp.45,173,178]

Cotinus coggygria **'Royal Purple'** PURPLE LEAVED SMOKE BUSH Shrub with deepest plum-red foliage, fading to translucent red in fall. For the largest leaves and to contain the plant, prune back to the base in spring, but this will eliminate the feathery flowers that create a "smoke" over the mature shrub in summer. H and S 15ft (5m) Z4-8 [Ill.p.147]

Euphorbia dulcis **'Chameleon'** SPURGE Semi-evergreen perennial with foliage and flowers in variable shades of khaki, purple, and near-black. Tolerates sun or

partial shade in moist soil. H and S 30in (75cm) Z5-7

Heuchera micrantha var. *diversifolia* **'Palace Purple'** SMALL FLOWERED ALUMROOT Perennial that makes clumps of crinkled, heart-shaped leaves of deepest plum red; they are shiny and so reflect the light. Puts up diffuse sprays of small white flowers. H and S 18in (45cm) Z4-8 [ill.p.177]

Iresine herbstii BEEFSTEAK PLANT \BLOODLEAF A tender foliage perennial with tints of deep purple melding into pinks. Requires bright light for good leaf color, and loamy soil. H 2ft (60cm) S 18in (45cm) Z9-10 [Ill.p.173]

Ocimum basilicum var. *purpurascens* PURPLE LEAVED BASIL A tender culinary herb with purple foliage, usually used as an ornamental in containers. Requires sun. H 15in (40cm) S 12in (30cm) [ill.p.119]

Ophiopogon planiscapus **'Nigrescens'** Evergreen perennial producing clumps of grass-like foliage which is dark green at the base and shiny black elsewhere. Best in partial shade H and S 8in (20cm) Z6-9

Prunus cerasifera CHERRY PLUM Tree whose small white flowers are among the first of spring, but which is also grown for its dark purple foliage. Also useful hedging plant. Requires full sun and any but waterlogged soil.

Good varieties include *P. c.* **'Nigra'** [ill. p.179]; and *P. c.* **'Pissardii'** [ill.p.181] H and S 30ft (10m) Z5-8

Ricinus communis CASTOR OIL PLANT The dark-leaved varieties of this evergreen shrub provide bold, exotic foliage. The leaves are large and deeply cut. Spiky red seedpods follow the small red flowers in late summer. Requires sun. H 5ft (1.5m) S 3ft (90cm) Z9-11 [ill.pp.173,177]

Sambucus nigra **'Purpurea'** BLACK LEAVED ELDER Tree with divided purple leaves that make a contrast with the flattened pink-tinged, cream-colored flower-heads in early summer. Requires sun and moist soil. H and S 20ft (6m) Z5 [ill.p.57]

Veratrum nigrum BLACK FALSE HELLEBORE Perennial grown mainly for its fluted oval leaves, but also for its tall spires of tightly packed, near-black flowers. Requires partial shade and moist soil. H 6ft (1.8m) S 3ft (90cm) Z3-8

FALL

Sedum telephium subsp. *maximum* **'Atropurpureum'** PURPLE LEAVED ORPINE Perennial whose succulent purple foliage glows red in fall, when the small deep red-pink flowerheads mature. Requires sun. H 24in (60cm) S 18in (45cm) Z3-9 [ill.p.173]

Viola 'Bowles' Black' **(Summer)**

Anthriscus sylvestris **(Summer)**

Euphorbia dulcis 'Chameleon' **(Summer)**

Heuchera micrantha var. *diversifolia* 'Palace Purple' **(Summer)**

Sedum telephium subsp. *maximum* 'Atropurpureum' **(Fall)**

Pinks

Pinks comprise a huge family of colors. Ranging from palest blush pink to vivid magenta, pink flowers can be found to perform from early spring right through to fall. Pinks do not appear on the color wheel because they are mixtures of other colors. We can think of pink as red diluted with a varying proportion of white.

Like its close relative red, pink can lean toward either blue or yellow. Hues derived from crimson-reds make the cool blue-pinks (see pages 54–55). Colors deriving from orange-reds make warm peachy pinks (see pages 56–57). In general, avoid cool pinks with warm pinks. The two colors appear similar separately, but when placed together, the eye detects the contrast between the cool blue and warm yellow elements. The result can be jarring.

Pinks can appear warm or cool, depending on their setting. A pink opium poppy, for instance, looks like a warm outsider in a cool border of blue catmints and violet salvias, but will appear cool if it pops up in a bed of red roses. Changing light also nudges these chameleon pinks from warm to cool. The warm sun of sunset makes them look warm and yellowish, but as soon as the sun goes down, those same pinks will appear cool or bluish.

An all-pink planting is feasible on any scale, but a uniform pink planting needs variety to give it interest. Flowers of different shapes will add interest, as will plants of different habit. For example, there are plants that make a dense, compact mound, while others sprawl and send out long, lax shoots. In the planting *below center*, the daisylike shapes of the marguerites contrast well with the shining pink cups of a mallow, as do the willowy stems of Japanese anemones with bushy dendranthemums in the planting *below right*. An all-pink planting runs the risk of being cloying; a diversity of tints either within a cool or warm pink range with some related darker colors will keep your garden from appearing too sweet. In the planting of tulips, *opposite, below*, the porcelain-pink tulips appear less sugary thanks to the addition of the lilac-pink and purple tulips.

Pink and white often form a successful partnership but, despite their red content, pinks do not always combine well with reds. The white in the pink cools down the red, so a red-pink combination can come across as an unattractive hot-cool reaction. Deeper pinks, like magenta, however, can set up an exciting, almost dangerous relationship with reds (see pages 144–45).

LEFT Massed azaleas – up to twenty of each variety – in different pinks create dramatic drifts of late spring color in the dappled shade and lime-free conditions of a woodland garden.

BELOW Ribbons of the pink edged tulip 'Meissner Porzellan', with the lilac-pink tulip 'Pandour', and the purple tulip 'Queen of the Night' behind, echo the underplanting of lilac and pink pansies. Once the tulips are over, all the flowers will be lifted and replaced with summer flowering plants. Changing the planting twice or three times during the year would be very time-consuming on a scale like this, but a similar effect can be more easily achieved in a much smaller space, even in a container. One advantage of this labor intensive work is that the color scheme can be changed at the same time as the plants.

FAR LEFT Deep pink *Verbena* 'Sissinghurst' and *V.* 'Kemerton' overhang a wall, accompanied by pale pink twinspur (*Diascia vigilis*) and beard tongue (*Penstemon* 'Evelyn'). They are all vigorous plants that will flower throughout the summer. Below them are two varieties of pink phlox that have a short flowering season. Their place will be taken by showy stonecrop (*Sedum* 'Autumn Joy') which is still in bud.

CENTER LEFT The young flowers of this perennial marguerite have mid-pink centers that become paler as they mature. Here, they are planted with a fast growing mallow (*Lavatera* 'Rosea').

NEAR LEFT A late summer planting consists of hardy perennials: pale pink, semi-double Japanese anemones (*Anemone* x *hybrida*), pale pink and low growing rusty pink *Dendranthema*. The deeper pink stonecrop (*Sedum* 'Ruby Glow'), seen here in bud, will take the pink theme through the fall.

Cool Pinks

Cool pinks – those which have some blue in them – run the gamut from very pale pink to deep crimson and magenta. Most associate well together, the paler colors making calmer, sweeter harmonies than the deeper ones. The most vivid pinks make assertive statements in the garden. If you are unsure of including them in a permanent planting, put them in containers that are easy to move, as pictured *near right*.

Pansies, *left*, and perennial peas, *below*, have such diversity of color that you can achieve a range of tints and shades by growing several together.

ABOVE The perennial peas (*Lathyrus latifolius*), in colors ranging from deep to pale pink, need plastic netting or chicken wire to give them support. The flowers fade to bluish-gray as they age, so there seem to be at least four colors here.

LEFT Pansies and closely color matched deep pink drumstick primulas (*Primula denticulata*) make an underplanting for tulips in spring. When this planting has finished flowering, it will be removed and its place taken by summer flowering plants. The perennial primulas can be saved for the following year by planting them out in a shady corner of the garden, and the tulip bulbs stored in a dark, dry place until the fall. The pansies will need replacing.

LEFT The newly introduced Japanese Surfinia trailing petunias accompany purple petunias and the pink *Verbena* 'Sissinghurst' in a collection of terracotta pots. To maintain container plantings through the summer, deadhead the plants every day or two, water daily, and give a liquid feed once a week.

BELOW Feathery leaved annual *Cosmos* 'Imperial Pink' has flowers of the same color but contrasting shape as those of perennial *Salvia involucrata* 'Bethellii'. To make such a close color match, you need to see the flowers together, so grow the annuals to flowering size in pots before you plant them.

BOTTOM Spikes of Byzantine gladiolus (*Gladiolus communis* subsp. *byzantinus*) grow through Armenian geranium (*Geranium psilostemon*) in a summer border. The geranium will die back in winter, and in all but mild climates the gladioli corms should be lifted and stored for the following year.

Warm Pinks

BELOW The rambling rose 'Albertine' is the perfect partner for the woodbine honeysuckle (*Lonicera periclymenum* 'Belgica'). Both are distinctly scented; both do best if they are not confined to too small an area, but allowed to grow to their natural mature size; and both are prone to aphids so need regular spraying.

Warm pinks contain a touch of yellow, and the more yellow they contain, the closer they come to apricot or pale orange. This yellow content makes them the only pinks to harmonize with pale yellows. Many flowers appear warm pink because of their orange or yellow centers, such as the coneflower and daylily, *opposite, right below*, or because they are bicolored, like the honeysuckle, *below*. Relatively few flowers come in tones of warm pink, making it difficult to create a large-scale planting using just this range. An interesting feature of this elusive color is that many flowers change as they mature, or contain a good deal of tonal variation. The black leaved elder, *right*, is pink in bud and cream in flower, and the rambling rose 'Albertine', *below*, has orange-red buds that open to flowers of warm pink with a hint of copper.

ABOVE The deciduous black-leaved elder (*Sambucus nigra* 'Purpurea') helps to provide the right conditions for the shade-loving foxgloves (*Digitalis* 'Sutton's Apricot') to thrive. The elder will grow to a tree unless you cut it back almost to ground level in winter. Prune one-year shoots less drastically, cutting off about one third of their length, and these will provide flowers the following year.

RIGHT ABOVE A coppery-apricot pink perennial mullein (*Verbascum* hybrid) warms up its cool neighbors, the flowering tobacco plant (*Nicotiana* x *sanderae* 'Domino Salmon Pink') and the perennial bee balm (*Monarda* 'Beauty of Cobham') that has pink petals and purple bracts, as well as scented foliage.

RIGHT The rich orange centers of the purple coneflowers (*Echinacea purpurea* 'Bright Star') echo the yellow throats of the daylily (*Hemerocallis* 'Catherine Woodbery'). Both are hardy perennials, thriving in sunny situations.

Magenta and Deep Pinks

SPRING

Malus x *moerlandsii* 'Profusion' CRAB APPLE A good, vigorous crab apple tree, with wine-red flowers in great profusion, young leaves tinged red, and small ox-blood red fruits in fall. Requires full sun. H 25ft (7.5m) S 20ft (6m) Z4-7

Rhododendron 'Praecox' A compact shrub with slightly aromatic, small, dark green leaves, and bunches of rosy-purple flowers in very early spring. Best in neutral to acid conditions, with some protection from late frosts. H 4ft (1.2m) S 5ft (1.5m) Z5-8

SUMMER

Bougainvillea glabra PAPER FLOWER Vigorous woody-stemmed climber with glossy oval leaves. Rich magenta floral bracts in quantity in the summer. Requires full sun. H and S 15ft (4.6m) Z9-11

Clematis The following climbing varieties can be cut hard back in early spring to flower from midsummer onward: 'Jackmanii Rubra' with single velvety magenta flowers with cream stamens; 'Niobe' with rich purple-pink flowers with light greenish stamens [ill.p.66]; and 'Rouge Cardinal' with large magenta flowers. All H and S 10-13ft (3-4m) Z3-9

Geranium CRANESBILL Invaluable border perennials. *G. psilostemon* ARMENIAN GERANIUM has deep magenta flowers with black centers, forms a large clump of elegantly cut broad leaves that color brilliantly in fall. H and S 4ft (1.2m) Z4-8 [ill.pp.55,181,182, 184]. *G. sanguineum* BLOODY CRANESBILL has flowers of deep or paler pink, makes slowly increasing clumps of deeply divided dark green leaves. H 10in (25cm) S 12in (30cm) Z4-9 [ill.pp.116,183]

Gladiolus communis subsp. *byzantinus* BYZANTINE GLADIOLUS Corm producing prettily shaped purple and magenta flowers. Can seed itself about quite energetically in light soils. Needs sun. H 2ft6in (50cm) S 6in (15cm) Z7-10 [ill.pp.55,180]

Lychnis coronaria ROSE CAMPION Biennial or short-lived perennial has many-branched stems carrying a succession of simple deep magenta flowers, and downy gray foliage. Requires sun. H 20in (45cm) S 1ft (30cm) Z4-8

Malva sylvestris var. *mauritiana* TALL MALLOW A perennial that will produce rich purple flowers in its first year from seed. H 3ft (90cm) S 1ft (30cm) Z4-8

Petunia Surfinia cultivars Tender perennials grown as annuals that will flower all summer in shades of pink, purple, or white. Can be used as groundcover or to cascade out of pots. Overwinter with cuttings. H 8in (20cm) S 24in (60cm) [ill.pp.55,146]

Rosa ROSE Good shrub roses in this color range include 'Cerise Bouquet' which has a strong, graceful, arching habit, clusters of nearly double blooms of intense pink, and lots of prickles, H and S 6ft (1.8m) Z5-9; 'Charles de Mills' which has the strong scent of a Gallica rose and purplish magenta flowers, H 4ft (1.2m) S 3ft (1m) Z5-9 [ill.p.157]; 'Chianti' which is free-blooming with clusters of rich purple-maroon flowers, H and S 5ft (1.5m) Z5-9 [ill.p.163]; and 'William Lobb' which has mossy buds that open purple and fade slightly to lavender gray (peg down the long new growths to get the most flowers), H and S 6ft6in (2m) Z5-9 [ill.pp.7,119]

Verbena A number of perennial hybrid verbenas are grown for their continual flowering. The following are good for containers, for groundcover or for the border: 'Homestead Purple' which is a rich crimson purple; and 'Sissinghurst' which is deep pink [ill.pp.53,55, 121,182]. All H 12in (30cm) S 18in (45cm) Z6-9

Mid-Pinks

SPRING

Anemone coronaria St Brigid Group POPPY ANEMONE Corm producing lacy leaves and large double or semi-double flowers in a range of colors. Tolerates sun or partial shade. H 12in (30cm) S 6in (15cm) Z7-9 [ill.p.116]

Bellis perennis Pomponette ENGLISH DAISY Perennial. This cultivated daisy has fully double flowers in shades of red, pink or white. Requires sun. H and S 6in (15cm) Z4-9 [ill.p.144]

Cornus florida f. *rubra* FLOWERING DOGWOOD Large shrub or small tree with an open, spreading habit, rosy foliage in spring with pink bracts and reddish new growth. Best in light shade in deep, lime-free soil. H 20ft (6m) S 25ft (8m) Z5-8

Cyclamen Tubers of *C. coum* produce rounded, prettily marked leaves and delicate flowers in a range of pinks and white. Will spread if happy, for instance in light woodland. H 6in (15cm) S 4in (10cm) Z5-9 [ill.pp.27,113]. *C. repandum* has variously marbled and toothed leaves, and flowers with slightly twisted petals. Prefers deep shade. H 4in (10cm) S 6in (15cm) Z6-9

Daphne mezereum FEBRUARY DAPHNE Shrub wreathed in sweetly-scented rose-pink flowers in late winter, before the leaves appear. Tolerates sun and partial shade in moist, alkaline soil. H and S 4ft (1.2m) Z4-7

Erythronium Tuberous perennial that requires partial shade and moist soil. *E. dens-canis* DOG'S TOOTH VIOLET has green leaves spotted purple-brown, and pink or lilac flowers with reflexed petals. H and S 6in (15cm) Z4-8. *E. revolutum* TROUT LILY has gently mottled leaves and delicate pink flowers on taller stems. H 12in (30cm) S 6in (15cm) Z5-8

Primula denticulata DRUMSTICK PRIMULA Perennial with round flowerheads in white, lavender-blue, as well as pinks, on a stout stem that elongates as it develops. Tolerates sun or partial shade in moist soil. H 2ft (60cm) S 18in (45cm) Z5-9 [ill.p.54]

Tulipa TULIP Bulb needing a sunny position. Good tulips for late spring in this color range include Lily-flowered 'China Pink' H 22in (55cm) S 9in (23cm) Z3-9; and Triumph tulip 'Peerless Pink' H 15in (40cm) S 9in (23cm) Z3-9 [ill.p.112]

Bougainvillea glabra (**Summer**)

Lychnis coronaria (**Summer**)

Rosa 'Charles de Mills' (**Summer**)

Cyclamen repandum (**Spring**)

Erythronium dens-canis (**Spring**)

SUMMER

Allium ORNAMENTAL ONION
Perennial bulb needing sun.
A. carinatum subsp. **pulchellum**
KEELED GARLIC has graceful
miniature fountains of pink
flowers. H 2ft (60cm) S 4in
(10cm) Z6-9. **A. cernuum**
LADY'S LEEK is unusual in its
nodding flowerheads, varying
from pale pink to deep rose-
purple. Lacks the oniony smell.
H 28in (70cm) S 5in (12cm)
Z3-7

Armeria maritima THRIFT
Evergreen perennial forming
mats of threadlike foliage, with
fragrant pink flowers. Requires
sun. H 4in (10cm) S 12in
(30cm) Z4-8 [ill.p.176]

Astrantia maxima
Clump-forming perennial with
bold three-fingered red foliage,
and long-lasting pink flowers.
Best in sun. H 24in (60cm)
S 12in (30cm) Z5-7 [ill.p.178]

Cistus 'Peggy Sammons'
Evergreen shrub with pleasing
clear pink flowers and grayish
foliage. Requires sun. H and S
3ft3in (1m) Z8-10

Clematis
Most tolerate sun or partial
shade in alkaline soil, but need
a cool root run. Good climbing
varieties include **'Comtesse de
Bouchard'** with abundant
flowers, and should be cut back
hard in late winter, H and S 10ft
(3m) Z6-8; **C. montana** var.

rubens ANEMONE CLEMATIS
which produces vanilla-scented
flowers in spring, as the purplish
foliage appears; it does not
need pruning, H 40ft (12m)
S 10ft (3m) Z6-8; and **C. m.
'Tetrarose'** which has slightly
larger and richer foliage and
flowers, although is less
vigorous, H 25ft (7.5m) S 10ft
(3m) Z6-8

Cleome hassleriana (syn. *C.
spinosa*) SPIDER FLOWER Annual
with pretty, spidery flowers in
shades of rose, purple, and
white. Aromatic foliage and
spiny stems. Requires sun.
H 4ft (1.2m) S 3ft (90cm)

Cosmos bipinnatus
Annual with feathery foliage
and stout stems flowering in
various pinks and whites
[ill.p.163]. **'Imperial Pink'** is a
strong pink [ill.pp.11,55,114].
Requires sun and moist soil.
H 4ft (1.2m) S 30in (75cm)

Dianthus CARNATION/PINK
Evergreen perennial, ideally
grown in a sunny open position
over chalk [ill.p.7]. The alpine
hybrid **'Pike's Pink'** makes an
extensive, weed-smothering
mat of foliage, and has well-
scented pale pink double
flowers. H 6in (15cm) S 1ft
(30cm) Z4. Modern pinks such
as **'Gran's Favorite'** which has
laced flowers, raspberry on
white, have strong blue-gray
foliage. H 10in (25cm) S15in
(40cm) Z4-8

Diascia 'Ruby Field' TWINSPUR
Half-hardy perennial that makes
neat mats of small green leaves
with generous sprays of salmon-
pink flowers from midsummer.
Requires sun and soil that is not
too dry. H 6in (15cm) S 12in
(30cm) Z6-8 [ill.p.112]

Dicentra spectabilis BLEEDING
HEART Perennial with heart-
shaped rosy flowers that dangle
from elegantly arching stems
and prettily divided foliage. Best
in humus-rich soil. H 30in
(75cm) S 20in (50cm) Z3-8
[ill.pp.112]

Dierama pulcherrimum FAIRY WAND
Evergreen perennial with grassy
foliage and deep pink bell-like
blossoms that shower from tall,
wiry stems in late summer.
Requires a sheltered, sunny site
and moist soil. H 5ft (1.5m)
S 12in (30cm) Z7-9 [ill.p.116]

Digitalis FOXGLOVE
D. purpurea is biennial with tall
spikes of pink, purple or white
flowers, spotted on the inside.
H 5ft (1.5m) S 18in (45cm)
Z4-8 [ill.pp.113,175]. **D. x
mertonensis** STRAWBERRY FOXGLOVE
is perennial if divided after
flowering, and has much shorter
flower spikes of a buff rose color.
H 2ft (60cm) S 1ft (30cm) Z5-8
[ill.p.131]. Both do best in partial
shade and moist soil.

Echinacea purpurea PURPLE
CONEFLOWER Perennial for late
summer with robust daisy-
flowers, each with a distinctive,

prominent central boss.
E. p. 'Bright Star' (syn. *E. p.*
'Leuchstern') is a good cultivar
[ill.p.57]. Needs sun and a
humus-rich soil. H 4ft (1.2m)
S 18in (45cm) Z3-9

Geranium CRANESBILL
Invaluable border perennials.
G. cinereum 'Ballerina' makes
neat mounds of rounded,
gray-green foliage, and has
relatively large lilac-pink flowers
with darker veining. H 4in
(10cm) S 12in (30cm) Z4-9.
G. x oxonianum 'Claridge Druce'
is a vigorous spreader, making
weed-proof clumps and has rich
rose pink flowers over a long
season. H and S 3ft (1m) Z4-9.
**G. x riversleaianum 'Russell
Prichard'** has similar foliage but
is shorter, and has magenta
flowers over a very long period
from midsummer. H 9in (23cm)
S 3ft (90cm) Z7-9 [ill.p.119]

Helianthemum 'Wisley Pink'
(syn. *H.* 'Rhodanthe Carneum')
SUN ROSE Evergreen shrub that
makes a spreading mound of
silver-gray foliage with myriads
of short-lived pink flowers.
Needs sun. H 18in (45cm)
S 24in (60cm) Z6-9 [ill.p.180]

Lathyrus PEA
Perennial **L. grandiflorus**
EVERLASTING PEA has largish
flowers of deep magenta with
lighter pink. Suckers and can be
invasive. H 5ft (1.5m) Z6-9
[ill.p.163]. Perennial **L. latifolius**
PERENNIAL SWEET PEA has robust,

almost lush, flowers over a long
period, sadly lacking scent.
Strong magenta, pink, pale
pink, and white forms are
available. H and S 6ft (1.8m) Z5-
9 [ill.p.54]. Annual **L. odoratus**
SWEET PEA has a unique and
indispensable scent. Many
different color forms available
as seed. H and S 6ft (1.8m). All
need sun and humus-rich soil.

Lavatera MALLOW
L. trimestris 'Silver Cup' is a
bushy annual smothered in
large glowing pink trumpets.
H and S 24in (60cm). **'Rosea'**
TREE MALLOW is a quick-growing
shrubby plant with downy,
sage-green leaves, and soft pink
flowers in quantity through
summer and fall. H and S 10ft
(3m) Z7-9 [ill.pp.53,184]

Lilium LILY
Bulb. **L. martagon** TURKSCAP LILY
has nodding flowers with
reflexed petals in shades
ranging from white through
dull pink to wine-red and buff,
variously spotted. Will self-seed
if happy, in humus-rich soil.
H 4ft (1.2m) Z4-9. **L. speciosum**
var. **rubrum** has larger flowers,
carmine pink and white spotted.
H 5ft (1.5m) Z5-9. Good hybrids
include **'Journey's End,'** which is
also carmine pink and white,
H 5ft (1.5m) Z4-9; and the
Pink Perfection Group which
are pink with deep carmine
reverse, H 4ft (1.2m) Z4-9
[ill.p.184]

Allium carinatum subsp. *pulchellum*
(Summer)

Clematis montana 'Tetrarose'
(Summer)

Digitalis x *mertonensis* **(Summer)**

Geranium x *riversleaianum* 'Russell
Prichard' **(Summer)**

Lilium speciosum var. *rubrum*
(Summer)

Lupinus 'The Chatelaine' LUPINE Perennial with pretty palmate foliage and stout flower spikes in two-tone pink and white. Best in sandy, well-drained soil in sun. H 4ft (1.2m) S 18in (45cm) Z4-8 [ill.pp.2,184]

Nicotiana x *sanderae* FLOWERING TOBACCO The annual tobacco plants produce their five-pointed flowers profusely all summer, and have the bonus of being sweetly scented. Best in sun. H 30in (75cm) S 12in (30cm) [ill.p.163]

Osteospermum 'Pink Whirls' FREEWAY DAISY A half-hardy perennial making tufts of narrow, aromatic leaves, with soft old rose pink daisy flowers from early summer until the frosts. Requires sun. H and S 2ft (60cm) Z8-10 [ill.p.109]

Paeonia lactiflora PEONY In the wild this perennial has large single white flowers with silky petals and yellow stamens, but in cultivation a broad color range of blooms, single and double, has arisen. Good pink cultivars include single 'Bowl of Beauty' and double, paler pink 'Sarah Bernhardt'. Prefers sun. H and S 2ft (60cm) Z4-8 [ill.p.113]

Penstemon 'Evelyn' BEARD TONGUE Semi-evergreen perennial that makes a bushy plant covered in tubular pink flowers from midsummer. Requires sun. H 18in (45cm) S 15in (40cm) Z6-9 [ill.pp.53,157,181]

Phlox paniculata 'Bright Eyes' GARDEN PHLOX Perennial forming clumps of tall stout stems topped with large pink sweetly-scented flowerheads. Best in moist soil. Tolerates sun and partial shade. H 4ft (1.2m) S 2ft (60cm) Z4-8

Rehmannia elata CHINESE FOXGLOVE Perennial that makes a clump of soft, prettily-lobed leaves, and has surprisingly large foxglove-like flowers of a rich pink with orangey markings. H 3ft (1m) S 18in (45cm) Z8-10 [ill.p.112]

Rosa ROSE Good climbing varieties include: 'Mme Grégoire Staechelin', a vigorous climbing Hybrid Tea with good foliage and large pale pink flowers, deeper on the reverse, H 20ft (6m) S 12ft (3.7m) Z5-9 [ill.p.65]; and 'Zéphirine Drouhin', thornless, with fragrant flowers that repeat well H 8ft (2.4m) S 6ft (1.8m) Z5-9. Good shrub roses include: 'Complicata' with long arching stems with flat, single pink flowers all along their length, in midsummer, H 7ft (2.1m) S 8ft (2.4m) Z4-9; 'Comte de Chambord' with fragrant pinkish lilac flowers, and an erect habit, H 4ft (1.2m) S 3ft (90cm) Z5-9 [ill.pp.176,178]; 'De Rescht' with small brilliant flowers that verge on magenta. H 4ft (1.2m) S 3ft (90cm) Z5-9 [ill.p.162]; *R. gallica officinalis* APOTHECARY'S ROSE with soft light green foliage and deep pink flowers, generously borne although not repeated, H and S 3ft (90cm) Z5-9 [ill.p.116]; and *R. g.* 'Versicolor' ROSA MUNDI\ FRENCH ROSE is similar, but the flowers are splashed pink and white, H 30in (75cm) S 3ft (90cm) Z5-9 [ill.p.162]

Salvia involucrata 'Bethellii' Perennial with rich green, aromatic leaves and large spikes of bright cerise flowers with pink bracts: lovely in bud. Requires sun. H 5ft (1.5m) S 3ft (90cm) Z7-9 [ill.p.55]

Sidalcea malviflora 'William Smith' PRAIRIE MALLOW Perennial with silky flowers on stately branching spires. Requires sun. H 36in (120cm) S 15in (5cm) Z5-7

Silene dioica RED CAMPION Perennial with clear pink flowers over dark hairy leaves; the double *S. d.* 'Flore Pleno' has a blowsy charm H 2ft (60cm) S 1ft (30cm) Z4-8

Weigela florida Makes a large shrub, with a generous crop of deep pink, funnel-shaped flowers in early summer. Requires sun. H and S 8ft (2.5m) Z4-9

FALL

Colchicum speciosum AUTUMN CROCUS Also known as Naked Ladies, as this bulb flowers without its leaves. The large, shiny leaves appear in spring, then die down. Requires an open, sunny situation. H and S 6-8in (15-20cm) Z4-9 [ill.p.146]

Cyclamen hederifolium (syn. C. *neapolitanum*) HARDY CYCLAMEN Tuberous perennial with delicate pink or white flowers with re-flexed petals followed by pretty heart-shaped leaves, variously marked with silver. Tolerates sun and shade and requires humus-rich soil. H 4in (10cm) S 6in (15cm) Z5-9 [ill.p.147]

Nerine bowdenii Bulb that throws up a cluster of bright pink flowers on a tallish stem in fall; the color is a wonderful shock so late in the year. Tolerates full sun and requires a light sandy soil. H 24in (60cm) S 6in (15cm) Z7-9

Schizostylis coccinea 'Mrs Hegarty' KAFFIR LILY Spreading rhizomes produce tufts of narrow leaves followed by strong stems of flowers of a pretty pale pink. Requires sun and moist soil. H 24in (60cm) S 12in (30cm) Z6-9

Sedum STONECROP Perennial requiring sun. 'Autumn Joy' (syn. 'Herbstfreude') has stout clumps of fleshy gray-green leaves and large flower-heads that turn rich pink and, gradually, coppery red. H and S 2ft (60cm) Z3-9 [ill.pp.146, 171]. 'Ruby Glow' is a sprawler, with deep crimson flowers and gray leaves. H to 9in (to 23cm) S 18in 45cm) Z5-9 [ill.p.53]

Pale Pinks

SPRING

Daphne x *burkwoodii* 'Somerset' Semi-evergreen shrub. Small, narrow leaves and gloriously scented flowers in late spring. Requires full sun but not dry soil. H and S 4ft (1.2m) Z5-8

Magnolia Shrub requiring neutral to acid soil, but tolerant of pollution. M. x *loebneri* 'Leonard Messel' has elegant, slender-petalled flowers that appear before the leaves. H 25ft (8m) S 20ft (6m) Z5-9. M. x *soulangeana* SAUCER MAGNOLIA is a wide-spreading shrub or small tree with large tulip-shaped flowers, white flushed purple, on bare branches. H and S 20ft (6m) Z5-9

Malus floribunda JAPANESE CRAB APPLE A gracefully spreading tree, early to flower. Deep pink buds open to pale pink, and are followed by small red and yellow fruits. Prefers full sun. H and S 30ft (10m) Z4-7

Tulipa TULIP Bulb that needs a sunny situation and appreciates summer baking. 'Angélique' is Peony-flowered. H 16in (40cm) [ill.p.111]. 'Elegant Lady' is Lily-flowered, cream edged with mauve-pink. H 18in (45cm). 'Meissner Porzellan' is ivory-flushed, apple blossom pink. H 15in (40cm) [ill.p.53].

Paeonia 'Bowl of Beauty' **(Summer)**

Rosa 'Zéphirine Drouhin' **(Summer)**

Sidalcea malviflora 'William Smith' **(Summer)**

Sedum 'Autumn Joy' **(Fall)**

Magnolia x *leobneri* 'Leonard Messel' **(Spring)**

'Pandour' appears pink although it is pale yellow flamed red, with mottled foliage. H 12in (30cm) [ill.p.53]. All Z3-9

SUMMER

Clematis
Climbing varieties that prefers partial shade with a cool root run include 'Duchess of Albany' with small tulip-shaped flowers; and 'Hagley Hybrid' with large rosy-mauve flowers with purplish anthers, produced in quantity for three months at midsummer. Both H and S 8ft (2.5m) Z3-9

Dianthus 'Doris' PINK
Evergreen perennial producing a succession of well-scented flowers, pink with a ring of deeper pink. Prefers an open, sunny situation in slightly alkaline soil. H and S 12in (30cm) Z4-8

Diascia TWINSPUR
Perennial requiring sun. *D. fetcaniensis* has creeping stems clothed in small rounded leaves and loose spikes of flowers. H 15in (40cm) S 18in (45cm) Z8-9. *D. rigescens* has a denser habit with stiffer flower stems crowded with coppery-pink flowers. H 9in (23cm) S 12in (30cm) Z8-9 [ill.p.131]

Erigeron karvinskianus (syn. *E. mucronatus*) FLEABANE Charming but untidy perennial producing dainty daisies throughout the summer. Likes to seed itself around warm, sunny walls and steps. H 8in (20cm) S 12in (30cm) Z4-8

Geranium CRANESBILL
Invaluable border perennials. *G. x oxonianum* 'Wargrave Pink' has small flowers over attractive, lobed, semi-evergreen foliage. H 18in (45cm) S 24in (60cm) Z4-8 [ill.p.180]. *G. macrorrhizum* 'Ingwersen's Variety' BIG ROOT GERANIUM makes particularly good groundcovering clumps of aromatic foliage. H 12in (30cm) S 24in (60cm) Z5-9. *G.* 'Mavis Simpson' has gray-green leaves, and clear pink flowers. H 18in (45cm) S 24in (6-60cm) Z7-9

Hemerocallis 'Catherine Woodbery' DAYLILY Semi-evergreen perennial with flowers of palest peach flushed crimson, and very fragrant. Requires full sun and moist soil. H 28in (70cm) S 30in (75cm) Z3-9 [ill.p.57]

Kolkwitzia amabilis BEAUTY BUSH
A graceful shrub with an arching habit, softly draped with masses of bell-shaped flowers in early summer. Requires full sun. H and S 10ft (3m) Z5-9

Lavatera 'Barnsley' TREE MALLOW
Shrub with soft gray-green foliage and an abundance of pale pink flowers with a red eye. Requires sun. H 6ft (1.8m) S 5ft (1.5m) Z4-9 [ill.p.176]

Lonicera periclymenum 'Belgica' WOODBINE\HONEYSUCKLE Climber with tubular flowers that are creamy inside, deep pink outside, and very fragrant in the evening. Tolerates sun and shade. H and S 10ft (3m) Z5-9 [ill.p.56]

Monarda 'Beauty of Cobham' BEE BALM/BERGAMOT Perennial with aromatic, purplish foliage, and pale pink tufts of flowers. H 3ft (1m) S 18in (45cm) Z4-9 [ill.p.57]

Papaver orientale ORIENTAL POPPY
Perennials that die back by midsummer, so careful siting is required. Petals emerge like crepe paper from furry buds. Good varieties include: *P. o.* 'Degas' which has salmon-pink flowers with black blotches; and salmon-pink *P. o.* 'Mrs Perry' [ill.p.180]. Best in full sun. H and S 3ft (90cm) Z3-8

Penstemon 'Apple Blossom' BEARD TONGUE Semi-evergreen bushy perennial producing pale pink tubular flowers all summer. Best in full sun. H and S 18in (45cm) Z5-8 [ill.p.176]

Rosa ROSE
Good climbing varieties include 'Albertine' with copper-pink buds and a fruity scent. H 15ft (5m) S 10ft (3m) Z5-9 [ill.p.56]; 'Blairii Numer Two' shell-pink and susceptible to mildew, H 12ft (3.5m) S 6ft (1.8m) Z5-9 [ill.p.114]; 'Francis E. Lester' with clusters of very pale scented, single flowers, tolerant of shade, and suitable for growing up trees, H 15ft (4.5m) S 10ft (3m) Z5-9 [ill.p.183];

'New Dawn' has palest silvery pink, well-formed flowers, and is tolerant of shade, H and S 15ft (5m) Z5-9 [ill.pp.176,178]; and 'Paul's Himalayan Musk' which makes a curtain of small, double sweet-scented flowers, H and S 30ft (10m) Z5-9. Good shrub roses include 'Céleste' (syn. *R.* 'Celestial') with flat, shell-pink flowers, good for hedging, H 5ft (1.5m) S 4ft (1.2m) Z5-9; 'Fantin-Latour' a blowsy, sweet-scented old rose, H 5ft (1.5m) S 4ft (1.2m) Z5; and 'Königin von Dänemark' with beautifully formed flowers, H 5ft (1.5m) S 4ft (1.2m) Z5-9

Verbena 'Silver Anne'
Vigorous trailing, tender perennial with small fragrant flowerheads, good for containers and raised beds. Requires sun. H 8in (20cm) S 18in (45cm) Z8-10 [ill.p.121]

FALL

Amaryllis belladonna BELLADONNA LILY Bulb with sweetly fragrant flowers that darken as they age, and broad strap-shaped leaves that appear later. Requires a sunny, sheltered situation. H 20in (50cm) S 12in (30cm) Z8-10 [ill.p.121]

Anemone x hybrida (syn *A. japonica*) JAPANESE ANEMONE
Perennial making hearty clumps of lobed, dark green leaves that throw up branching stems of rounded rose-pink flowers; a feature of late fall. Tolerates sun and partial shade and requires humus-rich soil. H 5ft (1.5m) S 2ft (60cm) Z5-8 [ill.pp.53,107]

Dendranthema (formerly *Chrysanthemum*) Perennial with daisy-like flowers that last from late summer through the fall. A vast number of varieties are available, in colors ranging from wine-red, through pinks to rust, yellow, and white, with different ones suitable for gardens or greenhouse. H from 12in (30cm) to 5ft (1.5m) [ill.p.53]

BERRIES

Sorbus vilmorinii
Tree with elegant, ferny foliage that colors in the fall. Hanging clusters of rosy fruits gradually fade to pinky-white. Tolerates sun and partial shade in moist soil. H and S 20ft (6m) Z6-7

WINTER

Prunus x subhirtella 'Autumnalis Rosea' AUTUMN FLOWERING CHERRY Tree that produces semi-double blush pink flowers intermittently throughout the winter. H and S 15ft (8m) Z6-8

Viburnum x bodnantense 'Dawn'
Erect, arching shrub, with clusters of fragrant rose pink flowers over a long period. Tolerates sun and partial shade in not too dry soil. H 10ft (3m) S 6ft (1.8m) Z5-7 [ill.p.171]

Erigeron karvinskianus (**Summer**)

Hemerocallis 'Catherine Woodbery' (**Summer**)

Rosa 'Paul's Himalayan Musk' (**Summer**)

Rosa 'Königin von Dänemark' (**Summer**)

Viburnum x botnantense 'Dawn' (**Winter**)

Violets

Violet is one of the richest colors in the garden. Deep violet flowers create a serious mood and have a somber quality that can be used to offset the exuberance of brighter flower colors. True violet is the color on the edge of the rainbow; it actually extends over the edge, merging with ultra-violet that the human eye cannot detect. Bees and other insects can perceive it, and this explains why they are most attracted to violet and related colors that reflect ultra-violet.

Violet is a cool color, almost as cool as blue, and so in the garden it may tend to recede and take a background role. Like the wayside flower from which it takes its name, violet can be discreet and retiring. It is also a fugitive color, in the sense that the slightest addition of another hue tips the color away from violet. Add red to violet and it becomes purple. Add a touch of blue, and the violet appears more blue than violet. As if to emphasize the transient nature of these colors, violet and blue flowers sometimes appear far pinker in photographs than they do to the eye.

Because it is so recessive, violet needs to be isolated from stronger colors to maximize its effect. As in the planting *opposite, above left*, devote a sunny bed to deep violet aubrieta and a single variety of velvet-petalled bearded iris; enjoy the depth of color of the darker pansies and violets by planting them *en masse* with spring vetchling for a mid-spring show as pictured *opposite, above right*; or entwine two violet clematis on a trellis obelisk, *right*.

For subdued harmonious associations, partner violet and lilac flowers with blue and blue-pink flowers. The horned violet for instance, looks marvellous as an underplanting for old-fashioned pink roses. The cottage garden annual clary comes in seed mixtures of violet, pink, and cream, which harmonize well together and look equally good mixed with blue larkspurs and cornflowers. For a much richer color incident in the garden, deep violet flowers can make a sumptuous combination with strong reds and oranges. Try planting violet pansies with fierce red tulips such as *Tulipa praestans*.

Violet is also the darkest color in the color wheel and therefore the nearest to black. Its complementary color is yellow, the lightest of the rainbow colors. But when you exploit this relationship and place a dark violet heliotrope, say, with a golden marguerite, the light-dark contrast makes a louder statement than the color contrast. For a more balanced contrast of the two colors, use unsaturated versions of each: the pale violet milky bellflower, for instance, will make a good partner for pale yellow dusty meadow rue.

ABOVE Two clematis, the purple-violet C. 'Etoile Violette' and the blue-violet C. 'Perle d'Azur', make good partners because they both flower in midsummer, and both do best if they are pruned back hard in the late winter. Here, together with an annual sweet pea of similar color, they clamber up a sturdy wooden obelisk stained dark green so that it merges with the foliage.

ABOVE The dwarf bearded irises are almost the same violet as the *Aubrieta* 'Doctor Mules', that accompanies them, but the camera distorts the relationship, giving the aubrieta a pink cast. Both plants enjoy similar sunny, dry conditions.

ABOVE RIGHT Violets and pansies together with two distinct varieties of the spring vetchling (*Lathyrus vernus*) make up this tightly knit spring grouping at the front of a border. The base color of this vetchling and of most violets is violet, but they can both be highly variable.

RIGHT Lying flat across the top of a wall, a clematis (*C.* 'Jackmanii Superba') makes a color link with the Black Knight delphinium, and with clumps of Brazilian verbena (*Verbena bonariensis*) in the border beyond. Clematis is usually grown vertically up walls and fences, but you can also encourage it to grow horizontally through a border, supported by other shrubs, where the color of its flowers can relate more closely with those of the other plants.

Soft Violets

BELOW LEFT An ancient wall supports a chinese wisteria (*W. sinensis*), and shelters the somewhat tender but fast-growing vine leaved flowering maple (*Abutilon vitifolium*). Prune both plants in midsummer: cut back the side shoots of the wisteria to three buds, and tidy the vine leaved flowering maple by reducing the laterals.

BELOW RIGHT The 'Lasurstern' clematis needs support, which it receives here from the semi-evergreen potato vine (*Solanum crispum* 'Glasnevin'). This, in turn, is supported by wires attached to the wall.

In its paler, unsaturated forms, violet becomes lilac, mauve, and lavender. Colors in this range can vary with the age of the flower: violet flowers often fade to mauve as they pass their prime. Light conditions also have an effect: in the cool light of deep shade or after sundown, lilac can seem quite blue; in warm light, as at sunrise and sunset, it appears pink.

Violet is a recessive color, and the shy charms of its paler, softer versions are even more easily overlooked. So plant it with closely related colors so that it does not have to compete for attention, and plant it abundantly to make a lasting impression. Curtain a wall with a combination of wisteria and vine leaved flowering maple, as pictured *below left*, or with a potato vine and clematis, *below right*. Or make the most of this retiring color in a whole planting, such as the herb garden *opposite*. Many herb flowers occur in soft violet, from the chives of early summer to the thymes, hyssop, lavender, sages, and catmints of high summer.

ABOVE An herb garden occupying the narrow space between a stone wall that supports a 'Mme Grégoire Staechelin' rose and a tunnel of apple trees, has been planned so that several lilac flowered herbs bloom simultaneously in summer. Chives (*Allium schoenoprasum*) have been partnered with their taller relatives, the Persian onion (*Allium aflatunense*) and color matched with a narrow leaved sage (*Salvia lavandulifolia*) and the alternate leaf butterfly bush (*BuddleJa alternifolia*).

Deep Purple-Violet

The slightest hint of red tips the color violet toward purple and magenta. You can exploit violet's range by putting together flowers that are close but not identical in hue, so that the colors shimmer together like a rich shade of shot silk. Large flowered clematis, like those pictured *right above,* are ideal candidates for this treatment because they include such a wide choice of hybrids with similar flowers but subtly different hues. Petunias offer similar opportunities for close color matching. You may prefer to put together flowers of contrasting shapes, in which case violet irises with the Persian onion – as in the planting *right below* – or Michaelmas daisies with salvias would make stimulating pairs.

To introduce a color that will make an attractive contrast to deep purple-violet, try muted yellows such as the lime-yellow of spurge flowers, or the palest lemons of evening primrose or of the mullein, *Verbascum* 'Gainsborough'.

RIGHT ABOVE To grow clematis together, like the violet 'The President' shown here with the magenta 'Niobe', you should plant them about 3ft/90cm apart so that their roots do not compete for nourishment. Weave the young shoots together by regularly tying them onto a support of wire mesh or wires attached to a wall or fence.

RIGHT Encourage bearded irises to flower by making sure that their rhizomes are undisturbed on the surface of the soil and letting them bake in the sun after flowering. The Persian onion (*Allium aflatunense* 'Purple Sensation') is an appropriate companion plant because there is room for its bulbs between the iris rhizomes, and its foliage dies back in summer, and does not compete for light and heat.

Deep and Mid Violets

SPRING

Aquilegia vulgaris COLUMBINE
Perennial with intriguing crown-shaped flowers with long spurs. The colors are higly variable, coming in violet, blue, pink and cream which cross and mix promiscuously. Needs sun or partial shade. H 3ft (90cm) S 20in (50cm) Z5-9 [ill.pp.73,183]

Aubrieta 'Doctor Mules'
Evergreen perennial to fill cracks between stones. Use to soften the edges of walls and steps. Best in full sun. H 6in (15cm) S 18in (45cm) Z5-7 [ill.p.63]

Crocus tommasinianus 'Whitewell Purple' TOMMASINI'S CROCUS The flowers of this corm open in full sun, revealing bright orange stamens. It will naturalize in undisturbed ground. H 4in (10cm) S 3in (8cm) Z5-9

Lathyrus vernus SPRING VETCHLING
Non-climbing perennial pea that makes a compact mound. Highly variable with pale pink and creamy forms as well as violet. Needs humus-rich soil and full sun. Difficult to transplant. H and S 12in (30cm) Z5-9 [ill.p.63]

Tulipa 'Negrita' TULIP
Bulb that produces a good tall, sturdy, late-flowering tulip. H 20in (50cm) S 9in (23cm) Z3-9 [ill.p.112]

Viola VIOLET
The wild violets are best, but good cultivated evergreen perennial violets include *V. riviniana* Purpurea Group PURPLE DOG VIOLET with dark purple foliage, H 4in (10cm) S 8in (20cm) Z3-8; and *V. odorata* SWEET VIOLET H 3in (7cm) S 10in (25cm) Z5-8 [ill.p.136] All tolerate both sun and shade.

SUMMER

Allium ORNAMENTAL ONION
Bulbous perennials with eye-catching spherical flowerheads that like an open, sunny position. Good varieties include *A. aflatunense* PERSIAN ONION H 30in (75cm) S 8in (20cm) Z4-8 [ill.pp.65,139,176,183]; and deeper violet *A. a.* 'Purple Sensation' H 30in (75cm) S 8in (20cm) Z4-8 [ill.pp.11,66,108]

Brachyscome iberidifolia SWAN RIVER DAISY Prolifically flowering annual, useful in containers. Needs a sunny, sheltered position. H and S 18in (45cm)

Buddleja davidii BUTTERFLY BUSH
Late-summer flowers in pointed racemes are irresistible to butterflies. Regular dead-heading needed to make the shrub look tidy. Requires full sun. H and S 15ft (5m) Z5-9

Campanula BELLFLOWER
Good perennial varieties include *C. lactiflora* MILKY BELLFLOWER which makes dense clumps covered with a mass of open bell-shaped flowers, H 4ft (1.2m) S 2ft (60cm) Z3-8; and *C. persicifolia* PEACH-LEAF BELLFLOWER which has tall spires of flowers that self-seed freely, H 3ft (1m) S 12in (30cm) Z3-8 [ill.p.174]. All tolerate both sun and shade, and benefit from regular division and replanting.

Clematis
Good summer-flowering climbing varieties include 'Etoile Violette' which is covered with small velvet-textured flowers in late summer, H and S 12ft (4m) Z5-9 [ill.p.62]; 'Jackmanii Superba' with large flowers with sepals lightly striped purple. S 10ft (3m) Z3-9 [ill.p.63]; 'The President' with large flowers with pointed sepals, H and S 10ft (3m) Z3-9 [ill.p.66]; and late-flowering *C. viticella* ITALIAN CLEMATIS that produces a mass of small, bell-shaped flowers H and S 10ft (3m) Z5-8 [ill.p.150]. Most like sun but a shaded root run.

Delphinium
Violet and lilac varieties of this perennial that carries its flowers on spires include King Arthur Group, 'Honey Bee' and 'Purple Triumph'. Requires an open, sunny position. H 6ft (1.8m) S 2ft (60cm) Z3-9

Erigeron 'Darkest of All' OREGON FLEABANE Perennial producing a mass of daisy flowers with yellow eyes. Needs sun and moist soil, but resents winter damp. H 32in (80cm) S 24in (60cm) Z2-9

Erysimum 'Bowles' Mauve'
Makes a mound of blue-green foliage, covered prolifically with flower-spikes through the season. A somewhat short-lived perennial that needs to be propagated by cuttings and replaced every three or four years. Requires sun. H 30in (75cm) S 4ft (1.2m) Z5-8 [ill.p.109,116,132]

Galega orientalis GOAT'S RUE
Perennial member of the pea family, with pea-like flowerheads surmounting mounds of dense foliage which may need staking with peasticks. After flowering cut to the ground to encourage fresh foliage. Requires an open, sunny position. H 4ft (1.2m) S 2ft (60cm) Z3-9 [ill.p.181]

Geranium CRANESBILL
Indispensable perennial for the border, easy to grow, resistant to disease, and producing densely-covered domes of flowers. *G. x magnificum* needs sun, and tolerates any but waterlogged soil. H 2ft (60cm) S 3ft (90cm) Z4-8 [ill.pp.11,184]. *G. clarkei* 'Kashmir Purple' has rich purple flowers with reddish veins and deeply cut leaves. H and S 2ft (60cm) Z4-8. *G. pratense* 'Plenum Violaceum' MEADOW CRANESBILL has clusters of double flowers. H 30in (75cm) S 24in (60cm) Z4-8 [ill.p.183]. *G. sylvaticum* 'Mayflower' WOOD CRANESBILL has bright flowers with white centers, and prefers shade. H and S 24in (60cm) Z4-8

Hebe 'Autumn Glory'
Evergreen shrub that provides a reliable, if not particularly glamorous touch of violet for late summer. Grows well in coastal areas and likes full sun. H 2ft (60cm) S 30in (75cm) Z8-10

Heliotropium arborescens HELIOTROPE An evergreen shrub that is propagated by cuttings, or that may be used as an annual, grown from seed. Sweet-scented and tender, suited to planting out in pots, or growing in a conservatory where it can be trained as a standard. Likes full sun. A good variety is *H.* 'Marine'. H and S 2ft (60cm) Z9-10 [ill.p.147]

Iris
Several tall bearded varieties of this rhizomatous perennial are of such deep violet as to be near black. They include 'Dusky Challenger'. Their rhizomes need to bake in sun, and although the flowers are short-lived, fans of blue green sword shaped foliage are an asset H 3ft (90cm) S 18in (45cm) Z4-9 [ill.p.136]. The following irises prefer partial shade and water or bog garden conditions: *I. ensata* 'Royal Purple' JAPANESE WATER IRIS H 3ft (90cm) S 20in (50cm) Z5-9; and *I. laevigata* RABBIT EAR IRIS H 3ft (90cm) S 20in (50cm) Z5-9

Crocus tommasinianus 'Whitewell Purple' **(Spring)**

Brachyscome iberidifolia **(Summer)**

Clematis 'Jackmanii Superba' **(Summer)**

Geranium pratense 'Plenum Violaceum' **(Summer)**

Iris ensata 'Royal Purple' **(Summer)**

Lathyrus odoratus SWEET PEA
Many violet, purple and mauve varieties of this annual climber are available. Grow plants of a single color in a container to move around a border to augment a color scheme. Needs full sun and rich soil. H and S 10ft (3m) [ill.pp.62,175]

Lavandula LAVENDER
A gray-leaved aromatic shrub. Tender varieties can be grown in pots, to overwinter indoors. All require full sun and enjoy poor soil. *L. stoechas* subsp. *pedunculata* SPANISH LAVENDER has violet flowers that form little "topknots." H and S 18in (45cm) Z8-10 [ill.p.109]. *L. angustifolia* 'Hidcote' has dense spikes of very aromatic violet-blue flowers. H and S 2ft (60cm) Z5-9

Linaria purpurea TOADFLAX
Slender violet flower spikes provide useful vertical incidents. Perennial, but self-seeds freely in light soil. Tolerates full sun or light shade. H 3ft (1m) S 2ft (60cm) Z4-9

Lunaria annua (syn. *L. biennis*) HONESTY Biennial with violet-mauve flowers in summer followed by dainty wafer-thin seed-pods, surviving on the plant well into winter. Prefers light shade. H 30in (75cm) S 12in (30cm) [ill.p.167]

Papaver somniferum OPIUM POPPY
Varying in color from near-black purple through mauve to pink, and available in single and double forms, this annual poppy also produces a "pepperpot" seedpod. Tolerates sun or partial shade in moist soil. H 30in (75cm) S 1ft (30cm)

Penstemon BEARD TONGUE
Reliable producers of spires of foxglove-like flowers in a broad range of colors. Most need full sun. Good evergreen perennial varieties include *P. fruticosus* 'Purple Haze' which is suitable for rock gardens, H and S 12in (30cm) Z5-8; 'Midnight' H 2ft (60cm) S 15in (40cm) Z6-9

Rosa ROSE
Good climbing roses include 'Veilchenblau' which is especially suitable for arches and combines well with violet or blue. H 12ft (3.7m) S 7ft (2.1m) Z5-9. Good shrub roses include '**Reine des Violettes**' H 6ft (1.8m) S 5ft (1.5m) Z5-9

Salvia SAGE
Good perennial varieties include *S. lavandulifolia*, the narrow-leaved sage, with spikes of hooded flowers, H and S 2ft (60cm) Z8-10 [ill.p.65]; *S. nemorosa* '**East Friesland**' which puts up racemes of tightly packed small flowers, and looks best grown in generous clumps, H 30in (75cm) S 18in (45cm) Z5-9 [ill.p.119]; *S. pratensis* **Haematodes Group** MEADOW CLARY has branching spikes of larger, lilac-blue flowers, H 3ft (90cm) S 18in (45cm) Z7-9 [ill.p.175]; and *S. x superba* H 3ft (90cm) S 18in (45cm) Z5-9 [ill.p.183]. *S. officinalis* **Purpurascens Group** PURPLE SAGE is an evergreen shrubby herb grown for its velvety purple foliage. H 2ft (60cm) S 3ft (90cm) Z5-9 [ill.pp.149,182]. Most prefer sun.

Solanum crispum 'Glasnevin' POTATO VINE Semi-evergreen climber whose yellow-eyed flowers look like those of a potato. Requires full sun. H 20ft (6m) S 10ft (3m) Z7-9 [ill.p.64]

Verbascum phoeniceum PURPLE MULLEIN Annual or short-lived perennial that produces spires of small flowers of variable color; the best are reddish purple. Tolerates shade but prefers an open sunny site. H 3ft (90cm) S 18in (45cm) Z6-8

Verbena
Good varieties of this perennial, which prefers sun, include *V. bonariensis* BRAZILIAN VERBENA, a "see-through" plant, with small bobbles of violet flowers that wave in the wind, atop impossibly narrow stems. It will seed itself in sun-baked paths and terraces, H 5ft (1.5m) S 20in (50cm) Z7-10 [ill.p.146]; *V. rigida* RIGID VERBENA, often grown as an annual, has flowers slightly pinker and on shorter stems, but otherwise similar to *V. bonariens.*, H 24in (60cm) S 12in (30cm) Z8-10 [ill.pp.19, 63,139]

Viola VIOLET\PANSY
Good evergreen perennial varieties include '**Purple Showers**', '**Maggie Mott**' [ill.p.133] and '**Vita**' H 10in (25cm) S 15in (40cm) Z6-9; '**Prince Henry**' is deepest violet, verging on black and smaller, H 6in (15cm) S 10in (25cm) Z6-9. Good annual varieties include '**Universal Purple**' PANSY which will flower all through the winter in mild conditions. H and S 10in (25cm). All tolerate sun or shade and prefer cool conditions.

FALL

Callicarpa bodinieri var. *giraldii* 'Profusion' A shrub producing a mass of small violet berries that stand out dramatically against the yellow foliage of fall. Likes full sun. H 6ft (1.8m) S 5ft (1.5m) Z5-8

Liriope muscari BLUE LILYTURF
Evergreen, rhizomatous perennial whose small, round flowers, clustered in spikes among the grassy foliage, resemble berries. Useful as an edging plant. Requires sun. H and S 18in (45cm) Z5-9

Soft Violets

SPRING

Anemone blanda GRECIAN WINDFLOWER Tuberous perennial that will naturalize to make a soft violet carpet on the edge of woodland. Likes a humus-rich soil and will tolerate both full light and partial shade. H 4in (10cm) S 6in (15cm) Z4-8 [ill.p.136]

Clematis
Good spring-flowering climbers include *C. alpina* with single, nodding lantern-shaped flowers with white centers, H 10ft (3m) S 5ft (1.5m) Z3-9; and *C. macropetala* which has similar, but semi-double flowers, H 10ft (3m) S 3ft (1m) Z3-9. Both prefer partial shade.

Crocus tommasinianus TOMMASINI'S CROCUS The first crocus of spring, it may poke up through snow. Bright orange stigmas light up the wispy flowers when they open in sun. The corms need a sunny site to naturalize well. H 4in (10cm) S 3in (8cm) Z5-9 [ill.pp.27,113]

Hepatica nobilis LIVERLEAF
Semi-evergreen perennial, with three-lobed leaves. Cut away old foliage to expose the shy clumps of elegant, many-petalled cup-shaped flowers of variable color. Requires partial shade and deep, humus-rich soil. H 6in (15cm) S 10in (25cm) Z4-8

Tulipa TULIP
Good cultivars include '**Blue Parrot**' H 2ft (60cm) S 9in (23cm) Z3-9; and '**Lilac Perfection**' H 18in (45cm) S 9in (23cm) Z3-9. The bulbs need a sunny, open position and appreciate a good summer baking.

Lavandula angustifolia 'Hidcote' (**Summer**)

Salvia pratensis Haematodes Group (**Summer**)

Verbena bonariensis (**Summer**)

Liriope muscari (**Fall**)

Hepatica nobilis (**Spring**)

SUMMER

Abutilon vitifolium VINE LEAVED RED FLOWERING MAPLE Try growing this stately, fast-growing shrub against a sheltered wall on which you have trained a harmonizing wisteria. Tolerates sun and partial shade. H 12ft (4m) S 8ft (2.4m) Z8-10 [ill.p.64]

Allium ORNAMENTAL ONION Bulbous perennial that likes an open, sunny position. *A. christophii* DOWNY ONION, STAR OF PERSIA has large flowerheads that dry well. H 15in (40cm) S 8in (20cm) Z4-8 [ill.pp.175,182]. *A. rosenbachianum* has globe-shaped flowerheads on long stems, like bubbles of soft lilac in the border. H 3ft (1m) S 12in (30cm) Z4-8 [ill.p.10]. *A. schoenoprasum* CHIVES makes a good edging plant, not necessarily confined to the herb garden. H 10in (25cm) S 4in (10cm) Z3-9 [ill.p.65]. *A. schubertii* needs a sheltered spot to produce its enormous umbels of up to 18in (45cm) wide. H and S 30in (75cm) Z4-9

Buddleja BUTTERFLY BUSH Good varieties of this shrub include the early-summer flowering *B. alternifolia* ALTERNATE-LEAF BUTTERFLY BUSH that is usually trained as a standard, and produces long, arching wands of violet flowers. H and S 12ft (4m) [ill.p.65]. *B. davidii* var. *nanhoensis* has

flowers of a subtle pale violet-blue. H and S 10ft (3m). The more tender *B. davidii* 'Glasnevin' has felty gray-green foliage. H and S 6ft (1.8m) [ill.p.139]. All require full sun and cutting back hard in spring. All Z5-9

Campanula lactiflora 'Loddon Anna' MILKY BELLFLOWER Perennial producing clouds of milky lilac-pink flowers. Tolerates both sun and shade. H 4ft (1.2m) S 2ft (60cm) Z4-8 [ill.p.181]

Erigeron alpinus ALPINE FLEABANE Perennial that looks good colonizing a wall or raised bed, where it can bake in the sun. Resents winter damp, but do not allow to dry out in the summer. H 10in (25cm) S 8in (20cm) Z4-8

Galega officinalis GOAT'S RUE Very variable perennial, with lilac flowers usually bicolored with white. Requires an open, sunny site. H 5ft (1.5m) S 2ft (60cm) Z3-9

Hesperis matronalis DAME'S ROCKET Perennial that self-seeds through the border, producing frothy sweet-scented flowerheads. Will tolerate poor soil but does best in full sun. H 30in (75cm) S 2ft (60cm) Z4-9 [ill.p.109]

Hydrangea aspera Villosa Group Shrub with "lacecap" flower-heads that have pinkish central flowers and pale lilac outer ones. Likes moist soil in either sun or partial shade. H 10ft (3m) S 9ft (2.7m) Z7-9

Lantana montevidensis SHRUB VERBENA The flowers of this evergreen perennial have a sparkling yellow "eye". A conservatory plant in most climates, it needs full light. H 3ft 3in (1m) S 5ft (1.5m) Z8-10

Lavandula angustifolia COMMON LAVENDER Shrub with gray foliage that harmonizes with its own flowers. Amenable to shaping, it makes a good edging plant beside a path, because it releases its scent as you brush past. Requires full sun. H and S 30in (75cm) Z6-9

Limonium latifolium SEA LAVENDER Perennial producing a diaphanous cloud of tiny lilac flowers. Likes full sun. H 12in (30cm) S 18in (45cm) Z4-9 [ill.p.134,151]

Penstemon BEARD TONGUE Valuable for their long flowering season, which can be extended by cutting back finished flower-spikes. Good evergreen perennial varieties, which prefer full sun, include 'Stapleford Gem' H 20in (50cm) S 12in (30cm) Z6-9 [ill.pp.119,175,181]; 'Sour Grapes' H 15in (40cm) S 12in (30cm) Z8-9; and *P. virens* H 15in (40cm) S 12 (30cm) Z4-8

Prostanthera ovalifolia OVAL LEAVED MINT BUSH An evergreen shrub that will flower over a long period in a conservatory. Will grow in full sun or partial shade. H 6ft (1.8m) S 7ft (2.1m) Z9-10

Salvia SAGE *S. sclarea* var. *turkestanica* CLARY, a biennial grown as an annual, produces many spikes of hooded lilac and white flowers, making a soft cloud of color. It thrives in dry soil and needs sun. H 30in (75cm) S 12in (30cm) [ill.p.181]. *S. leucantha* MEXICAN BUSH SAGE, an evergreen shrub, has white flowers hung on purplish sepals to give a lilac haze. Needs sun. H and S 2ft (60cm) Z8-9

Syringa LILAC Good varieties that make small trees or large shrubs include *S. vulgaris* COMMON LILAC that has countless cultivars including 'Katherine Havemeyer' and 'Pocahontas' H 12ft (3.5m) S 10ft (3m) Z4-8. *S. x persica* PERSIAN LILAC has more delicate sprays of flowers, still with characteristic lilac scent. H and S 6ft (1.8m) Z4-7. All require sun and slightly alkaline soil.

Thalictrum MEADOW RUE Perennials with sprays of tiny flowers, suspended on slender stems, that create a haze of thin color. All require sun or light shade. Good varieties include *T. aquilegiifolium* COLUMBINE MEADOW RUE H 4ft (1.2m) S 18in (45cm) Z5-8; *T. delavayi* YUNNAN MEADOW RUE H 6ft (1.8m) S 2ft (60cm) Z5-8; *T. rochebruneanum* H 7ft (2.1m) S 30in (75cm) Z5-8

Verbena tenuisecta MOSS VERBENA Good perennial for a raised bed

or a container, where it can be allowed to hang down over the edge. Prefers sun. H 15in (40cm) S 30in (75cm) Z8-10 [ill.pp.109,181]

Viola cornuta HORNED VIOLET Prolifically flowering perennial that makes good under-planting for roses. Cut back to the ground when it begins to look shaggy and it will reward you with new growth and a further flush of flowers. Tolerates sun or partial shade. H 15in (40cm) S 24in (60cm) Z6-9 [ill.pp.114, 176,184]

Wisteria Slow-growing at first, this climber is unlikely to flower in the first ten years. With support it can be trained to make a weeping standard tree. Needs sun. Both *W. floribunda* JAPANESE WISTERIA H and S 30ft (9m) Z4-9 and *W. sinensis* CHINESE WISTERIA H and S 100ft (30m) Z5-9 [ill.p.64] have fragrant lilac- to violet-blue flowers on racemes followed by velvety pods in late summer.

WINTER

Iris unguicularis (syn. *I. stylosa*) ALGERIAN IRIS An evergreen rhizomatous perenial, this iris is better planted in clumps rather than singly. Requires a sunny, sheltered position and will tolerate lime and poor soil. H 15in (40cm) S 30in (75cm) Z7-9

Allium schoenoprasum (**Summer**)

Hesperis matronalis (**Summer**)

Penstemon 'Sour Grapes' (**Summer**)

Syringa 'Pocahontas' (**Summer**)

Iris unguicularis (syn. *I. stylosa*) (**Winter**)

ABOVE The palest blue striped squill (*Puschkinia scilloides* var. *libanotica*) with a blue stripe along each of its near white petals, is combined with the upward-facing star shaped glory-of-the-snow (*Chionodoxa luciliae*) and darker blue Armenian grape hyacinths (*Muscari armeniacum*) to make a glorious spring carpet. These, and other blue bulbs such as Siberian squill (*Scilla siberica*) are good for underplanting deciduous shrubs. In early spring the bare branches allow light to reach the bulbs' foliage, while in summer the dormant bulbs enjoy being shaded by the foliage above them, and being kept dry by the surrounding roots competing for moisture.

Blues

Blue is the quintessential cool color. Just the sight of sparkling blue water offers relief in the heat of summer. Blue also suggests space and distance, like the sky that stretches to infinity, and hills that seem bluer the farther away they are.

In the garden, blue carries similar connotations, suggesting coolness, space, and distance. Blue flowers act like frames in the garden picture, giving their neighbors a visual nudge forward while appearing to recede themselves. Put a bank of dark blue delphiniums at the back of a deep border, and you can imagine space stretching back far beyond them.

Along with green, blue is the most agreeable of colors in the garden. It associates well with all other colors; it makes gentle harmonies with closely related cool colors, such as violets and blue-greens, and it has a calming influence in contrasting partnerships, even with orange or bright yellow.

Unlike red, blue retains its character when diluted with white. Blue with a touch of red is slightly warmer; the more pronounced the red, the more it tips the color toward violet and blue-pink; yet it remains essentially a cool color.

Blues can be found in foliage too, though the "blue" is actually blue-green and much more muted than the blue found in flowers. To enhance the blueness of foliage, combine it with yellow-green leaves or creamy flowers. The yellow in the Alaska fringecups' foliage and flowers, for example, makes the blue-green hostas and grasses of the planting *opposite, right* look quite blue by comparison.

Blues appear coolest and most blue in shade. Take advantage of this and, as *left*, create a blue pool by allowing spring-flowering bulbs to naturalize beneath trees. You could repeat the effect in summer with the shade-tolerant peach leaf bellflower. Sunlight, on the other hand, makes blue flowers seem warmer and slightly pinker. To exploit this, partner blue with pink flowers in sunny situations to give a warmer version of a cool harmony.

At dusk, blue flowers have a special value. Together with whites, they remain visible longer than any other color. This is because the eye is more sensitive to blue in dim conditions, and also because the light after sunset has a blue cast. You can take advantage of this by concentrating blue and white flowers around the area where you like to sit on summer evenings.

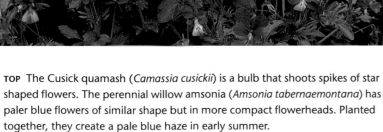

TOP The Cusick quamash (*Camassia cusickii*) is a bulb that shoots spikes of star shaped flowers. The perennial willow amsonia (*Amsonia tabernaemontana*) has paler blue flowers of similar shape but in more compact flowerheads. Planted together, they create a pale blue haze in early summer.

ABOVE A blue violet makes a successful marriage with the common bugleweed (*Ajuga reptans*). Both thrive in partial shade. The two will compete for the same ground, the bugleweed spreading by runners and the violet by seed, but you can easily remove plants of the dominant partner.

ABOVE The creeping perennial navelwort (*Omphalodes cappadocica* 'Cherry Ingram') weaves between the hosta (*H.* 'Halcyon'), the blue fescue (*Festuca glauca*), silvery lavender cotton (*Santolina*), and creamy Alaska fringecups (*Tellima grandiflora*). The plants here thrive best in different conditions, making this arrangement a bit tricky. The hosta likes damp soil and shade to keep its blue color through the summer; the fringecups also prefer shade, while the fescue and the lavender cotton prefer drier soil and more sun. A garden can often accommodate all these needs: well drained soil with mulch and shade for the hostas and fringecups during the hottest part of the day.

All-Blue Plantings

Because blue is so versatile and makes pleasing harmonies with pinks and violets as well as satisfying contrasts with yellow and cream, it provides a good base for garden plantings that change color through the year, perhaps being all blue for only one season. Blue flowered shrubs might form the framework, beginning with lilac, Californian lilac, and clematis in the late spring, and continuing into late summer with blue mist shrub, hardy plumbago, hydrangea, and blue hibiscus, for example. The informal planting of blue flowered shrubs, underplanted with bulbs, perennials and self-seeders, *opposite, right*, is yellow and white with hellebores and narcissi in early spring before becoming blue in late spring.

For an all-blue planting – as with any planting – it is vital to choose plants that will flourish where you want them to grow. Pictured *left* is a sheltered walled garden with areas of sun, shade, and semi-shade, divided into small boxwood-edged beds to allow plants with varied needs to flourish. Each bed can be planted with flowers for different seasons, and the soil conditions can be tailor-made for the plants' requirements. Plants that require a lot of attention, such as Himalayan blue poppies, can be put in one bed, and balanced with a bed of plants that need less rigorous care.

LEFT Mountain knapweed (*Centaurea montana*) and Jacob's ladder (*Polemonium caeruleum*) fill the foreground; beyond is a good stand of the Himalayan blue poppy (*Meconopsis betonicifolia*). This most treasured of blue flowers is very fussy, needing semi-shade, protection from wind, and a rich lime-free soil that does not dry out. It is a short-lived perennial and unless it is prevented from flowering in its first two seasons, will only flower once during its life.

RIGHT The framework for this informal planting includes a Californian lilac (*Ceanothus*) with rich blue flowers to the left of the path, and an unusual blue lilac (*Syringa vulgaris* 'Firmament') with a white flowered viburnum (*V. opulus* 'Xanthocarpum') to the right. In the foreground is Jacob's ladder (*Polemonium caeruleum*), which comes true to color when it seeds itself, and columbine (*Aquilegia vulgaris*), which spreads equally prolifically but varies between blue, pink, and purple. Farther back, beyond the foliage of ferns, daylilies and hellebores, is the mourning widow's cranesbill (*Geranium phaeum*) and Alaska fringecups (*Tellima grandiflora*).

BELOW By clipping off the dead heads of the violets like these on the edge of a sunny border, you can prevent them from forming seed and they will go on flowering throughout the summer. The same applies to the mountain knapweed (*Centaurea montana*) in the foreground, but the forget-me-nots only flower once in late spring. Leave them to seed before removing straggly plants in early summer.

Blues

SPRING

Ajuga reptans COMMON BUGLE
Semi-evergreen perennial that makes mats of shiny dark green foliage, with short spires of dusky blue flowers. Good groundcover for sun or shade. H 4in (10cm) S 15in (40cm) Z3-8 [ill.pp.71,151]. *A. r.* 'Atropurpurea' has dark purple foliage. H 6in (15cm) S 15in (40cm) Z3-8 [ill.p.133]

Brunnera macrophylla SIBERIAN BUGLOSS Perennial with flowers like those of forget-me-nots, and the added bonus of attractive heart-shaped leaves. Prefers light shade. H 18in (45cm) S 24in (60cm) Z3-9

Ceanothus CALIFORNIAN LILAC
The best of all blue-flowered shrubs [ill.p.73]. Evergreen *C. arboreus* makes a mound of almost uninterrupted blue if left to its own devices. Usually trained against a wall for frost protection and to contain its size. Also effective trained into an arch, but new growth needs pruning regularly, as plant will not regenerate if cut into old wood. Favors light soil and partial shade. H and S 12ft (4m) Z8-10 [ill.p.132]

Chionodoxa luciliae GLORY-OF-THE-SNOW An early-flowering bulb whose upward-facing flowers, blue with white centers, open to

the sun. Will seed itself and spread in undisturbed ground. H 4in (10cm) S 2in (5cm) Z4-9 [ill.pp.5,70]

Clematis alpina
Climbers that are small enough to be grown in containers and through wall trained shrubs. Normally left unpruned, most alpina types tolerate partial shade. *C. a.* 'Frances Rivis' has flowers with long sepals, like a tensed claw. *C. a.* 'Pamela Jackman' has lantern-shaped flowers with white centers. Both H and S 8ft (2.5m) Z3-9

Gentiana verna subsp. **balcanica** SPRING GENTIAN Evergreen perennial with incomparable jewel-blue flowers. It prefers sun and needs humus-rich soil with sharp drainage. H and S 2in (5cm) Z6-9

Hyacinthoides hispanica SPANISH BLUEBELL If left undisturbed, the bulbs will spread into clumps, and will ultimately make sheets of blue. In borders it can become invasive. Prefers heavy soil and requires partial shade with plenty of moisture. H 15in (40cm) S 4in (10cm) Z4-9

Iris (dwarf varieties)
Good varieties of these early flowering bulbous perennials include *I. histrioides* 'Major' with dark blue flowers, H S 4in (10cm) S 3in (7cm) Z5-9; and *I.* 'Cantab' with paler, clear blue flowers, H 4in (10cm) S 2½in (6cm) Z5-9

Lithodora diffusa
Shrubby perennial that makes a low carpet of vivid blue flowers. Best varieties include intense blue *L. d.* 'Heavenly Blue' and paler blue *L. d.* 'Cambridge Blue'. Resents root disturbance and requires full sun and acid soil. H 2ft (60cm) S 3ft (90cm) Z7-9

Muscari GRAPE HYACINTH
These small bulbs with dense flower spikes require a sunny situation. Good varieties include *M. armeniacum* ARMENIAN GRAPE HYACINTH with deep blue flowers, H 6in (20cm) S 3in (8cm) Z3-8 [ill.pp.5,70]; and *M. latifolium* with blue flowers that open from violet buds, H 6in (15cm) S 3in (8cm) Z3-8

Myosotis alpestris FORGET-ME-NOT
A self-seeding biennial, but over generations the flower color becomes progressively more insipid. For the brightest blue, use bought seed. Prefers full sun but tolerates light shade. H 6in (15cm) S 12in (30cm) Z5-8 [ill.pp.10,73,141,142]

Omphalodes cappadocica NAVELWORT Perennial with exquisite blue flowers, that spreads by creeping stems. It is useful for giving color in open shade. H 8in (20cm) S 10in (25cm) Z6-9 [ill.p.71]

Phlox stolonifera CREEPING PHLOX
Short-lived perennial, with pale blue flowers, pink at the center. It makes attractive clumps, but does not spread. *P. s.* 'Blue Ridge'

spreads by creeping shoots making a pale blue carpet under deciduous trees. Requires moist, acid soil. H 6in (15cm) S 12in (30cm) Z3-8

Pulmonaria LUNGWORT
Early flowering perennial that prefers shade and moist soil. *P. angustifolia* BLUE LUNGWORT and *P. a. azurea* have intense blue flowers with un-patterned mid-green foliage. H 9in (23cm) S 12in (30cm) Z3-8. *P. longifolia* 'Bertram Anderson' LONG LEAF LUNGWORT has long dark green leaves spotted with white. H 12in (30cm) S 18in (45cm) Z3-8. *P. saccharata* 'Roy Davidson' BETHLEHEM SAGE has pale blue flowers. H 12in (30cm) S 18in (45cm) Z3-8

Puschkinia scilloides var. **libanotica** (syn. *P. libanotica*) STRIPED SQUILL Early-flowering bulbs, needing sun. They are most effective planted *en masse*. Delicate looking, the flower petals are near-white, with a blue midline that makes them appear pale blue overall. H 6in (15cm) S 2in (5cm) Z4-9 [ill.p.70]

Rosmarinus officinalis 'Benenden Blue' ROSEMARY Evergreen shrubs that require sun, rosemaries are usually grown for their aromatic foliage, but this one also has rich blue flowers. The plants can be shaped and even used as a hedge, if only new growth is clipped after flowering. H and S 5ft (1.5m) Z6-9

Scilla
Early-flowering bulbs that need an open site in sun or partial shade. *S. siberica* SIBERIAN SQUILL has down-turned mid-blue flowers. H 6in (15cm) S 2in (5cm) Z2-8. *S. mischtschenkoana* has palest blue flowers. H 4in (10cm) S 2in (5cm) Z2-8.

SUMMER

Aconitum napellus COMMON MONKSHOOD Tuberous perennial with spikes of hooded, dusky blue flowers and deeply cut leaves. Prefers sun, but will tolerate partial shade. H 5ft (1.5m) S 1ft (30cm) Z5-8 [ill.p.181]

Agapanthus AFRICAN LILY
Perennial, with globes of blue flowers atop long stems, and strap-like leaves. The plants like to bake in the sun, so a place in front of a border, or at the foot of a sunny wall or in a container is ideal. *A. campanulatus* has narrow leaves and good blue flowers. H 3ft (90cm) S 20in (50cm) Z8-10 [ill.p.116]. **Headbourne Hybrids** have slightly larger flowers of a more variable blue. H and S 3ft (1m) Z7-10 [ill.p.181]

Amsonia tabernaemontana WILLOW AMSONIA Perennial with dainty flowerheads of pale sky-blue on a rounded plant. The flower color is discreet, and dominated by the mass of lance-

Brunnera macrophylla (**Spring**)

Gentiana verna subsp. *balcanica* (**Spring**)

Lithodora diffusa (**Spring**)

Pulmonaria angustifolia (**Spring**)

Aconitum napellus (**Summer**)

shaped leaves. Best if left undisturbed for years. Needs partial shade. H 24in (60cm) S 12in (30cm) Z4-8 [ill.p.171]

Anchusa azurea 'Loddon Royalist' ITALIAN BUGLOSS One of the most desirable of all blue flowers, giving generous spires of intense blue. Although perennial, it may be short-lived, and can be propagated by root cuttings. Requires sun and dislikes winter damp [ill.pp.116,184]. For a lighter, forget-me-not blue, try *A. a* 'Opal'. Both H 4ft (1.2m) S 2ft (60 cm) Z3-8

Aquilegia 'Hensol Harebell' COLUMBINE The best of the blue aquilegias. Prefers sun. H 30in (75cm) S 20in (50cm) Z5-9 [ill.p.183]

Aster* x *frikartii 'Mönch' One of the best of the perennial late summer daisies, valuable for its good lavender-blue flowers (with yellow centers) and long flowering season. Prefers sun or partial shade. H 28in (70cm) S 15in (40cm) Z5-8

Baptisia australis BLUE WILD INDIGO Perennial with blue flowers like small lupins, though less compact, and pretty lupin-like foliage. It needs staking, likes full sun and deep, neutral to acid soil, and is best left undisturbed. H 30in (75cm) S 2ft (60cm) Z4-9

Borago officinalis BORAGE This herbaceous annual, an ornamental and culinary asset to any herb or vegetable garden,

has clear blue, star-shaped flowers and attractive downy gray foliage. It self-seeds profusely, and so may become invasive. Prefers sun. H 3ft (90cm) S 1ft (30cm)

Buddleja 'Lochinch' BUTTERFLY BUSH With only a suggestion of lilac in its pale flowers, this is the closest a buddleja comes to blue. The foliage is slightly hairy, giving the shrub a silvery look. It requires full sun, and should be cut back hard in spring. H and S 10ft (3m) Z6-9 [ill.p.181]

Camassia cusickii CUSICK QUAMASH Spikes of starry mid-blue flowers grow from a fringe of strap-like foliage. The bulbs will multiply in the right conditions, and they may naturalize in damp meadows. Tolerates shade or partial shade in a clay soil. H 30in (75cm) S 12in (30cm) Z3-8 [ill.p.71]

Campanula BELLFLOWER Good perennial varieties include *C. latiloba* which makes spreading groundcover under trees, where the shady light intensifies the blueness of the flowers, H 4ft (1.2m) S 2ft (60cm) Z4-8 [ill.p.180]; *C. portenschlagiana* is mat-forming, H 6in (15cm) S 18in (45cm) Z4-8 [ill.p.116]; *C. poscharskyana* SIBERIAN BELLFLOWER is similar, with slightly paler flowers, shaped like deeper bells, and has a tendency to creep up low walls, H 6in (15cm)

S 18in (45cm) Z3-8 [ill.p.133]. All tolerate sun and partial shade.

Catananche caerulea CUPID'S DART Flowers of this perennial are cornflower-like, with papery white bracts around their bases. Needs staking. Does best in sun and light soil. H 30in (90cm) S 18in (45cm) Z4-8

Centaurea CORNFLOWER Good varieties include annual *C. cyanus*, which has intense blue flowers, though there are varieties available in white, pink or deepest purple. Keep them dead-headed to ensure repeat-flowering. H 3ft (1m) S 1ft (30cm) [ill.p.164]. *C. montana* MOUNTAIN KNAPWEED is a spreading and potentially invasive plant, but rewarding for its intense blue flowers, larger than the annual, and for its gray-green foliage. H 20in (50cm) S 2ft (60cm) Z4-8 [ill.p.184]. All are best in full sun.

Clematis Climbing varieties that tolerate both sun and shade so long as they have a shaded root run include:'Lasurstern' with large flowers in midsummer, H 10ft (3m) S 3ft (1m) Z3-9 [ill.pp.64,114]; 'Perle d'Azur', vigorous with large pale blue flowers, H 15ft (4.6m) S 3ft (1m) Z3-9 [ill.pp.11,62,164];and 'Prince Charles', smaller flowered and less vigorous, H 8ft (2.4m) S 3ft (90cm) Z3-9

[ill.p.151]. Good semi-herbaceous varieties include *C. heracleifolia* var. *davidiana* H 3ft (90cm) S 30in (75cm) Z3-9; and *C.* x *durandii* H 6ft (1.8m) S 3ft (90cm) Z4-9. Both can be trained into other shrubs.

Consolida ambigua (syn. *C. ajacis*) LARKSPUR Very similar to their perennial cousins, the delphiniums, only these are annuals growing to full size in a season. Effective when the seed is scattered in open ground between perennials. Requires sun. H 2ft (60cm) S 1ft (30cm)

Convolvulus *C. sabatius* (syn. *C. mauritanicus*) GROUND MORNING GLORY An evergreen perennial, good for a container. Will trail elegantly over the side and produce a profusion of small, funnel-shaped blue-violet flowers. H 8in (20cm) S 1ft (30cm) Z8-9. *C. tricolor* (syn. *C. minor*) DWARF MORNING GLORY, is an annual with intense blue, saucer-shaped flowers with bright yellow throats. H 12in (30cm) S 8in (20cm). Both need full sun.

Corydalis flexuosa BLUE CORYDALIS A perennial with delicate flowerheads of sky blue combined with intricately cut foliage. Ideal for naturalizing under deciduous trees, where a massed planting looks like a blue pool. Requires a loose, leafy soil in shade or partial shade. H 12in (30cm) S 15in (40cm) Z5-8

Cynoglossum amabile CHINESE FORGET-ME-NOT A sun-loving biennal with intense turquoise-blue flowers among downy gray-green foliage. H 2ft (60cm) S 15in (40cm) Z7-8

Delphinium Star performers of the blue galaxy, these perennials are available in all tints and shades of blue, as well as white, cream and violet [ill.pp.8,180,182]. Good blue ones include Black Knight Group H 6ft (1.8m) S 15in (40cm) [ill.pp.63,143]; 'Chelsea Star' H 6ft (1.8m) S 2ft6in (75cm);*D. grandiflorum* 'Blue Butterfly', usually grown as an annual, H 18in (45cm) S12in (30cm); Pacific Hybrids H 6ft (1.8m) S 15in (40cm) [ill.pp.176,183]; Summer Skies Group H 6ft (1.8m) S 15in (40cm). All require sun. All Z3-9

Echinops ritro GLOBE THISTLE A reliable perennial with spiky, compact globes of tiny blue flowers surmounting tall clumps of hairy, jagged-edged foliage. Best in sun and in poor soil. H 4ft (120cm) S 15in (40cm) Z3-9 [ill.p.11]

Echium 'Blue Bedder' VIPER'S BUGLOSS Annual that produces mounds of mid-blue flowers that ultimately become untidy, and because they are shy of re-flowering if cut right back, it is best to remove them altogether after flowering. Requires sun. H 1ft (30cm) S 8in (20cm)

Baptisia australis (**Summer**)

Campanula poscharskyana (**Summer**)

Catananche caerulea (**Summer**)

Corydalis flexuosa (**Summer**)

Echinops ritro (**Summer**)

Eryngium SEA HOLLY

Good perennial varieties include *E. alpinum* ALPINE SEA HOLLY which has a flowerhead like a pin-cushion surrounded by a prickly fringe of bracts of dusky blue, H 3ft3in (1m) S 2ft (60cm) [ill.pp.25,157]; *E. x oliverianum* has less elaborate bracts, H 36in (90cm) S 24in (60cm); *E. x tripartitum* has much smaller flowers but more of them, arranged in clusters, all flower-parts suffused with blue, H 4ft (1.2m) S 20in (50cm) [ill.p.108]. All require sun. All Z5-8

Felicia amelloides 'Santa Anita' BLUE MARGUERITE Since this evergreen shrub with daisy-like flowers is tender, it is best for containers or for a summer bedding scheme. Requires full sun. H and S 1ft (30cm) Z9-10

Geranium CRANESBILL

Reliable perennials that tolerate sun and partial shade. 'Johnson's Blue' makes a lovely mound of rounded blue flowers above cut foliage. H 12in (30cm) S 24in (60cm) Z5-8 [ill.pp.11,151]. *G. pratense* 'Mrs Kendall Clark' MEADOW CRANESBILL has palest blue-gray flowers with pink stamens. H and S 2ft (60cm) Z4-8 [ill.p.7]. *G. pratense* 'Plenum Caeruleum' has double mid-blue flowers. H and S 30in (75cm) Z4-8 [ill.p.175]

Hibiscus syriacus 'Blue Bird' (syn. *H. s.* 'Oiseau Bleu') ROSE OF SHARON The blue flowers of this

shrub have magenta throats and close up in damp weather. May be planted in a row and clipped to make a hedge. Requires sun. H 10ft (3m) S 6ft6in (2m) Z5-9

Hydrangea macrophylla 'Blue Wave' (syn. *H.m.*'Mariesii Perfection') BIG LEAF HYDRANGEA This shrub is best in partial shade and moist soil, and it needs acid soil if the elegant "lacecap" flowerheads are to be bright blue. In neutral to alkaline soils they become quite pink. H 6ft6in (2m) S 8ft (2.4m) Z6-9

Ipomea tricolor 'Heavenly Blue' (syn. *I. rubrocaerulea* 'Heavenly Blue') MORNING GLORY Fast-growing, this annual climber has intense blue funnel-shaped flowers, made all the more scintillating by their ephemeral-ity. Barely open at breakfast, they are over by lunch. Requires full sun. H and S 10ft (3m)

Iris

The following rhizomatous perennial irises need a sunny position: *I. cristata* CRESTED IRIS, a miniature that spreads to form a blue mat in gravel or on the rock garden, H 4in (10cm) S 12in (30cm) Z4-8; *I. ensata* 'Favorite' (syn. *I. kaempferi* 'F.') JAPANESE WATER IRIS which thrives in water or bog gardens, H 3ft3in (1m) S 15in (40cm) Z5-9; and *I. pallida* DALMATIAN IRIS, evergreen with bluish sword-shaped leaves, H 4ft (1.2m) S 18in (45cm) Z6-9. *I. missouriensis* (syn *I. tolmieana*)

MISSOURI FLAG IRIS needs sun or partial shade, and resents being moved. H 30in (75cm) S 15in (40cm) Z3-9. *I. sibirica* SIBERIAN IRIS needs sun and moist soil, and forms clumps of grass-like foliage,with tall flowering stems carrying relatively small rich blue flowers. H 4ft (1.2m) S 18in (45cm) Z4-9 [ill.p.11].

Linum perenne PERENNIAL FLAX Perennial that makes a clump of narrow, grass-like leaves, surmounted by small, open saucer-shaped flowers of exquisite blue, which appear in succession through the summer. Requires sun. H 24in (60cm) S 6in (15cm) Z5-9

Lobelia erinus TRAILING LOBELIA An annual stalwart for the edges of bedding schemes, and for containers, especially window boxes and hanging baskets, where the tiny, trailing blue flowers can be used to greatest effect. Requires moist soil in either sun or partial shade. Good varieties include trailing *L. e.* 'Blue Cascade' H 8in (20cm) S 6in (15cm); and *L. e.* 'Cambridge Blue' which is more compact.

Meconopsis

These most desirable of perennial plants are very choosy about their living conditions. The privileged minority of gardeners will be rewarded with enviable drifts of blue poppies in broken shade and moist, acid soil. *M. betonicifolia* HIMALAYAN

BLUE POPPY H 4ft (1.2m) S 18in (45cm) Z6-8 [ill.p.72]; *M. grandis* H 5ft (1.5m) S 1ft (30cm) Z6-8

Nemophila menziesii BABY BLUE EYES Annual with little scalloped blue flowers with white centers to add a touch of lightness for the blue border. Tolerates both sun and partial shade. H 8in (20cm) S 6in (15cm)

Nepeta CATMINT

Perennial with aromatic foliage that is irresistible to cats and indispensable for creating a diaphanous haze of lavender-blue [ill.p.6]. Useful varieties include *N. x faassenii* H and S 18in (45cm) Z4-9 [ill.p.119, 175,180]; *N. nervosa* H 2ft (60cm) S 15in (40cm) Z4-9 [ill.p.21]; *N. sibirica* H and S 3ft (90cm) Z3-9; and, most desirable of all, *N. sibirica* 'Souvenir d'André Chaudron' with shorter habit but larger flowers [ill.p.172]. 'Six Hills Giant' is one of the most vigorous. It is floppy in habit and useful as an edging to a broad walkway where you can brush it as you pass. If you cut it right back after flowering, the plant will quickly regenerate. H 30in (75cm) S 4ft (1.2m) Z3-9 [ill.pp.7,106,141,174,176]. All do best in sun and moist soil.

Nigella damascena LOVE-IN-A-MIST The semi-double flowers of this annual are intriguingly shaped and framed by spindly bracts. The seedpods are shapely too,

and useful for dried flower arrangements – but leave some *in situ* so the plant will self-seed. Best in sun. H. 24in (60cm) S 8in (20cm). Good cultivars include *N. d.* 'Miss Jekyll' H 18in (45cm) S 8in (20cm) [ill.p.143]

Parahebe perfoliata DIGGER'S SPEEDWELL The stems of the branching sprays of small blue flowers are clasped by evergreen oval blue-green leaves. A sub-shrub that requires sun, and peaty and sandy soil, it tends to flop and needs the discreet support of peasticks. H 18-24in (45-60cm) S 18in (45cm) Z8-10

Penstemon heterophyllus BEARD TONGUE This perennial and its varieties are the best of the blue penstemons, giving a succession of spikes of tubular flowers, if flowering stems are cut back when they are over. All do best in sun. H 15in (40cm) S 12in (30cm) Z6-9 [ill.pp.11,114,183]

Perovskia 'Blue Spire' RUSSIAN SAGE Spires of small blue flowers, combined with small, silvery, toothed leaves, create a late-season haze of color. This aromatic sub-shrub needs full sun and very well-drained soil. H 3ft3in (1m)S 2ft8in (80cm) Z5-9

Phacelia campanularia CALIFORNIA BLUEBELL Deep blue bell-shaped flowers on reddish stems combine with oval serrated foliage on this annual that needs sun. H 8in (20cm) S 6in (15cm)

Geranium pratense 'Mrs Kendall Clark' **(Summer)**

Ipomea tricolor 'Heavenly Blue' **(Summer)**

Iris sibirica **(Summer)**

Nemophila menzeisii **(Summer)**

Phacelia campanularia **(Summer)**

Phlox

P. divaricata subsp. *laphamii* **'Chattahoochee'** is a short-lived perennial making clumps of bright lavender-blue flowers with crimson throats. Best in sun. H 15in (40cm) S 12in (30cm) Z4-9. *P. drummondii* **'Blue Beauty'** is an annual with rounded flowerheads of open, clear lavender-blue flowers. Best in sun. H 6in (15cm) S 4in (10cm)

Platycodon grandiflorus BALLOON FLOWER This perennial has striking balloon-shaped buds, which open into shallow bell-shaped flowers with fused petals. Likes sun and light, sandy soil. H and S 18in (45cm) Z3-9

Polemonium caeruleum JACOB'S LADDER Forms a clump, with finely divided foliage and clusters of clear blue flowers with contrasting yellow stamens. A perennial, it spreads by self-seeding. Requires sun. H and S 2ft (60cm) Z3-8 [ill.pp.72,73]

Plumbago auriculata (syn. *P. capensis*) CAPE PLUMBAGO South African evergreen climber for conservatories and summer containers in cooler climates. Makes long-lived clouds of pale blue flowers in summer. Requires sun. H and S 20ft (6m) Z9-11

Salvia SAGE

Those with the best blue flowers are mostly perennials or annuals. *S. farinacea* **'Victoria'** MEALY CUP SAGE has spikes of small dark blue flowers, reminiscent of lavender.

It is a perennial that can be grown as an annual. Likes sun. H 18in (45cm) S 12in (30cm) Z8-9. *S. guaranitica* is a perennial that becomes quite shrubby in appearance, with dark green leaves and claw-shaped flowers of an intense blue. H 5ft (1.5m) S 2ft (60cm) Z7-9. *S. viridis* **'Blue Beard'** (syn. *S. horminum* 'B.B.') is an annual, with totally different attractions. Its color interest comes from the terminal bracts, which are blue-violet and long lasting; the flowers themselves are modest. Does best in sun. H 18in (45cm) S 8in (20cm) [ill.p.132]. *S. patens* GENTIAN SAGE is a perennial with bright blue flowers. Requires sun. H and S 18in (45cm) Z8-9; *S. p.* **'Cambridge blue'** has pale blue flowers. H 18in (45cms) S 24in (60cm). *S. x sylvestris* **'Blue Hill'** is a clump-forming perennial with spikes of clear blue flowers. H 20in (50cm) S 30in (75cm) Z5-9

Scabiosa caucasica 'Clive Greaves' SCABIOUS Perennial whose round flowers with fluffed petals and creamy centers wave in the wind on long stems. Requires sun and prefers alkaline soil. H and S 18in (45cm) Z4-9

Stokesia laevis 'Blue Danube' STOKE'S ASTER This evergreen perennial, which tolerates sun and partial shade, bears its cornflower-like flowers on short

stems above narrow mid-green leaves. H and S 18in (45cm) Z5-9

Syringa vulgaris 'Firmament' LILAC The bluest of the lilacs, with good scent, this tree requires sun or partial shade. Prune to keep within bounds. H and S 24ft (7m) Z4-8 [ill.p.73]

Teucrium fruticans BUSH GERMANDER The lipped pale blue flowers look well against the shrub's own evergreen, gray-green leaves, which are aromatic. There is a desirable variety with dark blue flowers called *T. f.* **'Azureum'**. Both require full sun. H 6ft 6in(2m) S 12ft (4m) Z8-10

Veronica SPEEDWELL

Among the best varieties of this sun-loving perennial are *V. austriaca* **'Crater Lake Blue'** making a mound of spikes of small flowers of an intense blue, lightened by tiny white eyes, an ideal plant for the front of the border, H and S 20in (50cm) Z5-8 [ill.p.133]; *V. gentianoides* GENTIAN SPEEDWELL which puts out spikes of palest blue flowers, H and S 18in (45cm) Z4-8 [ill.p.141]; and *V. peduncularis* **'Georgia Blue'** with intense blue flowers on a compact plant, H 9in (25cm) S 18in (45cm) Z5-8

Viola VIOLET, PANSY

Good varieties that tolerate both sun and shade include the perennial **'Boughton Blue'** that

flowers throughout the summer. Cut back when it begins to look tired, and it will sprout and flower again if new growth is kept fed and watered. H 10in (25cm) S 15in (40cm) Z6-9

FALL

Aconitum carmichaelii AZURE MONKSHOOD The hooded dark blue flowers of this perennial are an unexpected feature of the fall garden and so more prized than they would be in competition with summer flowers. Prefers sun, but tolerates some shade. H 5ft (1.5m) S 3ft (1m) Z3-8

Caryopteris x clandonensis BLUEBEARD Attractive throughout the summer, this small shrub has blue-green lance-shaped leaves, and pointed racemes of clear blue flowers in late season. Good named varieties are *C. c.* **'Heavenly Blue'** with the deepest blue flowers; and *C. c.* **'Kew Blue'** with paler flowers. H and S 3ft (90cm) Z5-9. All require full sun.

Ceratostigma PLUMBAGO

Rich blue flowers combine well with the shrub's own orange and red fall foliage. It requires sun and prefers some shelter. *C. plumbaginoides* LEADWORT is a low, spreading plant, good for groundcover, H 18in (45cm) S 30in (75cm) Z5-8; *C. willmottianum* is a more substantial shrub, H and S 3ft3in (1m) Z5-8

Crocus speciosus CROCUS Corm with blue-violet flowers and bright orange stigmas that appear in advance of the leaves. The best blue variety is *C. s.* **'Oxonian'**. H 4in (10cm) S 3in (8cm) Z5-9. Both need sun.

Gentiana sino-ornata GENTIAN A creeping evergreen perennial, with large, strong blue trumpet-shaped flowers. Thrives in an alpine trough or on the edge of woodland, provided it has lime-free soil, a cool root-run and is not allowed to dry out. H 2in (5cm) S 12in (30cm) Z5-9

Geranium wallichianum 'Buxton's Variety' CRANESBILL A creeping perennial with blue flowers with pink veins and bright white centers. Tolerates sun, shade and any except waterlogged soil. H 12in (30cm) S 3ft (90cm) Z4-8

Salvia uliginosa BOG SAGE A lovely "see-through" perennial for late fall, its flower-heads of the most intense pale blue are suspended on insubstantial stems that wave prettily in the wind. Requires sun. H 6ft6in (2m) S 18in (45cm) Z8-10

WINTER

Viola **'Universal Blue'** PANSY Annual that flowers in mild winter spells. Tolerates sun or shade. Grow a few in pots or on the edge of borders to bring a little winter cheer. H and S 10in (25cm)

Plumbago auriculata (**Summer**)

Salvia patens (**Summer**)

Veronica peduncularis 'Georgia Blue' (**Summer**)

Caryopteris x *clandonensis* 'Kew Blue' (**Fall**)

Crocus speciosus (**Fall**)

Greens

Green is the natural backdrop to all other colors in the garden. But it is not an entirely neutral background, as a mid-gray screen would be. It plays an active part in color associations and has an effect on its neighbors, contrasting most strongly with its complementary – red – and harmonizing most closely with the hues adjacent to it on the color wheel – yellow and blue. Green also has a calming influence on other colors and for this reason it is often associated with peace and tranquility.

In the garden, we often strive for "color," forgetting, perhaps, that green is a wonderful color in itself and is all that we need to create a mood of tranquility and peace. Foliage has a purely practical advantage over flowers too, in that it is longer-lived and generally easier to maintain, often needing only an occasional weed and trim. If you use evergreen plants, you can create foliage effects that last throughout the year.

Mid-greens are neutral in terms of color temperature and tone. They lie on the borderline between hot and cold colors, and near the middle of the scale of dark and light tones. That is why green foliage works so well as a transition between other colors, softening contrasts that would appear too intense if colors were placed side by side without its intervening influence. Bear in mind too that many foliage greens are fairly dark on the tonal scale, and so help to show up light colored flowers, while dark colored flowers, such as violets, purples and deep blues, will merge with the similar dark tones of their green background.

Greens offer the gardener greater diversity than any other color family. They range from the fresh lime-green of emerging leaf buds in spring to the near black evergreen foliage of yew, and from the bright yellow-green leaves of golden privet, to the blue-green foliage of the hosta, *H.* 'Halcyon'. There is also an extraordinary range of shapes, sizes, and textures from which to choose. Even when restricted to those plants that will grow in containers, they can form a rich tapestry of greens, as in the planting of aromatic herbs and grasses, *left*. Here, yellow-green is represented by Bowles' golden grass, boxleaf honeysuckle, and golden thyme, while cream-edged variegated holly picks up the yellow-green. The planting also includes mid-green boxwood, blue-green tanacetum, dark green bush germander, and feathery bronze fennel.

Patterned foliage adds yet another dimension to the greens. The possibilities include white striped grasses or irises with cream striped leaves, spotted lungwort, white splashed dogwood, Italian arum, or the white or yellow margined hostas. Variegation like this gives the effect of broken color and fragmented shape and form. When you

ABOVE Positioned so the warmth of the sun enhances their scent, herbs and grasses in terracotta pots enliven a paved patio. Bowles' golden grass (*Milium effusum* 'Aureum') is planted with young fennel against a backdrop of boxleaf honeysuckle (*Lonicera nitida* 'Baggesen's Gold'). Miniature boxwood globes are underplanted with golden lemon thyme (*Thymus* x *citriodorus* 'Aureus') and germander (*Teucrium* x *lucidrys*). The variegated holly (*Ilex aquifolium* 'Silver Queen') has blue-green tanacetum (*T. densum amani*) at its foot.

look at a green and white striped leaf, it is as if several leaves are shimmering together, rather than one single leaf. Pale spots and smudges on leaves can give the impression of sunbeams filtering through the foliage. Capitalize on this and bring the illusion of dappled light to a shady area by using variegated plants, such as deadnettles or hostas.

Using variegated foliage also presents opportunities for subtle color associations. You could plant the white edged hosta, *H.* 'Albomarginata' with green and white striped 'Spring Green' tulips. Or grow a yellow variegated ivy, like the English ivy, *Hedera helix* 'Goldheart', on a trellis screen with the clematis, *C. tangutica*, whose exotic yellow dangling flowers in mid to late summer will echo the yellow variegations in the ivy leaves.

One important point to remember when growing variegated plants is that they are not usually as vigorous as their unvariegated relations. And since some variegations are caused by viruses, patterned foliage can look sickly. Use them with restraint. The single variegated holly in the planting, *opposite*, helps to break up the greens

of the portable garden of herbs and grasses and makes a visual link with the white painted bench beyond.

With such a range of greens available in foliage, it is easy to forget that there are some choice plants with green flowers. Green flowers are an acquired taste and novice gardeners tend not to notice them. But as the gardening passion takes hold, green flowers reveal their special charms. Like green foliage, they are useful in any plant association; they look good with any other flower color and they provide a buffer between stronger and brighter flowers.

Green flowered hellebores are among the first flowers to appear in early spring. They sometimes accompany snowdrops, whose flowers have echoing touches of green. Green catkins of the evergreen silk-tassel bush are followed by lime-green spurges. A few months on, the foamy green flowered lady's mantle provides the perfect foil for all the other colors of the summer garden. Among the annuals, bells of Ireland and the flowering tobacco plants (*Nicotiana langsdorffii* and *N.* x *sanderae* 'Lime Green') have flowers that are only slightly lighter green than their leaves.

ABOVE The English ivy (*Hedera helix*) is immensely variable. Create a patterned green drape over a low wall by planting two different varieties together. Here, the yellow leaved *H.h.* 'Buttercup' mingles with the grayish variegated variety, *H.h.* 'Glacier'. Ivy thrives in most conditions and may need regular trimming to keep it from choking other plants.

ABOVE In early summer, a clever combination of perennials and shrubs – many of them evergreens – shows the broad range of greens that can be used. The lime-yellow of the long-flowering cushion spurge and of the Bowles' golden grass dominate, and enhance the blueness of the foliage of the polemonium and the artemisias. Most of these thrive in semi-shade, making solid mounds of color and some good groundcover. (For a diagram of this planting, see page 173.)

Foliage Associations

A variety of green foliage is all that you need, especially on a small scale, to create color interest in the garden. To exploit the limitless repertory of greens, put yellow-greens with blue-greens, rusty greens with silvers, and spotted variegated patterns beside stripes. For shape and textural interest, combine plants with strong outlines – jagged against smooth, spear shapes against fuzzy ones, shiny surfaces against felty ones. The advantage of foliage plantings is that they are much longer-lived than floral plantings, and their color effects ebb and flow with the seasons.

LEFT, TOP The silver variegated sweet iris (*I.pallida* 'Argentea Variegata') grows through the feathery young foliage of annual love-in-a-mist (*Nigella*). To achieve this effect, sow the love-in-a-mist seeds among the iris rhizomes.

LEFT, BOTTOM In midsummer, the creamy veins of an ornamental cabbage are echoed by flowering tobacco (*Nicotiana* x *sanderae* 'Domino Lime'), plumes of squirrel tail grass (*Hordeum jubatum*), and variegated sage (*Salvia officinalis* 'Icterina'). Mallow (*Lavatera trimestris* 'Mont Blanc') and coral plume poppy (*Macleaya microcarpa* 'Kelway's Coral Plume') add darker tones.

FAR LEFT, TOP A purple grass palm (*Cordyline australis* 'Purpurea') and purple *Lobelia* 'Queen Victoria' grow through felty Grecian horehound (*Ballota pseudodictamnus*) and glossy green umbrella plants (*Darmera peltata*). Small-flowered alumroot (*Heuchera micrantha* var. *diversifolia* 'Palace Purple') in the foreground picks up the purple theme. These perennials all tolerate semi-shade but the horehound prefers a sunny spot.

FAR LEFT, BOTTOM Red mountain spinach and the frothy foliage of love-in-a-mist grow through the lower stems of the wall shrubs, golden leaved hop (*Humulus lupulus* 'Aureus') and brightly variegated *Euonymus fortunei* 'Silver Queen'.

ABOVE Ornamental rhubarb (*Rheum palmatum* 'Atrosanguineum'), archangel (*Angelica archangelica*), golden feverfew (*Tanacetum parthenium* 'Aureum'), plume poppy (*Macleaya*), golden ray (*Ligularia przewalskii*), and gardener's garters (*Phalaris arundinacea* var. *picta* 'Picta') all echo the colors of their neighbors. Take care with these plants: the rhubarb needs space, gardener's garters can be invasive, and archangel will die if its seedheads are left on.

TOP The shiny leaves of Japanese fatsia (*Fatsia japonica*) contrast with the foliage of the blue-green coral plume poppy (*Macleaya microcarpa* 'Kelway's Coral Plume') and the velvet foliage of Sargent's hydrangea (*Hydrangea aspera* subsp. *sargentiana*). The fatsia keeps its variegation best in sun.

ABOVE In early summer, autumn fern (*Dryopteris eythrosora*) embraces the felty young leaves of a rhododendron (*R. yakushimanum*), the bright green as well as the purple-tinged bugbane (*Cimicifuga racemosa* and *C. simplex* Atropurpurea Group), and *Polygonatum campanulatum*. Dappled shade and moist soil provide the best conditions for these plants.

TOP In early summer, green fennel (*Foeniculum vulgare*) softens the link between the blue hostas (*H.* 'Halcyon' and *H.* 'Krossa Regal') and *Hosta fortunei* var. *aureomarginata* whose cream margins tie in with the flower spikes of Alaska fringecups (*Tellima grandiflora*). This group of perennials with highly decorative leaves has the bonus of giving excellent groundcover.

All-Green Gardens

BELOW Its strict geometry softened by the silvery boughs of a willow-leaf pear tree, this formal garden retains its structure through the year with little maintenance. The boxwood domes, hedges, and obelisks need trimming twice during the growing season, as does the ivy on the arbor to keep it from filling the spaces in the trellis.

No color is as peaceful as green. By restricting your palette to green plants, you can create a garden – or corner of a garden – of absolute tranquility, whether it is formal and highly structured, or informal and natural looking.

The formal garden, *below left*, relies on year-round geometric structure. Its sense of ordered calm depends upon its symmetry. A low maze has been created from clipped boxwood. Topiary and ivy-covered treillage add vertical emphasis, and a seat has been placed for silent contemplation. A very limited range of color has been used in this

garden, but it could be extended by infilling the parterre with other evergreens such as variegated ivy or Japanese spurge, or gray leaved lavender cotton, and by using dark bottlegreen yew for the obelisks instead of lightly variegated boxwood. If you wish to add a little more color, you could introduce pale flowers in pots that can be changed when they fade.

Ferns and hostas and other shade-tolerant plants have been used to imitate nature in the garden *below right*. There aren't any blue-greens, and the yellow-greens are largely the result of the sun filtering through the young foliage. Although it looks entirely natural, a lot of skill and effort are needed to maintain the lushness, while keeping the less vigorous plants from being swamped.

BELOW Later in the summer, the leaves of the giant rhubarb (*Gunnera manicata*) will swell to meet the overhanging branches of the Japanese maple (*Acer palmatum*) and Indian horse chestnut (*Aesculus indica*). The extra shade will make the groundcover foliage more attenuated, as the hostas, ferns, and dinner-plate leaves of shieldleaf rodgersia (*Astilboides tabularis*) compete for the remaining light.

Dark Greens

EVERGREEN

Camellia japonica JAPANESE CAMELLIA Handsome shrub with glossy leaves and flower color ranging from pure white through pinks to deep mauve and red. Requires neutral to acid soil and a cool root-run. H 15ft (4.6m) S 12ft (3.7m) Z7-9

Ilex aquifolium 'J. C. van Tol' ENGLISH HOLLY Hardy shrub with glossy, almost spineless leaves, and a reliable crop of red berries. Can be clipped to make a solid hedge. Tolerates sun or shade. H 12ft (3.7m) S 10ft (3m) Z6-8

Laurus nobilis SWEET BAY Culinary herb with aromatic foliage. Fierce winters can cut it to the ground but it will come again. Clipped specimens need winter protection. **L. n. f. angustifolia**, the narrow-leaved form, is slightly hardier and more elegant. Tolerates sun and partial shade. H 20ft (6m) S 15ft (4.6m) Z8-10

Mahonia japonica JAPANESE MAHONIA An imposing shrub with deep green, pinnate, spiny leaves and long lax racemes of fragrant lemon-yellow flowers over a long period from late fall to spring. Tolerates sun and partial shade. H and S 8ft (2.4m) Z6-8

Osmanthus x burkwoodii Shrub with neat, shiny dark foliage that will make a substantial hedge. Flowers freely in a sunny position. **O. delavayi** has flowers with an even sweeter scent. Both H and S 10ft (3m) Z8-10

Phillyrea latifolia MOCK PRIVET Will make an elegant small tree with glossy masses of foliage. **P. angustifolia** has longer, narrower leaves, and can be clipped to make a good compact hedge, or topiaried forms. Requires full sun. H and S 25ft (8m) Z7-9

Prunus lusitanica PORTUGAL LAUREL A beautiful tree, given room. Can be shaped. Tolerates sun or shade in any except waterlogged soil. H and S 20ft (6m) Z7-9

Taxus baccata ENGLISH YEW Essential hedging material, dark and dense; the backbone of so many fine gardens. Can be cut back very hard. Tolerates sun or shade and any soil. H and S to 30ft (9m) Z6-7 [ill.pp.128, 178,184]

Teucrium x lucidrys GERMANDER Sub-shrub densely clothed with small, dark, toothed leaves, small deep pink flowers appearing in quantity in late summer. Can be clipped to make a dwarf hedge. Requires sun. H 1ft (30cm) S 2ft (60cm) Z6-8 [ill.p.78]

Viburnum davidii Shrub that generally makes a wide-spreading mound of glossy, dark green foliage. Plant at least one male in a group of female plants to ensure a good crop of the bright blue berries in winter. Requires sun or partial shade. H 4ft (1.2m) S 5ft (1.5m) Z8-10

SPRING AND SUMMER

Cotoneaster horizontalis ROCK SPRAY COTONEASTER If planted against a wall, the fan-like growth of this shrub will send its "herringbone" branches climbing high. The small leaves color richly in fall and last well, as do the red berries. In summer it is a buzz of bees (and wasps). Tolerates sun or partial shade. H 20in (50cm) S 5ft (1.5m) Z5-7

Hydrangea aspera subsp. **sargentiana** SARGENT'S HYDRANGEA The huge, velvety leaves of this shrub are a fine setting for the wide heads of white flowers in mid summer. Tolerates sun and partial shade. H 8ft (2.5m) S 6ft6in (2m) Z7-9 [ill p.81]

Mid-greens

EVERGREEN

Asplenium scolopendrium HART'S TONGUE FERN Perennial fern with strap-like leaves that unfurl from spirals in spring. Requires moist soil and partial shade. H 2ft (60cm) S 18in (45cm) Z4-8

Bergenia cordifolia HEART-LEAF BERGENIA Perennial with clumps of rounded leaves, tinted red in winter. Useful groundcover in shade. Panicles of pink flowers in spring. Tolerates sun and shade and poor soil. H 18in (45cm) S 2ft (60cm) Z4-8 [ill.pp.96,170]

Buxus sempervirens COMMON BOXWOOD Slow-growing shrub or small tree with small shiny leaves. Amenable to training and clipping. The perfect plant for compact hedging. Requires sun or partial shade, and any but water-logged soil. H and S 15ft (5m) Z6-8 [ill.pp.39,82,176, 183]

Choisya ternata MEXICAN ORANGE BLOSSOM Shrub with shiny three-lobed leaves, aromatic when cut or crushed, with scented white flowers in late spring. Requires sun or partial shade. H and S 10ft (3m) Z7-9

Epimedium pinnatum subsp. **colchicum** BARRENWORT Perennial with heart-shaped leaves coloring in fall and winter. Cut the foliage down in late winter to reveal the delicate yellow flowers in spring. Requires partial shade and humus-rich soil. H and S 12in (30cm) Z4-9

Fatsia japonica JAPANESE ARALIA Shrub with elegant, large shiny divided leaves. Produces sprays of white flowers in fall, followed by black fruits. Ideal for sheltered town gardens away from cold winds. Tolerates sun or shade. H and S 10ft (3m) Z7-10 [ill.p.81]

Griselinia littoralis Wind-resistant shrub with luxuriant apple-green foliage. Requires sun. H 20ft (6m) S 15ft (4.6m) Z9-10

Hedera helix ENGLISH IVY Excellent climber for covering sound walls or the ground, with a wide variety of leaf forms, color, and vigor. Tolerant of shade and poor soil. A good variety is **H. h. 'Gracilis'** H and S 15ft (5m) Z5-9

Ligustrum ovalifolium CALIFORNIA PRIVET Justly popular shrub for hedging, the privet will also make a lovely soft mass of greenery whether in shade or sun and whatever the soil, although it will flower more freely in the sun. H 12ft (3.7m) S 10ft (3m) Z6-9

Lonicera pileata PRIVET HONEYSUCKLE Spreading shrub with small, narrow leaves. Useful for groundcover and as a substitute for boxwood for low hedging. Tolerates sun or shade. H 4ft (1.2m) S 3ft (90cm) Z6-8

Prunus laurocerasus CHERRY LAUREL Large-leaved shrub or small tree, useful for screens and hedges. May also be shaped into cones and domes, but not fine topiary. White flower spikes in spring. Tolerates sun and shade. H 20ft (6m) S 30ft (9m) Z6-8

Tellima grandiflora ALASKA FRINGECUPS Semi-evergreen perennial forming spreading clumps of hairy, lobed leaves that make pretty groundcover. The long stems of pale cream flowers

Mahonia japonica (**Spring**)

Phillyrea latifolia (**Summer**)

Asplenium scolopendrium (**Spring**)

Epimedium pinnatum subsp. *colchicum* (**Spring**)

Hedera helix (**Winter**)

smell of honey. Seeds itself generously but not invasively. Requires a cool position in partial shade. H and S 2ft (60cm) Z4-8 [ill.pp.81,139]

Vinca major GREATER PERIWINKLE A rampant spreader, with glossy green oblong leaves. Bright blue, violet, or white flowers through spring and early summer. Tolerates sun and shade in all except dry soils. H 18in (45cm) S 3ft (90cm) Z5-8

SPRING AND SUMMER

Acanthus spinosus SPINY BEAR'S BREECHES Perennial producing clumps of arching broadly-cut leaves, and tall, spiky, purple and white flowers in summer. Best in full sun, but tolerates light shade. H 4ft (1.2m) S 5ft (1.5m) Z6-10

Angelica archangelica ARCHANGEL Tall statuesque biennial that produces in its second year a stout stem ending in rounded pale green umbels. Cut off the seedheads to prevent it seeding itself everywhere. Tolerates sun and shade. H 7ft (2.1m) S 3ft (90cm) Z4-9 [ill.p.157]

Astilboides tabularis (syn. *Rodgersia tabularis*) SHIELDLEAF RODGERSIA Perennial with creamy-white plumes of flowers held above the bold, circular leaves, which can be 3ft (90cm) wide. Requires sun or partial shade in moist soil. H 5ft (1.5m) S 6ft (1.8m) Z5-7 [ill.p.83]

Carpinus betulus COMMON HORNBEAM Can either be grown as a specimen tree, or for hedging, where it resembles beech, but with finer, ribbed, ovate leaves. Tolerates sun and partial shade. H 80ft (25m) S 70ft (20m) Z5-8

Darmera peltata (syn. *Peltiphyllum peltatum*) UMBRELLA PLANT Bog-loving and waterside perennial with umbrella-like leaves. Pink flowers appear in spring before foliage. Tolerates sun or shade. H 3ft3in (1m) S 2ft (60cm) Z6-8 [ill.p.80]

Dryopteris FERN Perennial fern that requires shade and moist soil. Good varieties include the deciduous *D. erythrosora* AUTUMN FERN H 18in (45cm) S 12in (30cm) Z5-8 [ill.pp.81,178]; and semi-evergreen *D. filix-mas* MALE FERN H 4ft (1.2m) S 3ft (90cm) Z4-8 [ill.p.178]

Epimedium x *versicolor* BARRENWORT Perennial with heart-shaped leaves; spring growth tinted red. Useful for groundcover in shade or partial shade. Grows best in moist soil. H and S 12in (30cm) Z5-9

Ferula communis GIANT FENNEL This unscented fennel makes a huge mound of perennial, finely cut dark foliage. The umbels of yellow flowers in late summer can be as tall as 12ft (3.7m) Requires sun. H 6ft6in (2m) S 4ft (1.2m) Z8-10

Foeniculum vulgare FENNEL Perennial herb with sprays of fine, wire-like aromatic foliage. Needs an open, sunny position. H 6ft6in (2m) S 18in (45cm) Z4-9 [ill.pp.81,172]

Gunnera manicata GIANT RHUBARB Waterside and bog-loving perennial with immense leaves and curious green flower spikes. Requires a sunny position in moist soil. Needs shelter from high winds and the crowns need extra protection during the colder months. H 6ft6in (2m) S 8ft (2.4m) Z7-10 [ill.p.83]

Hosta PLANTAIN LILY Perennials. Most grow best in shade in rich, moist soil. Slug and snail control is essential. [ill.p.83] *H. lancifolia* makes good groundcovering clumps of shining, dark green pointed leaves, with lilac flowers freely produced in late summer. H 18in (45cm) S 30in (75cm) Z3-9. *H. plantaginea* is, untypically, a sun-loving hosta with glossy pale green leaves and fragrant white flowers in late summer. H 2ft (60cm) S 4ft (1.2m) Z3-9. *H. ventricosa* has broad heart-shaped ribbed leaves of dark glossy green and rich violet flowers held well above the mound of foliage. H 2ft4in (70cm) S 3ft (90cm) Z3-9

Kirengeshoma palmata YELLOW WAXBELLS A beautiful perennial for light shade with clear green vine-like leaves on purple stems.

Cool yellow waxy flowers appear in fall. Prefers moist, lime-free soil. H 3ft (90cm) S 2ft (60cm) Z5-8

Matteuccia struthiopteris OSTRICH FEATHER FERN Has arching, feathery fronds, with a pale green shuttlecock of lacy fronds emerging from the top of a short stem. Best with some protection and in moist, even wet, conditions. H 2ft (60cm) S 18in (45cm) Z2-9 [ill.p.9]

Miscanthus sinensis EULALIA GRASS Perennial that slowly forms a clump of narrow leaves with paler midriffs. Sends up tall, soft inflorescences in late summer that persist through winter. H 4ft (1.2m) S 18in (45cm) Z4-9

Myrrhis odorata SWEET CICELY Perennial with leaves smelling of anis. Fragrant creamy white flowers in early summer. Tolerates sun or shade. H 3ft (90cm) S 2ft (60cm) Z4-9

Osmunda regalis ROYAL FERN Tall, graceful perennial that tolerates sun but prefers shade. Needs wet conditions and lime-free soil. H 6ft 1.82m) S 3ft (90cm) Z4-9 [ill.pp.32,172]

Polypodium vulgare POLYPODY Perennial with mid-green deeply cut leaves that makes effective groundcover. Needs partial shade and fibrous, well-drained soil. H and S 12in (30cm) Z5-8

Polystichum setiferum SOFT SHIELD FERN Unusually tolerant evergreen fern, fresh and

luxuriant even in relatively dry conditions. H and S 3ft (90cm) Z5-8

Rheum palmatum ORNAMENTAL RHUBARB Perennial with large, decorative deeply-cut leaves, and tall plumes of muted red flowers in summer. Requires sun or partial shade in deep, rich soil. H and S 6ft6in (2m) Z5-9 [ill.pp.81,177]

Rodgersia pinnata BRONZE LEAF RODGERSIA Perennial with heavily ribbed, divided leaves which have a bronze sheen. Panicles of cream or pink flowers appear in summer. Tolerates sun or partial shade if in a sheltered position, and needs moist soil. H 4ft (1.2m) S 30in (75cm) Z5-7 [ill.p.38]

Selinum tenuifolium A tall, elegant perennial sending up many stems with lacy foliage and flat white umbels in summer. Prefers sun and will tolerate any well-drained soil. H 5ft (1.5m) S 2ft (60cm) Z5-8

Vitis GRAPEVINE A number of varieties of grapevine have been selected for their ornamental value: 'Brant' colors particularly well in fall; *V. vinifera* 'Ciotat' has attractively divided leaves; *V. v.* 'Purpurea' has claret-colored foliage contrasting with blue-black grapes [ill.p.20]. They require fertile chalky soil in sun or partial shade. H and S 23ft (7m) Z6-9

Angelica archangelica (**Summer**)

Darmera peltata (**Summer**)

Gunnera manicata (**Summer**)

Miscanthus sinensis (**Summer**)

Vitis vinifera (**Summer**)

Yellow-Greens

EVERGREEN

Carex elata 'Aurea' BOWLES'
GOLDEN SEDGE Perennial that
forms clumps of bright foliage in
spring, greener in summer. Likes
sun and moist soil. H 3ft3in (1m)
S 4ft (1.2m) Z6-8 [ill.p.172]

Choisya ternata 'Sundance'
MEXICAN ORANGE BLOSSOM The
foliage is bright yellow in good
light but will scorch in hot sun.
Best in partial shade. H and S 6ft
(1.8m) Z7-9

Hedera helix 'Buttercup' ENGLISH
IVY Climber with variable heart-
shaped leaves, yellow in sun but
green in shade. Good for
cutting. Like all ivies, prune back
to avoid maturation to
arborescent form. Tolerates sun
or shade and prefers alkaline
soil. H and S 8ft (2.4m) Z5-9
[ill.pp.79,184]

Ligustrum ovalifolium 'Aureum'
GOLDEN PRIVET Gives best color in
full sun. H 12ft (3.7m) S10ft
(3m) Z6-9 [ill.pp.18,147]

Lonicera nitida 'Baggesen's Gold'
BOXLEAF HONEYSUCKLE Small-leaved
shrub, amenable to clipping into
low hedges or simple shapes.
Leaves are yellow in summer,
greener in winter. Requires sun
or partial shade. H and S 5ft
(1.5m) Z7-9 [ill.pp.32,78,167,
172]

Phormium cookianum 'Cream
Delight' NEW ZEALAND FLAX

Perennial with long, lax, shiny
leaves and a tall spike of
yellowish brown flowers that
provides a good contrast to
more rounded shapes. Requires
sun. H 6ft (1.8m) S 1ft (30cm)
Z8-10 [ill.p.143]

Rhododendron yakushimanum
A compact shrub with leathery
leaves, dark above and rusty
beneath, carrying a truss of bell-
shaped pale pink flowers in early
summer. Requires partial shade
and will tolerate neutral to acid
soil. H 3ft (90cm) S 5ft (1.5m)
Z5-8 [ill.p.81]

Taxus baccata 'Aurea' GOLDEN
ENGLISH YEW Slow-growing
conifer with needle-like leaves.
Amenable to hard pruning.
Tolerates shade. H and S 15ft
(4.6m) Z6-7 [ill.pp.139,181]

SPRING AND SUMMER

Acer shirasawanum 'Aureum' (syn.
A. japonicum) FULL MOON MAPLE
Slow-growing shrub or small
tree with fan-like leaves of light
greenish gold. Best in partial
shade. H and S 20ft (6m) Z5-8
[ill.p.143]

Berberis thunbergii 'Aurea' GOLDEN
LEAVED JAPANESE BARBERRY
Compact shrub with vivid yellow
little leaves in spring, greener in
late summer. Pale yellow flowers
appear in early summer;
Tolerates sun or partial shade in
any but water-logged soil. H and
S 5ft (1.5m) Z5-8

Cornus alba 'Aurea' TATANIAN
DOGWOOD Shrub with pointed
yellow leaves and reddish bark
on young stems. Prune back to
base in spring to encourage new
growth with larger leaves and
bright stems. Tolerates sun and
partial shade. H and S 10ft (3m)
Z2-7 [ill.pp.122,184]

Gleditsia triacanthos 'Sunburst'
SUNBURST HONEY LOCUST Tree
with elegant foliage, bright
yellow when young. Likes sun.
H 44ft (13m) S 25ft (7.5m)
Z4-9 [ill.p.178]

Helichrysum petiolare 'Limelight'
LICORICE PLANT Tender sub-shrub
with white woolly stems and
yellowy-green woolly leaves held
on long, wide-spreading
branches. Can be trained up a
support to give a more vertical
effect. Requires sun. H and S 5ft
(1.5m) Z9-10

Hosta 'Gold Standard' GOLDEN
PLANTAIN LILY Perennial with
deeply veined leaves, thinly
edged with green, becoming a
deeper yellow as they mature.
Requires partial shade and moist,
neutral soil. H and S 30in
(75cm) Z3-9

Humulus lupulus 'Aureus' GOLDEN
LEAVED HOP Climber with soft
divided leaves. Ideal for covering
unsightly buildings, but may be
invasive. Tolerates sun and
partial shade. H and S 20ft (6m)
Z5-9 [ill.pp.80,143,184]

Milium effusum 'Aureum' BOWLES'
GOLDEN GRASS Perennial grass

with dainty foliage and slender
yellow flowerheads in summer.
H and S 18in (45cm) Z6-9
[ill.pp.11,78,79,167,173]

Origanum vulgare 'Aureum'
GOLDEN MARJORAM Perennial
herb, forming low clumps of
aromatic pointed leaves and
inconspicuous flowers in
summer. Useful for long-term
summer color. Prefers sun and
alkaline soil. H 10in (25cm) S 2ft
(60cm) Z4-8 [ill.p.147]

Philadelphus coronarius 'Aureus'
MOCK ORANGE A substantial shrub
with lovely fresh yellow foliage
in spring and creamy, fragrant
flowers in early summer. Needs
protection from full sun. H 8ft
(2.4m) S 5ft (1.5m) Z5-8
[ill.pp.10,184]

Physocarpus opulifolius 'Dart's
Gold' NINE BARK One of the best
yellow-green shrubs, with lobed
leaves, colored best when young
in spring. Clusters of greenish-
white flowers in early summer.
Needs sun and prefers acid soil.
H 13ft (4m) S 10ft (3m) Z3-7

Robinia pseudoacacia 'Frisia'
GOLDEN LEAVED BLACK LOCUST One
of the best yellow-leaved trees,
not fading to green later in the
season. Elegant pinnate foliage.
Requires sun and tolerates poor,
dry soil. H 35ft (11m) S 20ft
(6m) Z4-9 [ill.pp.11,169,184]

Sambucus racemosa 'Plumosa
Aurea' RED ELDER Shrub with
deeply divided golden leaves
with serrated leaflets; the richest

effect is achieved by cutting
older growths nearly to the
ground in early spring, and then
feeding. Likes sun. H and S 10ft
(3m) Z4-9

Spiraea japonica 'Goldflame'
BRIDALWREATH Shrub with
spectacular rich golden orange
foliage in spring, and somewhat
unfortunate deep pink flower
heads in late summer. Needs sun
and prefers moist soil. H and S
3ft (90cm) Z4-9 [ill.p.10]

Tanacetum parthenium 'Aureum'
GOLDEN FEVERFEW Semi-evergreen
perennial with lime-yellow, finely
divided aromatic foliage and
sprays of little white daisies
through the summer. Self-seeds.
Requires sun. H and S 12in
(30cm) Z4-9 [ill.pp.81,172,179]

Valeriana phu 'Aurea'
Perennial with rosettes of bright
yellow-green foliage in spring,
turning green in summer.
Requires sun. H 15in (40cm)
S 12in (30cm) Z5-9

Blue-Greens

EVERGREEN

Arctostaphylos patula GREEN
MANZANITA This medium-sized
shrub has neat foliage and pinky
white flowers in spring. Requires
full sun and acid soil. H and S 6ft
(1.8m) Z7-9

Eucalyptus gunnii CIDER GUM
Although this gum will make a

Hedera helix 'Buttercup'
(**Summer**)

Berberis thunbergii 'Aurea'
(**Spring**)

Milium effusum 'Aureum'
(**Summer**)

Physocarpus opulifolius 'Dart's
Gold' (**Summer**)

Valeriana phu 'Aurea' (**Summer**)

large tree with pretty sage-green leaves if left to its own devices, it can be stooled and thus kept to shrub size, with round, silver-blue juvenile foliage, lovely for cutting. H 80ft (25m) S 23ft (8m), or H and S 7ft (2.1m) Z8-10

Euphorbia characias SPURGE
The stiff stems are crowded with narrow blue-gray leaves, and from late winter the drooping heads begin to look up and open their heads of lime-green flowers, which last in beauty until early summer. Cut the flowered stems close to the ground to encourage next year's flowering shoots. Tolerates sun or partial shade. H 4ft (1.2m) S 3ft (90cm) Z7-9

Festuca glauca BLUE FESCUE
Perennial tufts of steely blue-green grass, good for edging. H and S 8in (20cm) Z4-9 [ill.pp.71,90,91]

Picea pungens 'Koster' KOSTER'S BLUE SPRUCE A conical tree with stout leaves of an intense silvery blue. Tolerates sun or shade in any soil except overlying chalk or limestone. H 20ft (6m) S 10ft (3m) Z3-8

Ruta graveolens 'Jackman's Blue' RUE Shrub with divided leaves of a good blue-green and bright yellow flowers in summer. Cut hard back in late spring to keep the mound compact and reduce flowering. Requires sun. H 20in (50cm) S 30in (75cm) Z4-9 [ill.p.181]

SPRING AND SUMMER

Acaena 'Blue Haze' NEW ZEALAND BURR Makes a nearly evergreen mat of finely cut bluish leaves on bronze stems. The flowers are little brown spiny burrs, in summer. Tolerates sun and partial shade. H 8in (20cm) S 30in (75cm) Z5-8

Hosta PLANTAIN LILY
Perennials that do best in partial shade and rich, moist soil. Good "blue" leaved varieties include *H.* 'Halcyon' with heart-shaped glaucous leaves, and lilac-gray flower spikes in summer, H 8in (20cm) S 12in (30cm) Z3-9 [ill.pp.71,81]; and *H. sieboldiana* var. *elegans* with deeply puckered leaves and near white flowers in summer, H 3ft (90cm) S 5ft (1.5m) Z3-9 [ill.pp.94,139]

Macleaya microcarpa 'Kelway's Coral Plume' CORAL PLUME POPPY An impressive perennial with a running rootstock. Beautiful lobed leaves, gray-green above and nearly white beneath, and fluffy plumes of coral flowers in summer. Requires sun. H 8ft (2.4m) S 4ft (1.2m) Z4-9 [ill.pp.80,81]

Melianthus major HONEYBUSH
Perennial with sumptuous frilled and incised blue-green foliage. Can be cut to the ground in colder winters but will generally sprout again from the base. Requires sun. H and S 4ft (1.2m) Z8-10 [ill.p.182]

Mertensia simplicissima (syn. *M. mertensia* subsp. *asiatica*) Perennial with very blue leaves that are pretty with the bunches of drooping pale blue flowers in early summer. Tolerates sun and shade in deep soil. H and S 12in (30cm) Z5-8 [ill.p.175]

Green Flowers

Alchemilla mollis LADY'S MANTLE
Perennial with round, furry leaves, and sprays of lime-green flowers in summer. Useful for edging paths and borders. Cut back after flowering to encourage fresh new foliage. Tolerant of sun or shade in any but boggy soil. H and S 20in (50cm) Z3-7 [ill.pp.166,172]

Astrantia major
Perennial forming clumps of divided leaves that throw up many-branched stems of pincushion-shaped flowerheads, of a pleasing greenish-white with a hint of pink. Tolerates sun and partial shade. H 24in (60cm) S 18in (45cm) Z5-7

Bupleurum fruticosum SHRUBBY HARE'S EAR Evergreen shrub with dark green glossy foliage and umbels of yellow-green flowers that last all summer long. Requires full sun. H 6ft (1.8m) S 8ft (2.4m) Z7-9

Eucomis bicolor PINEAPPLE FLOWER
In late summer this bulbous

plant produces substantial spikes of starry pale green flowers edged with dark red, making a strong contrast with the broad dark green leaves. Requires full sun. H and S 18in (45cm) Z8-10

Euphorbia SPURGE
Apart from *E. characias* – *see above* – other good varieties with lime-green flowers include *E. amygdaloides* var. *robbiae* WOOD SPURGE which is rampant but useful for shade, even in poor soil, with rounded flowerheads in spring. H 18in (45cm) S 24in (60cm) Z7-9. *E. characias* subsp. *wulfenii* has large flowers and good blue-green evergreen leaves. H and S 3ft3in (1m) Z7-10 [ill.pp.142, 172,184]. *E. palustris* needs deeper soil, but rewards with brilliant yellow-green flower heads in summer, and foliage coloring in fall. H and S 3ft (90cm) Z7-9. *E. polychroma* makes tidy mounds of bright yellow-green in early spring, lasting well. H and S 20in (50cm) Z3-9 [ill.pp.79,184]. *E. schillingii* is a strong plant that produces its impressive yellow flowers late in summer. H and S 3ft (90cm) Z7-9

Garrya elliptica SILK TASSEL BUSH
A well-furnished shrub with leathery evergreen leaves and long catkins of grayish green flowers in late winter. The good male form *G. e.* 'James Roof' has the longest catkins, purple-

tinted. Will be happy on a shady wall, and tolerates poor soil. H 16ft (5m) S 10ft (3m) Z8-10

Helleborus HELLEBORE
Evergreen perennial that requires partial shade and moisture-retentive soil.
H. argutifolius (syn. *H. corsicus*) forms a clump of stout stems with handsome three-fingered leaves of a cool green, producing its large clusters of apple-green cups from late winter. H 3ft (90cm) S 20in (50cm) Z6-8. *H. foetidus* STINKING HELLEBORE has much-divided, darkest green leaves, with clusters of flowers like pale green bells, edged with purple. H and S 18in (45cm) Z3-9

Itea ilicifolia HOLLY SWEETSPIRE
Evergreen shrub bearing mid-green holly-like leaves and long racemes of honey-scented flowers in profusion in late summer. Tolerates sun or partial shade. H and S 10ft (3m) Z7-9

Kniphofia 'Bet's Lemon' TORCH LILY
Evergreen perennial that forms a clump of long, thin, lax leaves and sends up tall "pokers" of cool jade green with a hint of cream in late summer. Requires full sun and moist soil. H 4ft (1.2m) S 30in (75cm) Z5-9

Moluccella laevis BELLS OF IRELAND
Annual that sends up long spires of cool emerald green bells that are good for cutting. Requires sun and rich soil. H 24in (60cm) S 8in (20cm)

Ruta graveolans 'Jackman's Blue' **(Summer)**

Melianthus major **(Summer)**

Eucomis bicolor **(Fall)**

Garrya elliptica **(Winter)**

Heleborus argutifolius **(Spring)**

Nicotiana FLOWERING TOBACCO
Perennials grown as annuals that require sun and rich soil.
N. x *sanderae* 'Lime Green' has bright yellow-green flowers in profusion over a long period. H 24in (60cm) S 8in (20cm) [ill.pp.44,180,182].
N. langsdorffii is a tall, open plant, with panicles of drooping green flowers; it self-seeds willingly but not oppressively. H 3ft3in (1m) S 1ft (30cm)

Veratrum viride INDIAN POKE
Perennial with gloriously pleated fresh green leaves followed by tall spikes densely packed with starry green flowers. Requires partial shade and fertile soil. H 4ft (1.2m) S 2ft (60cm) Z3-7

Green Variegated with White or Cream

EVERGREEN

Euonymus fortunei
These plants are normally semi-prostrate, but will climb if given support. They do best in sun.
E. f. 'Emerald Gaiety' has rounded leaves and the whitest variegation. H 3ft (90cm) S 5ft (1.5m) Z5-8. *E. f.* 'Silver Queen' makes an elegant, compact shrub when not climbing, with

yellow variegation becoming creamy white later. H 8ft (2.4m) S 5ft (1.5m) Z5-8 [ill.pp.80,143]

Hedera helix 'Glacier' ENGLISH IVY
Evergreen climber that makes a good background with clear markings in gray and white. H and S 10ft (3m) Z6-9 [ill.p.79]

Lamium galeobdolon 'Florentinum' DEADNETTLE
Perennial with dark green leaves, marbled with white. It roots as it spreads, and may be invasive, but not difficult to keep within bounds. Requires sun. H 10in (25cm) S 18in (45cm) Z3-9

SPRING AND SUMMER

Arum italicum subsp. *italicum* 'Marmoratum' ITALIAN ARUM
Tuberous bulb that produces glossy dark green spear-shaped leaves, veined with white, that are very effective in winter. Stalks of orange-red berries appear in late summer. Requires sun. H 10in (25cm) S 12in (30cm) Z6-9 [ill.p.146]

Brunnera macrophylla 'Dawson's White' VARIEGATED HEARTLEAF BRUNNERA Perennial that makes good groundcover, its large heart-shaped leaves boldly variegated with creamy white. Long sprays of forget-me-not blue flowers in spring. Requires partial shade and moist soil. H 18in (45cm) S 24in (60cm) Z3-9

Cornus alba 'Elegantissima' TATARIAN DOGWOOD Shrub with

pale green leaves edged with creamy white. Cut back half the shoots to the ground in early spring to get red stems for winter color. Requires sun. H and S 10ft (3m) Z2-7

Glyceria maxima var. *variegata* (syn. *G. aquatica* 'Variegata') VARIEGATED MANNA GRASS This spreading grass prefers pond margins or boggy soil, and has broad spiky leaves striped with white and cream. Best in sun but tolerates partial shade. H 2ft8in (80cm) S 2ft (60cm) Z5-9 [ill.p.32]

Holcus mollis 'Albovariegatus' VARIEGATED CREEPING SOFT GRASS Grass whose fresh growth in spring and fall gives the effect of a white carpet, the soft leaves having only a narrow central green stripe. The creeping rhizomes are easily uprooted. Requires partial shade. H 10in (25cm) S 18in (45cm) Z5-8 [ill.p.149]

Hosta PLANTAIN LILY
Perennials that do best in shade.
H. crispula has undulating leaf margins that are boldy edged with white. H 30in (75cm) S 3ft (90cm) Z3-9 [ill.p.18]. *H. fortunei* 'Marginata Alba' has rich sage-green leaves broadly edged with white H and S 2ft (60cm) Z3-9. *H. undulata* var. *albomarginata* (syn. *H.* 'Thomas Hogg') is a robust plant with smooth fresh leaves edged with cream, and tall lilac flowers in

summer. H 30in (75cm) S 3ft (90cm) Z3

Iris pallida 'Argentea Variegata' DALMATIAN IRIS Rhizomatous perennial with superb sword-shaped leaves, boldly striped blue-green and white. Tall blue flowering stems in summer. Requires sun. H 2ft (60cm) S 1ft (30cm) Z5 [ill.p.80]

Lunaria annua 'Alba Variegata' VARIEGATED HONESTY Biennial that produces loose spires of white flowers in spring, and leaves irregularly marked creamy white. Comes true from seed. Requires partial shade. H 3ft (90cm) S 1ft (30cm) Z6 [ill.pp.111,183,184]

Miscanthus sinensis 'Variegatus' VARIEGATED EULALIA GRASS Perennial that form clumps of ribbon-like leaves, prettily striped green and white. H 5ft (1.5m) S 3ft (90cm) Z6 [ill.p.176]

Phalaris arundinacea var. *picta* 'Picta' GARDENER'S GARTERS Dense, running grass with white-striped leaves. Can be cut to the ground in summer to make fresh growth for the fall. Needs partial shade and moist soil. H and S 3ft (90cm) Z4 [ill.pp.81,172,181]

Phlox paniculata 'Norah Leigh' GARDEN PHLOX Perennial with tall, willowy stems which have cream-variegated leaves, and palepink flowers in late summer. Requires sun and moist soil. H 3ft3in (1m) S 2ft (60cm) Z4

Pulmonaria LUNGWORT
Spring-flowering perennials.

P. longifolia LONGLEAF LUNGWORT
has narrow, dark green leaves with white spots, and deep blue flowers Z3-8. *P. officinalis* has heart-shaped spotted leaves and pink flowers that turn pale blue Z4-8 [ill.p.183]. *P. o.* 'Sissinghurst White' has white flowers Z4-8. All make good groundcover in moisture-retentive soil. All H 12in (30cm) S 18in (45cm)

Scrophularia auriculata 'Variegata' (syn. *S. aquatica*) VARIEGATED WATER FIGWORT Perennial, evergreen clumps with particularly good cream variegation. Cut off the flower spikes to prevent seeding. Requires partial shade and moist soil. H 30in (75cm) S 12in (30cm) Z6-9 [ill.p.131]

Silybum marianum HOLY THISTLE
Biennial with very prickly thistle leaves of dark green splashed with white. Reliable self-seeder. Requires sun. H 4ft (1.2m) S 2ft (60cm) Z7-9

Green Variegated with Yellow

EVERGREEN

Agave americana 'Variegata' CENTURY PLANT Perennial succulent that makes a huge

Nicotiana langsdorffii (**Summer**)

Cornus alba 'Elegantissima' (**Summer**)

H. undulata var. *albomarginata* (**Summer**)

Pulmonaria longifolia (**Spring**)

Silybum marianum (**Summer**)

rosette of sharply pointed striped gray-green and yellow leaves. Only hardy in the warmest gardens. Requires sun. H and S 6ft6in (2m) Z9-11

Carex hachijoensis 'Evergold' (syn. *C. oshimensis* 'E.') JAPANESE SEDGE Perennial that forms dense tufts of grass-like foliage, whiich are bright yellow with narrow green margins. Requires sun. H and S 12in (30cm) Z5-8

Cortaderia selloana 'Aureolineata' (syn. *C. s.* 'Gold Band') PAMPAS GRASS Perennial with large, luxuriant clumps of yellow-striped leaves, and creamy, erect plumes from late summer. Requires sun. H 6ft (1.8m) S 4ft (1.2m) Z7-10

Elaeagnus pungens 'Maculata' THORNY ELAEAGNUS Shrub at its cheerful best in winter sunlight. The new growth is brownish in color, maturing to dark green, leathery leaves with bright yellow centers. Requires sun. H 10ft (3m) S 12ft (3.7m) Z7-9

Euonymus fortunei 'Emerald 'n' Gold' A good groundcovering shrub, densely covered with small very dark green leaves with bright variegation. Requires sun. H 2ft (60cm) S 3ft (90cm) Z5-8 [ill.p.178]

Hedera IVY
Climbers that do well in sun or shade, good or poor soil. They will grow horizontally for groundcover, as well as vertically.
H. colchica 'Dentata Variegata'

COLCHIS IVY has large elliptic leaves, shaded green and margined creamy-yellow Z6-9.
H. c. 'Sulphur Heart' (syn. *H. c.* 'Paddy's Pride') has dark green margins and deep yellow and paler green centers Z6-9 [ill.p.170]. *H. helix* 'Oro di Bogliasco' (syn. *H. h.* 'Goldheart') ENGLISH IVY has neat dark green leaves with a central yellow splash Z5-9. All H and S 10ft (3m)

Ilex aquifolium 'Aurea Marginata' HOLLY A very solid shrub, or small tree, with spiny leaves broadly edged with creamy yellow. Red berries. Amenable to shaping. Tolerates both sun and partial shade. H 20ft (6m) S 16in (5m) Z7-9 [ill.p.181]

Pleioblastus auricomus (syn. *P. viridistriatus*) STRIPED BAMBOO Bamboo whose leaves are bright yellow with irregular green striping. A runner, but can be controlled. Needs sun. H 4ft (1.2m) S indefinite Z5-9

Salvia officinalis 'Icterina' SAGE This shrub's soft, rounded leaves are light green variegated with yellow, and strongly aromatic. Requires sun. H 2ft (60cm) S 3ft (90cm) Z4-9 [ill.p.80]

Vinca major 'Variegata' VARIEGATED GREATER PERIWINKLE A carpeting shrub with glossy dark green leaves splashed with cream. Lavender-blue flowers in spring. Requires partial shade and moist soil. H 15in (10cm) S 5ft (1.5m) Z5-8

SPRING AND SUMMER

Cornus alba 'Spaethii' TATARIAN DOGWOOD Shrub with brilliant yellow variegation in the leaves in summer and deep red stems that show best after leaf fall in winter. Requires sun. H 8ft (2.4m) S 6ft (1.8m) Z2-7

Hakonechloa macra 'Alboaurea' HAKONE GRASS Perennial grass that makes slowly increasing clumps of arching leaves variegated cream and yellow, coloring russet-yellow in fall. H and S 18in (45cm) Z7-9

Hosta PLANTAIN LILY
Perennial that tolerates sun and partial shade in moist soil.
H. fortunei var. *aureomarginata* (syn. *H.* 'Yellow Edge') has sage-green pointed leaves edged with yellow and spires of lavender flowers in midsummer. H 12in (30cm) S 18in (45cm) Z3-9 [ill.p.81]. *H. sieboldiana* 'Frances Williams' has puckered glaucous leaves with a bold yellow margin, and pale mauve spikes . H 2ft (60cm) S 3ft (90cm) Z3-9

Iris
Rhizomatous perennials.
I. pallida 'Variegata' VARIEGATED SWEET IRIS, which needs a sunny position, has sword-shaped leaves striped blue-green and yellow, and tall blue flowers in early summer. H 2ft (60cm) S 1ft (30cm) Z6-9 [ill.pp.136,157].
I. pseudacorus 'Variegata' VARIEGATED YELLOW FLAG IRIS Is

best in a moist position. The dramatic foliage has bold yellow stripes in spring, turning green later, and yellow flowers in early summer. H 4ft (1.2m) S 1ft (30cm) Z5-9 [ill.p.32]

Mentha suaveolens 'Variegata' APPLEMINT Like all mints, this can be invasive, but is a very fresh groundcover with creamy white variegation. Requires sun. H 18in (45cm) S 24in (60cm) Z5-9

Symphoricarpos orbiculatus 'Foliis Variegatis' INDIAN CURRANT\CORAL BERRY A graceful shrub with small leaves irregularly edged with yellow, coloring best in full sun. H 3ft (90cm) S 5ft (1.5m) Z3-7 [ill.p.166]

Green Variegated with Reds and Pinks

EVERGREEN

Berberis thunbergii 'Rose Glow' ROSEGLOW JAPANESE BARBERRY Generally the leaves of this shrub open purple and become more and more variegated with pink as the season progresses. Good fall color. Tolerates both sun and partial shade. H and S 4ft (1.2m) Z5-8 [ill.p.130]

Brassica oleracea Acephala Group 'Red Peacock' ORNAMENTAL KALE

These annual kales are grown for their fall value: they need low night temperatures before they color up well, but a severe frost will finish them off. Requires sun and fertile, lime-rich soil. H and S 18in (45cm) [ill.p.109]

Trifolium repens 'Purpurascens' WHITE CLOVER Semi-evergreen perennial that makes effective groundcover with good foliage that is dark green mottled with chocolate brown. Requires sun. H 5in (12cm) S 12in (30cm) Z5-8 [ill.p.131]

SPRING AND SUMMER

Acer negundo 'Flamingo' BOX ELDER The trifoliate leaves of this tree are pinkish green, turning white. Requires sun. H 50ft (15m) S 26ft (8m) Z2-8

Actinidia kolomikta KOLOMIKTA ACTINIDIA Twining climber with large leaves that are variously splashed in shades of pink, white and green as they develop in early summer, but revert to green as the season progresses. Needs full sun. H and S 16ft (5m) Z4-9

Houttuynia cordata 'Chameleon' Perennial with pungent heart shaped leaves in shades of dark green, red, yellow and bronze, bearing single white flowers in summer. The roots are invasive in moist ground. H and S 12in (30cm) Z6-9

Carex hachijoensis 'Evergold' (**Summer**)

Pleioblastus auricomus (**Summer**)

Hosta fortunei var. *aureomarginata* (**Summer**)

Mentha suaveolens 'Variegata' (**Summer**)

Actinidia kolomikta (**Summer**)

Silver-Grays

Silver is often used as a setting for brilliant jewels, since it flatters its surroundings by reflecting them back. The color of silver is elusive, deriving its quality from its brilliance: without that sheen, silver would be gray. It is a near neutral color, almost as inert as white, though not so bright and assertive.

In the garden, silver foliage can be used like silver in jewelry as a background against which other colors are set. The leaves of many silver and gray plants, such as some artemisias and lavender cotton, are of such filigree fineness that they can give a glimmering impression. Other paler, gray plants have a soft, cloudy dustiness. Being lighter in tone than most green foliage, and more neutral, gray reacts less with other colors. Because of this, silver leaved plants make good "peacekeepers." Longer lasting than flowers, they can be used, like white flowers, to keep warring colors such as pink and yellow apart in a border, and can be even more effective than green foliage as a buffer between colors. Repeating incidents of silver in a border will hold together a diverse range of colors with a unifying strand of neutrality.

Silver is a particularly good foil for magenta flowers, such as the Armenian cranesbill or rose campion, two plants which many gardeners are nervous to use because their color is so intense. For a longer lasting planting of similar striking tonal contrasts, use silver leaved plants with the darkest available foliage plants, such as the plum colored and muted red varieties of plum, barberry, and smokebush (see pages 130–31).

Silver leaved plants are good components for pale harmonious plantings involving cream, blues, and pinks, because they will make the pastel colors seem brighter.

LEFT An obelisk has been painted silver-gray to forge a link with the silver spears of foliage in a black-painted terracotta pot. Bright green boxwood, clipped into spirals contributes to the geometric formality of the scene.

RIGHT The giant, many-fingered leaves of the cardoon (*Cynara cardunculus*) loom over blue fescue (*Festuca glauca*) and silver lamb's ears (*Stachys byzantina*), with the silver leaved shrub, Russian olive (*Elaeagnus angustifolia*) glimmering behind. All do best in sun, so try to place the cardoon where it will not shade the smaller plants for too much of the day.

Silver foliage, like white variegation, can also be valuable in the garden when used in an all-white planting. Here, it will enhance the overall impression of lightness made by the white flowers, and its intermediate tone, halfway between white and green, reduces what would otherwise be harsh tonal contrasts between white flowers and their own green leaves.

An exclusively silver planting can be effective on a relatively small scale, but will rely for interest on strong contrasts of shape and texture, because the color itself is so inert and the range of color so narrow. The majestic cardoon, *opposite, right*, makes an emphatic centerpiece for a combination that includes the fluttering leaves of a silver Russian olive and the woolly leaves of lamb's ears.

A silver garden would benefit, though, from a less purist approach. If you introduce a few blue or purple flowers or some blue-green foliage such as rue, or blue-green hostas, these will enhance the silver to give a cool, harmonious planting with much greater color interest. In the planting *below right,* the blue tinge to the fountain of fescue emphasizes the silver-gray of the curry plant. You can also lighten and sharpen a gray planting without adding bright color by introducing some white, or a clear mid-green. In the planting *below left,* the small white flowerheads of a hebe seem to shine out of the enveloping background of gray artemisias.

When using silver leaved plants it is important to bear in mind that most of them originate in arid climates, and so need dry and sunny conditions. Their silver sheen in fact comes from masses of tiny white hairs on the surface of the leaves, which have evolved to protect the plants from overheating in hot sun. But remember that this sheen is at its best in summer sunshine. Plants such as artemisias and lamb's ears that gleam like silver in the sun, seem transmuted into base metal in other lights. They can look leaden gray in damp or shade, or when lit by thin winter light – conditions in which they do not thrive.

LEFT In early summer, a hebe makes a white flowered mound surrounded by two kinds of artemisia, the filigree leaved *A.* 'Powis Castle' and white sagebush (*A. ludoviciana*) with lance-shaped leaves. The felty leaves and purple flower spikes of lamb's ears (*Stachys byzantina*) add textural and color interest. All will tolerate some shade, but do best in the sun in well drained soil.

RIGHT The blue fescue (*Festuca glauca*) mingles with the curry plant (*Helichrysum italicum*) against the border's loose stone edging – an ideal position since both these plants favor dry, well drained conditions.

Silvers and Grays

EVERGREENS

Anthemis punctata subsp. *cupaniana* DWARF CHAMOMILE A quick-growing perennial forming a low mound of finely cut silvery foliage. The white daisies should be cut back after flowering is over. Requires sun. H 12in (30cm) S 24in (60cm) Z5-9 [ill.pp.95,98]

Artemisia
Perennials and sub-shrubs that generally do best in open, sunny sites. *A. absinthium* 'Lambrook Silver' WORMWOOD has boldly divided silky gray leaves and tall sprays of tiny dirty yellow flowers in summer. H and S 30in (75cm) Z5-8. *A. arborescens* has beautiful silver filigree foliage. Given a warm wall and a dry position it will climb 6ft (1.8m), normally H 3ft (90cm) S 2ft (60cm) Z9-11. 'Powis Castle' has elegant silvery foliage and does not usually flower. H 30in (75cm) S 3ft (90cm) Z5-8 [ill.pp.91,176]. *A. stelleriana* 'Mori' BEACH WORMWOOD is a prostrate carpeter, with broadly cut leaves of silvery gray felt. H 1ft (30cm) S 3ft (90cm) Z3-8

Ballota pseudodictamnus GRECIAN HOREHOUND Sub-shrub that, from a woody base, throws up many long stems clothed in woolly gray green leaves, with bobbly flowers opening along the stem in midsummer. Requires full sun and very well drained soil. H 2ft (60cm) S 3ft (90cm) Z7-9 [ill.pp.80,180]

Brachyglottis 'Sunshine' (syn. *Senecio* 'Sunshine') Sprawling shrub with good gray foliage which can be pruned quite hard; either in spring to prevent its brassy yellow flowers, or in midsummer to remove the spent flower heads. Requires full sun. H 3ft (90cm) S 5ft (1.5m) Z8-10 [ill.p.172]

Convolvulus cneorum BUSH MORNING GLORY A neat shrub well-clothed in narrow, silky leaves, producing its white trumpets over a long period in summer. Requires sun. H and S 30in (75cm) Z8-10

Cortaderia selloana 'Pumila' PAMPAS GRASS A dwarf form of the perennial that makes a large clump of lax, sharp-edged leaves, with tall, silvery plumes in early fall. Requires sun. H and S 5ft (1.5m) Z7-10 [ill.p.130]

Dianthus PINK
The pinks make evergreen mats of gray leaves, with very sweetly scented flowers in shades of white, pink, red and purple. Named varieties include 'Her Majesty' with double white flowers, 'Robespierre' with deep crimson flowers flecked with pink, 'Mrs Sinkins' with double white flowers, richly scented, 'Old Spice' with double dark pink flowers, and 'Sweet Memory' with dusky pink flowers marked with white. All need sun. H and S 12in (30cm) Z4-8

Echeveria
These succulents are not hardy, but will make large clumps of neat rosettes in a range of grays and greens; shiny, matt, or furry. Spikes of drooping orange or red flowers appear in summer. Require sun. H 6in (15cm) S 12in (30cm) Z9-10

Hebe pinguifolia 'Pagei'
A densely creeping shrub with small, evergreen leaves of a leaden gray, and small white flowers in summer. Requires full sun. H 1ft (30cm) S 2ft (60cm) Z8-10

Helichrysum
Annuals, perennials and shrubs that are best in sun. *H. italicum* CURRY PLANT is a pungent sub-shrub that is best clipped in spring to prevent the lanky stems of yellow flowers. H 2ft (60cm) S 3ft (90cm) Z8-10 [ill.pp.91,176]. *H. petiolare* LICORICE PLANT is a shrub, usually grown as an annual with rounded gray leaves and a spreading habit. The vigorous growth can be trained vertically. H 18in (45cm) S 5ft (1.5m) Z8-10 [ill.p.121]

Helictotrichon sempervirens (syn. *Avena candida*) BLUE OAT GRASS Perennial making dense clumps of narrow blue-gray leaves, with waving flower plumes of gray in summer. Requires sun. H 3ft (90cm) S 2ft (60cm) Z4-9 [ill.p.179]

Lavandula LAVENDER
Shrub with fine gray foliage and strongly aromatic flower spikes in summer. It grows best in sun and well-drained soil [ill.pp.95, 173]. A good pink variety is *L. angustifolia* 'Loddon Pink'; good blue and violet varieties include *L. a.* 'Hidcote' and *L. a.* 'Munstead' H and S 30in (75cm) Z4-9. *L. stoechas* FRENCH LAVENDER has small violet flowers with prominant bracts like topknots; *L.s.* f. *leucantha* has white flowers. H and S 30in (75cm) Z4-9

Phlomis fruticosa JERUSALEM SAGE A Mediterranean shrub of a woolly, gray-green appearance; the deep yellow flowers have long-lasting seedheads. Requires sun. H and S 4ft (1.2m) Z7-9 [ill.pp.163,169]

Santolina chaemaecyparissus COTTON LAVENDER This shrub is best clipped tight in early spring, to make a mound of neat gray foliage which has a pleasant scent. The bright yellow flowers are usually clipped away. Requires sun and soil that is not too rich. H 30in (75cm) S 3ft (90cm) Z6-9 [ill.pp.71,127, 151]

Sedum spathulifolium STONECROP Evergreen perennial that makes a close mat of gray-green rosettes, often flushed red. Sprays of yellow stars appear through late summer. Tolerates shade. H 4in (10cm) S 12in (30cm) Z5-9

Senecio viravira (syn. *Cineraria*) DUSTY MILLER Sub-shrub, often grown as an annual. Exquisite woolly gray foliage, but not reliably hardy. The yellow flowers are best removed. Requires full sun. H and S 3ft (90cm) Z9-10

Stachys byzantina (syn. *S. lanata*) LAMB'S EARS Woody perennial making mats of velvety leaves that cover the ground well. Spikes of deep pink flowers are almost swamped in grey fluff. Best in sun and poor soil. H 12in (30cm) S 24in (60cm) [ill.pp.90, 1,98,178,183]. *S. b.* 'Silver Carpet' is similar but does not flower. Both Z4-8

Tanacetum argenteum (syn. *Achillea argentea*) Perennial that forms mats of silvery filigree foliage with small pure white daisies. Requires sun. H 9in (23cm) S 8in (20cm) Z5-8

Teucrium fruticans BUSH GERMANDER Quick-growing, open shrub with an overall appearance of soft gray-white. Pale blue flowers are produced over a long period. Requires full sun. H 6ft (1.8m) S 12ft (4m) Z8-10

Thymus x *citriodorus* 'Argenteus' LEMON THYME Perennial with tiny silvery, lemon scented leaves. Requires sun. H 8in (20cm) S 15in (40cm) Z5-8

Artemisia 'Powis Castle' **(Summer)**

Dianthus 'Mrs Sinkins' **(Summer)**

Echeveria **(Summer)**

Lavandula stoechas f. *leucantha* **(Summer)**

Tanacetum argenteum **(Summer)**

SPRING AND SUMMER

Argyranthemum MARGUERITE
Perennials with gray-green leaves and a long season of flowering H and S 30in (75cm) Z9-10 [ill.pp.172,182,183]

Artemisia
Perennials and shrubs that are not evergreen include *A. alba* 'Canescens' which has extremely lacy, finely curving leaflets, giving it a rather spiky overall look, H 18in (45cm) S 12in (30cm) Z5-8 [ill.p.178].
A. ludoviciana 'Silver Queen' WHITE SAGEBUSH has lanceolate silver-gray leaves on running stems. H 30in (75cm) S 3ft (90cm) Z4-8 [ill.pp.91,130]
A. schmidtiana SILVER-MOUND ARTEMISIA has creeping shoots forming low cushions of soft greenish gray, hair-like leaves and nodding white flowerheads in early fall. H 6in (15cm) S 18in (45cm) Z5-8 [ill.p.182]

Astelia chathamica SILVER SPEAR
Perennial producing open tussocks of arching, sword-shaped, silver-gray leaves, with reddish scented flowers on short spikes in summer. Tolerates both sun and partial shade, requiring fertile soil that does not dry out H 4ft (1.2m) S 3ft (90cm) Z9-10

Athyrium niponicum var. *pictum*
JAPANESE PAINTED FERN Deciduous, glaucous fronds with purple flushed stalks and midrib. Requires shade and humus-rich,

moist soil. H 2ft (60cm) S 18in (45cm) Z3-9

Centaurea cineraria DUSTY MILLER
Quite a chunky plant, this perennial has loose rosettes of very beautiful, lacy, gray leaves. Best to remove the mauve thistle flower. Requires sun and will tolerate poor soil. H 30in (75cm) S 3ft (90cm) Z6-8

Cerastium tomentosum SNOW IN SUMMER Semi-evergreen perennial forming mats of gray foliage smothered in white flowers in late spring. Can be invasive. Requires full sun. H 3in (8cm) S 18in (45cm) Z3-8 [ill.p.109]

Cynara cardunculus CARDOON
A magnificent perennial with pointed, deeply divided leaves that can be 4ft (1.2m) long. In the summer stout stems carry prickly purple thistles. Requires sun. H 6ft6in (2m) S 3ft (90cm) Z6-8 [ill.pp.90,149,174,181]

Eryngium giganteum GIANT SEA HOLLY Biennial producing rosettes of lightly veined green leaves that throw up spiny silver flower spikes in their second year. Easy from seed. Requires sun. H 3ft (90cm) S 1ft (30cm) Z5-8 [ill.p.172]

Elaeagnus angustifolia RUSSIAN OLIVE Large shrub that can easily be pruned to make a small tree, with downy grayish green leaves and startling spines. Requires full sun and fertile soil. H and S 20ft (6m) Z3-7 [ill.p.90]

Hippophaë rhamnoïdes SEA BUCKTHORN A silvery shrub with an open habit, this needs to be planted in a group with at least one male plant, and the females will then develop masses of translucent orange berries. Requires sun and tolerates poor, dry or sandy soil. H and S 20ft (6m) Z4-7

Iris pallida DALMATIAN IRIS
Rhizomatous perennial. The strong fans of sword-shaped leaves remain glaucous blue throughout the summer, and tall stems of blue flowers are freely produced in early summer. Requires full sun and rich, preferably alkaline soil. H 4ft (1.2m) S18in (45cm) Z6-9

Lamium maculatum 'Beacon Silver' SPOTTED DEADNETTLE
Creeping and carpeting perennial with silver paterned leaves and deep puce flowers.
L. m. 'White Nancy' has white flowers. Tolerates full and partial shade and prefers moist soil. H 8in (20cm) S 3ft (90cm) Z4-8

Lotus hirsutus (syn. *Dorycnium hirsutum*) CANARY CLOVER Sub-shrub with small silky leaves, at its best from late summer when the white pea-flowers begin to mature into clusters of chocolate brown seedpods. Prune in spring to keep it dense. Requires full sun and dry soil. H and S 2ft (60cm) Z8-10

Lychnis coronaria ROSE CAMPION
Biennial or short-lived perennial

has a rosette of grayish leaves and many-branched stems carrying a succession of single flowers, commonly deep magenta or white (Alba Group). Requires sun. H 20in (50cm) S 12in (30cm) Z4-8 [ill.pp.98,175]

Onopordum acanthium SCOTCH THISTLE Splendid biennial with large prickly leaves covered with silver white hairs, topped in its second year with a spire of mauve thistles. Tolerates both sun and partial shade and prefers rich soil. H 6ft (1.8m) S 3ft (90cm) Z5-8.
O. nervosum will attain 8ft (2.4m) [ill.p.176]

Ornithogalum nutans DROOPING STAR OF BETHLEHEM Bulb that produces spikes of satiny pale green and silvery white flowers in early spring, in sun or partial shade. H and S 8in (20cm) Z5-9

Pyrus salicifolia 'Pendula' WILLOW LEAF PEAR A graceful, spreading silvery-gray tree, although sometimes it needs a stake to help a leader make a good height. Requires full sun. H 15ft (5m) S 12ft (3.7m) Z5-9 [ill.pp.82,130]

Rosa glauca (syn. *R. rubrifolia*) RED LEAF ROSE A very useful rose with reddish stems and gray-green foliage. Simple pink flowers are followed by charming oval hips. Often self-seeds. Requires an open, sunny position. H 6ft (1.8m) S 5ft (1.5m) Z4-9 [ill.pp.120,176]

Salix alba var. *sericea* (syns. *S. a. argentea*, *S.a.*'Splendens') SILVER WILLOW Although this willow, which has leaves of an intense silvery hue, will make a substantial tree, it takes kindly to coppicing and can be kept as small as 8ft (2.4m). Requires full sun and any but dry soil. H 50ft (15m) S 25ft (8m) Z2-7

Salvia argentea SILVER SAGE
Biennial that produces large flat rosettes made up of silky felted gray leaves in spring, followed by stems of white flowers. Requires sun. H 30in (75cm) S 18in (45cm) Z5-9

Tanacetum ptarmiciflorum (syn. *Pyrethrum p.*) SILVER LACE This perennial is usually grown as an annual, particularly in the variety 'Silver Feather'. It has feathery pale gray foliage. Requires sun. H and S 20in (50cm)

Verbascum MULLEIN
V. bombyciferum 'Polarsommer' (syn. *V.* 'Arctic Summer') has rosettes of large woolly leaves; though naturally biennial, it can be kept going for a few years if it is prevented from flowering. H 6ft (1.8m) S 2ft (60cm) Z6-8 [ill.p.142]. *V. olympicum* has large gray-felted leaves followed by statuesque flowering stems, branched like a candelabra, covered with bright yellow flowers for many weeks. H 6ft (1.8m) S 30in (75cm) Z6-8. Both tolerate shade but prefer an open, sunny site.

Athyrium niponicum var. *pictum* (**Summer**)

Eryngium giganteum (**Summer**)

Lamium maculatum 'White Nancy' (**Summer**)

Rosa glauca (**Summer**)

Verbascum olympicum (**Summer**)

Whites

White is the most mysterious of colors – is it a color at all? It can seem empty of color, yet white light is created when all the colors of the spectrum are combined, so it can be said to incorporate all colors. This is its greatest virtue for the gardener, since white will combine happily with any other color. It also has sufficient impact to stand on its own. White can be said to be an inert color, since it does not react with other colors or change them in any way. Because of this, it is capable of acting as a buffer between two patches of color in a border that might otherwise react uncomfortably together (see pages 162–63).

White also reflects all the light that strikes it. Its effect in the garden is to lighten it and make the mood more cheerful. Capitalize on this by using white flowers such as foxgloves, and shrubs such as viburnums to brighten any shady areas, as in the open woodland planting *below right*.

The brilliance of white means that the shapes and patterns that white flowers make catch the eye and so are more intrusive than those of other colors in a mixed-color planting. Because they are light-reflecting, flowers with a solid silhouette, such as lilies or phlox, tend to stand out among other, darker colors. Tiny white "misty" flowers like baby's breath, goat's beard or crambe also reflect light but they break it up. The result is a translucence that adds a shimmering quality to other colors.

Be sensitive to the subtle distinctions and degrees of whiteness – it is remarkable how few flowers are pure white, ranging from the ivory whites and creams of daffodils such as *Narcissi* 'White Lion',

ABOVE To keep the white strain of foxgloves pure, weed out any pink seedlings – recognizable by their pink-veined leaves. Their blue leaved companion, the hosta (*H. sieboldiana* var. *elegans*) also likes the shade and humus-rich soil of the woodland floor.

ABOVE Flowering together in open woodland in early summer, the European snowball (*Viburnum opulus* 'Roseum') and its relative, the doublefile viburnum (*V. plicatum* 'Mariesii'), introduce variety of shape as well as subtle color difference to a white planting. For a similar effect later in the year, plant hydrangeas such as smooth hydrangea (*H. arborescens* 'Grandiflora') with oak-leaf hydangea (*H. quercifolia*). You could also extend the season by growing a late flowering white clematis, such as the Italian clematis (*C.* 'Alba Luxurians') into shrubs that flower earlier.

or of shrubs such as the pom-pom flowerheads of the European snowball *opposite, right*, to the "blush-pink" whites of some roses and the bluish off-whites of the white flowered bellflowers. Be aware too of the fact that Nature decorates white in myriad ways, changing its overall appearance slightly. White lilies may be marked with crimson spots or blotches. The petals of white geraniums may have blue or purple veining. White daisies have an explosion of yellow florets at their centers. Match these details with other plants of the appropriate color. Blue or purple veined geraniums, for example, will set up "echoes" of color with blue or purple flowers, while the daisies will enhance a yellow and orange planting.

Green foliage provides a darker foil for white and looks good with it, but also consider planting silver-gray foliage with white flowers. This is an especially effective combination since silver and white are closely related. Silver chamomile and artemisias

make elegant filigree backdrops for the more solid white snapdragons and tulips, *below left* and *below right*. Similarly, white variegated foliage is useful with white flowers. Try the variegated grass *Holcus mollis* 'Albovariegatus', or the low-growing bamboo, *Pleioblastus variegatus,* with white flowered mallows or roses.

White is always a popular choice of color for garden furniture, but you should take care when using it. Its brightness can dazzle and eclipse other colors in nearby borders, with the result that it looks far too stark in comparison with them. It usually looks best with white and silver plantings, but even here it is easy to overdo it. The cast iron white bench with fine tracery, *below left,* looks elegant with a white and silver planting, but if the bench were more solid, it could easily overwhelm the delicate plants. In that case it would be better to paint it gray-green, to tone with the foliage of the lavender and dwarf chamomile

ABOVE An ornate cast iron bench makes a fetching centerpiece for a white and silver late spring planting that includes 'White Triumphator' tulips, white lavender, and clumps of dwarf chamomile (*Anthemis punctata* subsp.*cupaniana*). The tulips can be lifted after flowering and replaced with white summer bedding plants, but the feathery anthemis has a long flowering season, and even when not in flower its silvery-green foliage is attractive.

ABOVE The panicle hydrangea (*Hydrangea paniculata* 'Kyushu') which flowers in the late summer, and the white sagebush (*Artemisia ludoviciana*) form the perennial backbone of a white border. White snapdragons in the foreground take center stage in the summer.

All-White Plantings

An all-white planting is one of the classics of garden design. It is also one of the easiest single color plantings to achieve since there is such a wide range of white flowers available through the seasons. Because there is relatively little color interest, the eye will be drawn instead to the plants' shapes and sizes, and differing textures.

In the white border in a sunny situation, *below*, tight clusters of small flowers on tall delphinium spires contrast with the single, daisylike heads of the chrysanthemum. The crambe produces sprays of tiny white flowers that create a diaphanous effect in comparison with the more solid-seeming flowers of the roses.

All-white plantings can also be planned to perform over a long period of time. The border here reaches a new peak every three or four weeks throughout the summer. The rose, valerian, and verbena are in their first flush, while the crambe is just coming to an end, and the borage is over. White phlox is poised to dominate within a few weeks. For still later flowers, include white Japanese anemones.

All-white gardens often depend as much upon foliage as upon flowers. The large leathery leaves of the bergenia make an anchor for this border, while the piptanthus forms its backdrop. Shadier schemes are often actually studies in green with white highlights. In the planting *opposite, below*, the interest comes from the large scalloped leaves of the bloodroot, the fountains of grape hyacinth foliage, and the boxwood hedges that edge the lawn and snake away into the distance. The white azaleas and dogwood lighten the greens.

OPPOSITE BELOW This sunny midsummer border in rich, moist soil demonstrates the staying power of an all-white planting. To prolong the display and keep it looking fresh, deadhead every day, especially the valerian. Cut back the spent delphinium stems now and there is a good chance that they will put out new flowers later. The phlox will soon need staking, preferably with discreet hazel twigs, to prevent it from collapsing over the beautiful foliage of the bergenia. (For a diagram of this planting, see page 174.)

LEFT Introduce white flowers early in the season by using bulbs that receive the light they need before the leaves appear on the trees above. Here broad leaved snowdrops (*Galanthus elwesii*) grow with spring snowflakes (*Leucojum vernum*).

BELOW Flowering in early summer, azaleas and Eastern dogwood (*Cornus florida*) both thrive in well drained slightly acid soil, as does the bloodroot (*Sanguinaria canadensis*) whose leaves form a carpet beneath the dogwood. The bloodroot's white flowers would have appeared in the spring before the leaves, so setting the scene for the garden's white theme.

A White Rose Garden

A small, scented rose garden, complete with an arbor in which to sit, makes an idyllic summer retreat. White is a particularly good choice of color since there is a wide range of roses from which to choose, and the flowers will remain visible well after dusk. However, because many of the most beautiful, heavily scented roses flower only once, the glory of such a garden can be short-lived.

To make the rose garden into a bower of mixed scents, you might accompany the roses with self-seeding white dame's rocket (*Hesperis matronalis* var. *albiflora*), and edge the beds with white lavender and white pinks (*Dianthus*) such as 'Mrs Sinkins'. Terracing of natural stone sets off the white flowers. It also reflects and retains heat, helping to bring out the garden's scents.

BELOW In this sheltered site, silver leaved lamb's ears and dwarf chamomile tolerate the dry soil around the urn. Behind it, an arbor is masked by a rambling rose, and the path toward it is lined with mock orange (*Philadelphus* 'Belle Etoile'), foxgloves (*Digitalis purpurea* f. *albiflora*), and clematis (*C. recta*) underplanted with polyantha roses ('White Pet') and white campion. In the foreground are shrub roses ('Alba Maxima').

Whites

SPRING

Amelanchier SHADBLOW SERVICE BERRY Shrub that flowers in spring as the leaves, bronze when young, develop; good color in the fall. Best on moist, acid to neutral soil. *A. canadensis* is a suckering shrub with an erect habit. H 16ft (5m) S 10ft (3m) Z3-7. *A. lamarckii* makes a spreading shrub or small tree. H 30ft (9m) S 20ft (6m) Z3-7

Anemone
Tuberous perennials.
A. blanda 'White Splendour' WINDFLOWER has large glossy white flowers in early spring H and S 8in (20cm) Z4-8. *A. nemorosa* has prettily divided foliage and smaller flowers, a little later. Tolerates both full light and partial shade in humus rich soil. H 4in (10cm) S 6in (15cm) Z4-8

Arabis caucasica ROCKCRESS
A mat-forming, evergreen perennial. Happiest in sunny, dry places, like tops of walls. H 6in (15cm) S 10in (25cm) Z3-8

Camellia japonica 'Alba Simplex' Evergreen shrub with mass of single flowers in spring. Needs shelter and partial shade. H 10ft (3m) S 5ft (1.5m) Z7-9

Clematis armandii ARMAND CLEMATIS Evergreen climber with handsome tripartite foliage,

coppery when young, and clusters of scented white flowers, sometimes tinged pink, in early spring. Deserves a warm, sheltered spot. H 15ft (5m) S 10ft (3m) Z7

Convallaria majalis LILY-OF-THE-VALLEY Spreading rhizomes make a thick carpet of pointed green leaves in moist, leafy, shady conditions. The bell-like flowers have a wonderful fragrance. H 6in (15cm) S indefinite Z2-9 [ill.p.151]

Cornus florida DOGWOOD
Large shrub or small tree with white bracts surrounding the flowers in early summer. The leaves color before they fall, revealing the glaucous young stem growth. Best in sun and deep, lime-free soil. H 20ft (6m) S 25ft (8m) Z5-8 [ill.pp.97,148]

Crocus chrysanthus 'Snow Bunting' Corm with white flowers delicately feathered purple. Requires an open, sunny position. H 4in (10cm) S 3in (8cm) Z4-9

Epimedium x youngianum 'Niveum' YOUNG'S BARRENWORT Rhizomatous perennial with pointed, heart-shaped leaves, often flushed purple when young, contrasting with the small white flowers, held well above the clump of foliage. Requires partial shade and humus rich, moist soil. Useful as groundcover. H 6in (15cm) S 12in (30cm) Z4-9

Erythronium californicum 'White Beauty' MAHOGANY TROUT LILY Perennial bulb with creamy-white flowers and mottled leaves. Requires partial shade and humus-rich soil. H 12in (30cm) S 6in (15cm) Z5-8

Exochorda x macrantha 'The Bride' PEARLBUSH Somewhat lax, though graceful shrub; can be trained as a small tree. Chlorosis may be a problem in shallow, chalky soil. H 5ft (1.5m) S 6ft (1.8m) Z5-8

Halesia carolina SNOWDROP TREE Shrub or small tree with clusters of charming bell-shaped flowers that hang from the bare branches before the leaves open. Oblong winged fruits follow in the autumn. Requires sun and neutral to acid soil. H 25ft(7.6m) S 33ft (10m) Z5-8

Hyacinthus 'L'Innocence' Although hyacinth bulbs are often forced into early growth for pots indoors, they will flourish outside in an open, sunny position, where the flowerheads will become less dense. H 8in (20cm) S 4in (10cm) Z4-8

Iberis sempervirens CANDYTUFT Evergreen sub shrub that makes a carpet of small dark green leaves, covered in pure white flowers in spring. Requires sun. H 12in (30cm) S 24in (60cm) Z3-9

Leucojum
Bulb that does best in partial shade. *L. aestivum* SUMMER SNOWFLAKE has nodding bells with

green tips. H 24in (60cm) S 5in (12cm) Z4-9. *L. vernum* SPRING SNOWFLAKE appears a little earlier, and its scented flowers are much shorter. H 8in (20cm) S 4in (10cm) Z3-9 [ill.p.97]

Magnolia stellata STAR MAGNOLIA A very slow-growing, bushy shrub, covered in narrow-petalled white stars if late frosts do not catch the buds. H and S 6ft (1.8m) Z5-9

Malus hupehensis TEA CRAB APPLE One of the best crab apple trees, with large flowers, followed by small orange red fruit in autumn. Prefers full sun. H and S 26ft (8m) Z4-9

Narcissus DAFFODIL
Bulb that tolerates sun and light shade. Good cultivars include 'Actaea' a Poeticus type, scented, with broad white petals and a yellowy eye, H 15in (40cm) Z3-9; 'Thalia' a multi-headed Triandrus type, with a cluster of snow-white, fragrant flowers, H 12in (30cm) Z3-9; and 'White Lion' which has double blooms, white mingled with cream, H 15in (40cm) Z3-9

Ornithogalum umbellatum STAR OF BETHLEHEM Bulb. Pretty, starry flowers, but can be invasive. Tolerates both sun and partial shade. H 12in (30cm) S 6in (15cm) Z4-9

Osmanthus delavayi
A substantial shrub with small, neat evergreen leaves and abundant strongly-scented small

flowers. Tolerates sun and partial shade. H and S 10ft (3m) Z7-9

Prunus CHERRY
P. padus BIRD CHERRY TREE bears almond-scented flowers that appear after the leaves H 50ft (15m) S 25ft (7.5m) Z4-6. 'Shirotae' has a spreading habit; large flower clusters and soft green, serrated foliage H 18ft (5.5m) S 25ft (7.6m) Z5-7. 'Taihaku' GREAT WHITE CHERRY One of the largest of the flowering cherries, the young leaves emerge copper-colored. H 25ft (7.6m) S 30ft (10m) Z5-7. 'Ukon' has cream flowers, and its foliage colors well in the fall. H 22ft (7m) S 30ft (10m) Z5-7

Pulmonaria officinalis 'Sissinghurst White' LUNGWORT Perennial with heart-shaped spotted leaves that make good groundcover all year round. Requires shade. H 12in (30cm) S 18in (45cm) Z4-8

Sanguinaria canadensis BLOODROOT Rhizomatous perennial. The lobed leaves emerge vertically and gradually unfold after the white flowers, to make an attractive, broad clump. Tolerates sun and partial shade, and requires humus-rich soil. H 6in (15cm) S 12in (30cm) Z4-9

Spiraea 'Arguta' BRIDAL WREATH Shrub with tiny flowers borne in great profusion all along its fine, arching branches. Requires sun. H and S 8ft (2.4m) Z4-8

Anemone blanda 'White Splendour' **(Spring)**

Epimedium x *youngianum* 'Niveum' **(Spring)**

Erythronium californicum 'White Beauty' **(Spring)**

Magnolia stellata **(Spring)**

Prunus 'Shirotae' **(Spring)**

Tiarella wherryi FOAMFLOWER
Rhizomatous perennial with clumps of maple-like leaves that are often purplish in color, and starry white flowers that are pink in the bud. Tolerates deep shade. H 8in (20cm) S 12in (30cm) Z3-8

Trillium grandiflorum GREAT WHITE TRILLIUM Rhizomatous perennial with pointed, ovate leaves that grow in threes around the flowering stem. Tolerates both full and partial shade. H 15in (38cm) S 12in (30cm) Z4-9

Tulipa TULIP
Bulb that appreciates summer baking. **'Purissima'** is pure milky white. H 15in (40cm) S 9in (23cm) Z3-9. **'Spring Green'** has creamy flowers streaked green H 15in (40cm) S 9in (23cm) Z3-9. **'White Triumphator'** is a Lily-flowered type, with pointed petals on tall stems. H 30in (75cm) S 10in (25cm) Z3-9 [ill.p.111]

SUMMER

Achillea YARROW
Perennial that tolerates most soil conditions in a sunny position. Good varieties include **A. chrysocoma 'Grandiflora'** with finely cut, lacy gray foliage, topped with flat heads of white daisy flowers in late summer, H 5ft (1.3m) S 3ft (90cm) Z5-9 [ill.p.172]; and **A. ptarmica 'The Pearl'** which has a tendency to

be invasive, has stout, branching stems of neat button-flowers. H and S 30in (75cm) Z4-9 [ill.p.25]

Agapanthus campanulatus var. albidus AFRICAN LILY Perennial that forms clumps of fleshy, strap-shaped leaves in spring and in late summer throws up tall stems with round heads of white flowers. Requires full sun. H 3ft (90cm) S 20in (50cm) Z8-10

Allium ORNAMENTAL ONION
Bulb. Varieties with white flowers include **A. karataviense** which has a large sphere of pinkish white flowers, and generally only two, opulent gray-green leaves, H 8in (20cm) S 10 (30cm) Z4-8 [ill.p.109];and **A. triquetrum** THREE CORNERED ONION which carries a loose umbel of greenish-white flowers, the flowering stem is distinctively triangular in section. Likes a damp, shady position where it will self-seed invasively, H 15in (40cm) S 6in (15cm) Z5-9

Anaphalis triplinervis PEARL EVERLASTING Perennial with a mound of gray foliage covered with white "everlasting" flowers in late summer. Prefers sun but will grow in partial shade. H 18in (45cm) S 24in (60cm) Z3-9 [ill.p.181]

Anthemis
Good varieties of this perennial include **A. punctata** subsp. **cupaniana** DWARF CHAMOMILE

which quickly forms a low mound of finely cut silvery foliage, with white daisy-flowers, H 12in (30cm) S 24in (60cm) Z5-9 [ill.p.98]; and **A. tinctoria 'Alba'** which has ferny, dark green foliage and white daisies, H and S 3ft (90cm) Z4-8. Both need sun and tolerate dry soil.

Anthericum liliago ST BERNARD'S LILY Perennial. Grassy gray-green leaves and spikes of white trumpet flowers in early summer. Needs a sunny site and soil that dries out in summer. H 24in (60cm) S 12in (30cm) Z7-9

Antirrhinum SNAPDRAGON
An old faithful for the summer border, this annual has long-lasting flowers like closed lips that bees push through to reach the nectar. Seedsmen stock numerous varieties of different heights and flower forms including **'White Wonder'** which has a splash of yellow at the flower throat. H 18in (45cm) S 10in (25cm) [ill.p.95]

Argyranthemum foeniculaceum (of gardens) MARGUERITE Perennial with finely cut blue-green leaves and many white daisies which flower over a long period. It is pretty in a pot, and can be trained as a standard. Requires sun. H and S 3ft (90cm) Z9-10 [ill.p.151]

Aruncus dioicus GOAT'S BEARD
A hearty perennial, tolerant of most conditions except deep shade. Makes a handsome

clump of rich ferny leaves, with creamy plumes in early summer. H 6ft (1.8m) S 4ft (1.2m) Z3-9 [ill.p.166]

Astilbe 'Bridal Veil' (syn A. 'Brautschleier') Perennial that forms clumps of bright green, ferny foliage and throws up elegant sprays of pure white flowers. Requires partial shade and rich, damp soil. Best left undisturbed. H and S 30in (75cm) Z5-8 [ill.p.178]

Bellis perennis DOUBLE DAISY
The perennial cultivated daisy flowers over a long season. Tolerates sun and partial shade. H and S 8in (20cm) Z4-9

Camassia leichtlinii subsp. **leichtlinii** (syn. C. l. 'Alba') Bulb with flowers like ivory stars on slender stems; will naturalize in deep, moist soil. Tolerates sun and partial shade. H 3ft (90cm) S 12in (30cm) Z5-9

Campanula BELLFLOWER
Perennial that tolerates both sun and shade. **C. lactiflora alba** MILKY BELLFLOWER has large, branching flowerheads need staking in windy areas. H 5ft (1.5m) S 2ft (60cm) Z4-8 [ill.p.182]. **C. persicifolia alba** PEACH LEAF BELLFLOWER flowers for a long time; it makes a good companion for old roses. H 3ft (90cm) S 1ft (30cm) Z3-8 [ill.p.174]

Carpenteria californica BUSH ANEMONE Evergreen shrub whose heavy dark green foliage

is justified by the richness of its flowers, which have pure white petals around long stamens. Best against a sunny wall. H 6ft (1.8m) S 5ft (1.5m) Z8-10

Centranthus ruber albus WHITE VALERIAN Perennial with fleshy leaves and large flowerheads all summer. It can self-seed invasively and often naturalizes on limestone walls. Requires sun and will tolerate poor, alkaline soil. H 30in (75cm) S 24in (60cm) Z4-9 [ill.p.174]

Cerastium tomentosum SNOW IN SUMMER Perennial producing mats of gray foliage smothered in white in late spring. Needs sun, and does well on a dry bank. Can be invasive. H 3in (8cm) S 18in (45cm) Z3-8 [ill.p.109]

Choisya ternata MEXICAN ORANGE BLOSSOM Evergreen shrub with shiny three-lobed leaves, and white scented flowers in early summer. Requires sun or partial shade. H and S 10ft (3m) Z7-9

Cimicifuga BUGBANE
Perennial requiring partial shade and moist soil. **C. racemosa** BLACK SNAKEROOT has branching stems of bottlebrush flowers over divided, fresh green leaves. H 5ft (1.5m) S 2ft (60cm) Z3-8 [ill.p.81]. **C. simplex** is smaller, and flowers later, in the fall. H 4ft (1.2m) S 2ft (60cm) Z3-8

Cistus x hybridus (syn. C. corbariensis) WHITE ROCK ROSE Shrub with wavy-edged leaves and reddish buds which open to

Tulipa 'Spring Green' **(Spring)**

Allium triquetrum **(Summer)**

Argyranthemum foeniculaceum **(Summer)**

Carpenteria californica **(Summer)**

Cimicifuga racemosa **(Summer)**

white. Very floriferous. Requires sun. H and S 4ft (1.2m) Z8-10

Clematis
Cimbing varieties, which appreciate a shaded root run include: **'Alba Luxurians'** with flowers that are often green to begin with but later white, with a dark eye, H and S 12ft (3.7m) Z3-9; **'Huldine'** with greeny-white stamens, and white flowers that are mauve on the reverse, H and S 13ft (4m) Z3-9; **'Marie Boisselot'** (syn.'Mme le Coultre') with flowers like flat plates, flushed pink on opening but becoming pure white, H and S 10ft (3m) Z3-9; and **C. montana sericea** whose flowers have only four petals, and a large tuft of greenish yellow stamens, H and S 30ft (9m) Z6-8. Good herbaceous varieties include **C. recta** with pinnate foliage and panicles of small white flowers [ill.pp.98,166]; and **C. r. 'Purpurea'** which has purple young foliage. Both H 6ft (1.8m) S 20in (50cm) Z3-7

Cornus kousa var. **chinensis** KOUSA DOGWOOD An elegant spreading tree or large shrub. It is the bracts of the flowers which are conspicuously white. The glossy dark green foliage turns a rich reddish purple in the fall. Tolerates sun and partial shade. Dislikes shallow chalk soil. H 30ft (10m) S 20ft (6m) Z5-8

Crambe cordifolia COLEWORT Perennial that makes a mound

of rather coarse green foliage, from which arise bare branching stems, exploding in a cloud of white stars in midsummer. Requires sun. H 6ft6in (2m) S 4ft (1.2m) Z6-9 [ill.p.174]

Dahlia
Tuberous perennial that flowers late in the season and carries on until the first frost; then tubers need lifting and storing in frost-free conditions. Elegant white varieties include the Cactus-flowered **'My Love'**. H and S 30in (75cm) Z8-10 [ill.p.163]

Delphinium
Perennials invaluable for providing an eye-catching vertical thrust to a border. Young growth may need protection from slugs. Best in full sun. [ill.p.176]. Good white varieties include the **Galahad Group** [ill.p.174]; and **'Butterball'**. H 5ft (1.5m) S 15in (40cm) Z3-9

Deutzia gracilis SLENDER DEUTZIA
A dense, small shrub, flowering best in full sun but requiring protection from spring frosts H and S 3ft (90cm) Z5-8

Dicentra BLEEDING HEART
Perennial requiring partial shade and moist, rich soil. **D. eximia 'Snowdrift'** has gray-green, divided leaves, topped by stems of narrow white flowers H and S 12in (30cm) Z3-8. **D. spectabilis 'Alba'** has creamy-white lockets that dangle above finely cut foliage of a fresh green. H 30in (75cm) S 20in (50cm) Z3-8

Dictamnus albus GAS PLANT
Perennial with spires of white flowers, which become star-shaped seed pods The foliage is and lemon-scented Requires sun. H 3ft (90cm) S 2ft (60cm) Z2-8

Digitalis purpurea f. **albiflora** FOXGLOVE Biennial producing spires of flowers, spotted on the inside. Requires partial shade and moist soil. H 5ft (1.5m) S 18in (45cm) Z4-8 [ill.pp.94,98]

Epilobium angustifolium album WHITE FIREWEED Perennial with slender spires that open their flowers gradually; the seedpods forming below before the last buds are mature above. Roots can be invasive in light soils. Requires sun. H 5ft (1.5m) S 20in (50cm) Z3-8 [ill.p.19]

Galium odoraum (syn. **Asperula odoratum**) WOODRUFF Spreading perennial with ruffs of small spiky leaves topped by clusters of white stars from late spring. Tolerates sun but prefers partial shade. H 6in (15cm) S 12in (30cm) Z3-8

Galtonia candicans SUMMER HYACINTH Bulb making stems of drooping white bells on tall stalks in late summer. Needs sun. H 4ft (1.2m) S 9in (23cm) Z6-9

Gaura lindheimeri WHITE GAURA
Perennial whose pinkish-white flowers seem to flutter through the border; best staked or supported by a stouter plant

such as a sedum. Requires sun. H 4ft (1.2m) S 3ft (90cm) Z6-9

Geranium CRANESBILL
Invaluable, reliable perennials for the border with attractive foliage. **G. clarkei 'Kashmir White'** has prettily cut leaves and veined white flowers. Can spread rapidly by roots and seed. Best in sun. H and S 2ft (60cm) Z4-8. **G. renardii** makes a solid dome of quilted sage green leaves. Best in sun. H and S 1ft (30cm) Z6-8. **G. sylvaticum** f. **albiflorum** WOOD CRANESBILL makes clumps of fingered leaves and branching stems of small flowers in late spring. Requires partial shade. H 3ft (90cm) S 2ft (60cm) Z4-8 [ill.p.18]

Gladiolus callianthus 'Murieliae' (syn. **Acidanthera m.**) Perennial corm producing spikes of graceful, sweetly scented flowers with dark blotches. Requires sun and fertile soil. H 3ft (90cm) S 6in (15cm) Z8-10. Good varieties of the large-flowered **Gladiolus** hybrids include **G. 'Ice Cap'** H 5ft6in (1.7m) S 1ft (30cm) Z8-10

Gypsophila paniculata BABY'S BREATH Rhizomatous perennial making a mound of tiny white stars. Plant so it can froth forward and cover bare ground in late summer. Tolerates poor soil, so long as it is deep soil. Requires sun and resents being moved. H and S 3ft (90cm) Z4-8 [ill.p.25]

Hesperis matronalis var. **albiflora** WHITE DAME'S ROCKET Perennial with very fragrant, stock-like flowers on tall branching stems. Seeds itself freely. Does best in sun. H 30in (75cm) S 2ft (60cm) Z4-9

Hydrangea
Most of these substantial shrubs require partial shade and moist soil. **H. arborescens 'Grandiflora'** SMOOTH HYDRANGEA has globe-shaped heads of creamy flowers. H and S 6ft (1.8m) Z4-9. **H. paniculata 'Kyushu'** PANICLE HYDRANGEA has slender terminal panicles of sterile florets and almost glossy leaves. H 8ft (2.4m) S 3ft (90cm) Z4-8 [ill.p.95]. **H. anomala** subsp. **petiolaris** CLIMBING HYDRANGEA will climb up a sunless wall, as it prefers cool soil. Flattened, greenish-white flowers appear early summer, but not in quantity on young plants. H and S to 50ft (15m) Z5-8. **H. quercifolia** OAK LEAVED HYDRANGEA has large, lobed leaves that turn a good color in the fall if grown in the sun, although it will grow in full shade. H 5ft (1.5m) S 6ft (1.8m) Z5-9

Lamium maculatum album SPOTTED DEADNETTLE Creeping and carpeting perennial with silvery leaves and white deadnettle flowers. Tolerates sun and shade and prefers moist soil. H 8in (20cm) S 3ft (90cm) Z4-8 [ill.p.175]

Clematis 'Marie Boisselot' **(Summer)**

Dicentra spectabilis 'Alba' **(Summer)**

Gaura lindheimeri **(Summer)**

Gladiolus callianthus 'Murieliae' **(Summer)**

Hydrangea quercifolia **(Summer)**

Lathyrus PEA

L. latifolius 'Albus' PERENNIAL SWEET PEA is a perennial climber with robust, almost lush flowers over a long period, lacking scent. H and S 6ft (1.8m) Z5-9 [ill.p.149]. *L. odoratus* SWEET PEA is an annual climber with a unique scent. H and S 6ft (1.8m). Both require sun and rich soil.

Lavandula angustifolia 'Alba' WHITE COMMON LAVENDER Shrub with fine evergreen gray foliage and strongly aromatic flower spikes. Best in sun and well-drained soil. H and S 30in (75cm) Z5-9 [ill.p.95]

Lavatera trimestris 'Mont Blanc' Bushy annual smothered in large white trumpets. Requires sun. H 30in (75cm) S 18in (45cm)

Leucanthemum x *superbum* 'Esther Read' (syn *Chrysanthemum* x *s.* 'E. R.') SHASTA DAISY Perennial that produces glistening white double daisy flowers. Requires sun. H and S 18in (45cm) Z4-9 [ill.p.174]

Libertia grandiflora NEW ZEALAND SATIN FLOWER Rhizomatous perennial with clumps of long narrow leaves that send up stiff sprays of white flowers. H 30in (75cm) S 2ft (60cm) Z8-10

Lilium LILY

Summer-flowering bulbs that do best in sun. *I. candidum* MADONNA LILY has foliage that appears in autumn and lasts all winter, followed by fragrant white flowers with yellow

stamens in early summer. Prefers lime-rich soil Z4-9. 'Casa Blanca' has large, clear white blooms Z3-9. *L. martagon* var. *album* MARTAGON LILY has nodding flowers with reflexed petals, variously spotted Z3-8. *L. regale* Album Group REGAL LILY has a bewitching scent, particularly in the evening Z3-8 [ill.p.183]. 'Sterling Star' has clusters of upward-facing creamy white flowers that are spotted with brown Z3-9. All H 3ft (90cm).

Lobularia 'Snow Carpet' (syn. Alyssum 'S.C.') Annual that makes low mats of long-lasting tiny white flowers. Quick and easy to grow, soit is a good plant for children, and makes a frilly edging to a path or border. Requires sun. H 4in (10cm) S 12in (30cm)

Lychnis coronaria Alba Group WHITE ROSE CAMPION Biennial or short-lived perennial with much-branched stems carrying a succession of single white flowers above tufts of downy gray foliage. Requires sun. H 20in (50cm) S 12in (30cm) Z4-8 [ill.pp.98,175]

Lysimachia LOOSESTRIFE

Perennials that tolerate sun and partial shade in moist soil. *L. clethroides* GOOSENECK LOOSESTRIFE has arching spikes of tiny gray-white flowers in late summer. H 3ft (90cm) S 2ft (60cm) Z3-8. *L. ephemerum* has slender spires of close-set white flowers and

cool gray foliage. H 3ft (90cm) S 1ft (30cm) Z6-9

Malva moschata alba MUSK MALLOW Short-lived perennial easily raised from seed. Fresh green divided foliage and abundant cup-shaped white flowers. Requires sun. H 30in (75cm) S 2ft (60cm) Z3-9 [ill.p.176]

Myrrhis odorata SWEET CICELY Perennial with flat flowerheads and foliage that is finely cut and aromatic. Tolerates both sun and shade. H and S 2ft (60cm) Z4-9

Nicotiana FLOWERING TOBACCO

Perennials usually grown as annuals. Do best in sun. *N. affinis* has pure white star-shaped blooms that are particularly fragrant in the evening. H 30in (75cm) S 1ft (30cm). *N.* x *sanderae* comes in colors ranging from red and pink to white and pale green. H 24in (60cm) S 8in (20cm) [ill.pp.121,163]. *N. sylvestris* is a towering plant with drooping, tubular flowers, good for the back of a border. Often self-seeds. H 5ft (1.5m) S 30in (75cm) [ill.pp.107,163].

Olearia x *macrodonta* NEW ZEALAND HOLLY Evergreen shrub with sage-green, spiny leaves, which is smothered in broad heads of scented white daisies in mid-summer. Requires full sun. H and S 10ft (3m) Z8-10 [ill.p.179]

Osteospermum caulescens AFRICAN DAISY Evergreen perennial with large white daisies with a blue

eye. Requires sun. H and S 18in (45cm) Z9-10 [ill.p.132]

Paeonia PEONY

P. lactiflora 'Duchesse de Nemours' is a perennial, free-flowering double peony with a good scent. H and S 30in (75cm) Z4-8. *P. suffruticosa* subsp. *rockii* ROCK'S TREE PEONY has enormous white blooms with maroon blotches at the base of the petals, and a big bunch of yellow stamens. Very special but also very rare, as it is difficult to propagate. Prefers sun but will tolerate light shade H and S 7ft (2.1m) 74-9

Papaver orientale 'Black and White' ORIENTAL POPPY Perennial whose flowers have petals like white crepe paper with black blotches. Foliage dies back by midsummer. Does best in sun. H 3ft (90cm) S 1ft (30cm) Z3-8

Petunia

Annual requiring a sunny position sheltered from wind. [ill.p.150] A good variety is 'White Cloud'. H 8in (20cm) S 12in (30cm)

Philadephus 'Belle Etoile' MOCK ORANGE Shrub whose creamy white flowers have a mauve center, and scent that carries well around the garden. Cut out old, twiggy wood immediately after flowering. Requires sun and fertile soil. H and S 8ft (2.4m) Z5-9 [ill.pp.98,151]

Phlox paniculata GARDEN PHLOX Elegant border perennial with

large heads of fragrant white flowers. H 3ft (90cm) S 18in (45cm). *P. p.* 'Mount Fuji' is taller with larger flowers. H 5ft (1.5m) S 2ft (60cm). Tolerate both sun and partial shade Z4-8

Potentilla fruticosa 'Abbotswood' BUSH CINQUEFOIL Shrub with small gray-green leaves and frilly pure white flowers over a long season. Can be hard pruned if it gets leggy. Requires sun. H 30in (75cm) S 3ft (90cm) Z5-7

Romneya coulteri MATILIJA POPPY Perennial with glaucous, divided foliage on long stems, topped with huge white poppies. Needs a warm, sunny position and deep soil. Can be difficult to establish, and resents being moved. H and S 6ft (1.8m) Z7-10

Rosa ROSE

Most do best in an open, sunny position. Good climbing varieties include 'Bobbie James' a vigorous rambler with large trusses of creamy white flowers, H 30ft (9m) S 20ft (6m) Z5-9; 'Mme Alfred Carrière' which is vigorous, tolerates partial shade, and has full, blush white blooms that repeat well, H 13ft (4m) S 10ft (3m) Z5-9; 'The Garland' with clusters of many small, fragrant flowers, H and S 15ft (4.6m) Z5-9; and 'Wedding Day' with heads of single, creamy flowers and nice hips and tolerant of shade and poor soil, H 30ft (9m) S 15ft (4.5m) Z5-9. Good shrub varieties include

Lilium candidum (**Summer**)

Lysimachia ephemerum (**Summer**)

Olearia x *macrodonta* (**Summer**)

Papaver orientale 'Black and White' (**Summer**)

Rosa 'The Garland' (**Summer**)

'Iceberg' which has little scent but flowers reliably and constantly, H 5ft (1.5m) S 3ft (90cm) Z5-9 [ill.p.176]; 'Margaret Merril' with white scented flowers tinged pink, H 3ft (90cm) 2ft (60cm) Z5-9; and *R. soulieana* with neat gray foliage and the masses of single flowers that are followed by small orange hips, H 10ft (3m) S 6ft (1.8m) Z6-9

Rubus 'Benenden'
This relative of the blackberry makes a broad shrub with large lobed leaves and showy white flowers in great quantity in early summer. Best in sun. H and S 10ft (3m) Z6-8

Solanum jasminoides 'Album' POTATO VINE A vigorous wall shrub with neat, dark foliage that shows off the loose heads of white jasmine-like flowers. Blooms from earliest summer until the frosts. Requires full sun. H and S to 20ft (6m) Z7-9

Syringa vulgaris 'Mme Lemoine' LILAC Shrub with plump racemes of heavily fragrant, double white flowers in early summer. Needs sun and deep, preferably alkaline soil. H and S 13ft (4m) Z4-8

Verbascum chaixii 'Album' NETTLE LEAVED MULLEIN Perennial producing long spikes of white flowers with pink eyes over dark foliage. Often self seeds. Tolerates shade, but prefers an open sunny site. H 3ft (90cm) S 2ft (60cm) Z5-9 [ill.p.176]

Verbena tenuisecta f. *alba* MOSS VERBENA Perennial with finely cut leaves and dense flowerheads. Requires sun. H 15in (40cm) S 30in (75cm) Z8-10 [ill.p.174]

Viburnum
V. opulus 'Roseum' EUROPEAN SNOWBALL TREE has balls of creamy flowers in early summer and rich foliage color in the fall. H and S 16ft (5m) Z4-8 [ill.p.94].
V. plicatum 'Mariesii' DOUBLE FILE VIBURNUM has a very elegant horizontal pattern of growth, emphasized by flat flowerheads all along the branches. H and S 13ft (4m) Z5-8 [ill.p.94]. Both tolerate sun and partial shade.

Viola cornuta Alba Group WHITE HORNED VIOLET Perennial making good groundcover, with flowers in quantity in early summer. Cut over after flowering and a second crop will appear in late summer. Tolerates sun or partial shade. H 15in (40cm) S 2ft (60cm) Z6-9 [ill.pp.18,114,176]

Wisteria floribunda 'Alba' JAPANESE WISTERIA Vigorous twining climber, with long racemes of white pea flowers in early summer. Requires sun. H and S to 100ft (30m) Z4-9

Yucca gloriosa SPANISH DAGGER Evergreen shrub with bold spiky, succulent leaves and tall panicles of creamy white flowers. Makes a bold pot plant or architectural feature, and needs full sun. H 6ft (1.8m) S 5ft (1.5m) Z7-10

Zantedeschia aethiopica CALLA LILY Perennial with a preference for

having its toes in the mud of a pond. Glossy green leaves are the perfect backdrop to the great white spathes. H 3ft3in (1m) S 18in (45cm) Z7-11

FALL

Anemone x *hybrida* 'Honorine Jobert' JAPANESE ANEMONE Perennial making hearty clumps of lobed leaves which throw up branching stems of rounded white flowers. Tolerates sun and partial shade in humus-rich soil. H 5ft (1.5m) S 2ft (60cm) Z5-8

Aster divaricatus WIND WOOD ASTER Evergreen perennial with wiry dark stems that spray forth masses of starry white flowers with yellow centers. Tolerates sun and partial shade in moist soil. H and S 2ft (60cm) Z4-8

Leucanthemella serotina (syn. *Chrysanthemum uliginosum*) Perennial with erect stems that carry many white daisy-flowers which turn to follow the sun. Requires a sunny site. H 7ft (2.1m) S 2ft (60cm) Z6-9

BERRIES

Actaea alba (syn. *A. pachypoda*) WHITE BANEBERRY Shrub whose fluffy flowers turn into curious, poisonous white berries on stout red stalks. Requires shade and moist, peaty soil. H 3ft (90cm) S 20in (50cm) Z3-8

Sorbus cashmiriana KASHMIR MOUNTAIN ASH Drooping clusters

of large white berries remain on the tree long after the pinnate leaves have colored and fallen. Tolerates sun and partial shade. H and S 30ft (9m) Z3-6

Symphoricarpos albus SNOWBERRY Shrub whose suckering, wiry stems form a thicket liberally scattered with pulpy white berries in fall. Tolerates sun and partial shade H 4ft (1.2m) S 3ft (90cm) Z4-7

WINTER

Erica carnea 'Springwood White' WINTER HEATH Evergreen sub-shrub covered with clusters of tiny white tubular flowers for up to six months through winter and spring. Tolerates lime soil and some shade. Makes good groundcover. H 12in (30cm) S 18in (45cm) Z5-8

Galanthus SNOWDROP
Bulb which, if given a cool position in partial shade and moist soil, will naturalize well. *G. elwesii* has broad glaucous leaves, with inner petals marked green. H and S 8in (20cm) Z4-7 [ill.p.97]. *G. nivalis* 'Flore Pleno' DOUBLE COMMON SNOWDROP has many white petals with a sprinkling of green. H 6in (15cm) S 3in (8cm) Z3-7 [ill.p.113]

Helleborus niger CHRISTMAS ROSE Evergreen perennial with nodding flowers, often flushed pink on the outside, held well above the dark green leathery

leaves. Requires partial shade and moisture-retentive soil. H and S 12in (30cm) Z3-9

Lonicera x *purpusii* 'Winter Beauty' This deciduous shrub has gloriously fragrant creamy flowers in winter. Tolerates sun and partial shade. H and S 5ft (1.5m) Z5-8

Viburnum tinus LAURUSTINUS Shrub with dark evergreen leaves on reddish stems. Pink buds open to white flowerheads that last all through the winter. Tolerates partial shade, but flowers more freely in sun. *V. t.* 'Eve Price' has more plentiful flowers and buds of a richer pink. H and S 10ft (3m) Z8-10 [ill.p.170]

STEMS

Betula utilis var. *jacquemontii* WHITE BARKED HIMALAYAN BIRCH A graceful tree lightened by the effect of its peeling white bark that is best seen after leaf fall. Requires sun and moist soil. H 60ft (18m) S 30ft (9m) Z5-7

Rubus BRAMBLE
Shrubs for winter interest. *R. biflorus* has stout, prickly stems and angular branches covered with a white bloom, fully revealed after leaf fall. H and S 6ft (1.8m) Z6-9 [ill.p.171]. *R. cockburnianus* has arching gray stems also with a gray-white bloom that shows up well in winter. H 8ft (2.4m) S 12ft (3.7m) Z6. Both require full sun.

Rubus 'Benenden' **(Summer)**

Wisteria floribunda 'Alba' **(Summer)**

Sorbus cashmiriana **(Fall)**

Helleborus niger **(Winter)**

Lonicera x *purpusii* ' Winter Beauty' **(Winter)**

HARMONIES

Color harmonies are the result of putting together closely related colors, such as those that are next to each other on the color wheel (see page 15). Therefore, if you want to base a harmony on blue, you could add the adjacent mauves and violets. Similarly, you might start with red, and add orange and yellow. Another harmony might be based on pink. Pink does not appear on the color wheel since it is not one of the pure spectral colors, but is a mixture of red with white and traces of other hues such as blue or yellow. Pink is one of the most widespread flower colors, and it forms the basis of some of the most successful planting harmonies.

White and gray contribute to color harmonies in a more passive way. They are both inert colors, and so do not actively affect the hue of their neighbors. They both "go" with all other colors, making the overall effect of any planting lighter and brighter.

Color temperature also plays a part in harmonious relationships. When blues or blue-violets dominate, the planting is a "cold" one and is generally subdued and calming. When reds and oranges take the lead, the opposite is true: the harmony will be "hot" and vibrant and far from relaxing. These are the two extremes. Between them lies an enormous range of "cool" and "warm" schemes. Pinks, for instance, hover on the border that divides warm and cool colors. Pinks that contain blue harmonize with cool schemes of blues and violets, while yellow-pinks work better with warmer colors.

When all the colors in a planting are the same lightness or darkness, the result is a harmony of tone. Much foliage tends to be dark-toned, so for example, by putting together dark green holly with the deepest blue delphiniums and dark crimson roses, you will make a dramatic dark-toned harmony. At the other end of the scale, silver-gray with pastel pinks and blues will make a shimmering light-toned harmony. Silver foliage, which dominates the picture shown here, is not only lighter than most green foliage but also cooler, because it lacks the warming yellow that green contains. So, although silver is a neutral hue, it tends to cool down a scheme by replacing the slightly warmer green foliage color.

RIGHT The blue catmint in the foreground and echoing blue delphiniums in the border beyond the lawn establish this scheme as a cold harmony, which is underlined by the relatively cool silver foliage that dominates the border. The white flowers, which are of neutral color temperature, make the planting lighter overall, but in this cool context, they also resemble a dusting of snow. (For a diagram of this planting, see page 174.)

Harmonies with Blue

Harmonies dominated by cool blues or colors with a blue bias are subtle and unostentatious. These cool harmonies create a restful, even slightly contemplative mood. Combine blues with blue-violets and icy whites, perhaps including the occasional plant with blue-pink flowers or flowers of cool primrose yellow. Green foliage is neutral: its context determines whether it is going to be warm or cool. But to contribute to cool harmonies, select silver-green foliage plants and those with blue-green leaves, such as some hostas, bleeding hearts, and irises.

The cool blues, violets, and silvers seem to recede into the distance, suggesting space that is not really there. Use this to make a border appear deeper than it actually is, by putting your cool colors at the back and warm ones, which appear to come forward, toward the front. To make the whole garden look bigger, mass the cool harmonies at the far ends.

In shade, light has a blue cast which enhances cool colors, while sunlight tends to warm them up, making blues look violet and violet look pink. So for the best effects, plant your cool harmonies in the shade. For the same reason, in the bluish light of dusk, cool colors remain visible longer than warm ones, so it is also a good idea to place cool plantings in a part of the garden that you see at that time of day.

But the color relationships in a garden are constantly changing. A planting that is a cool harmony one week may easily become a warm harmony the next, when the cool blue plants decline and their role is taken over, say, by warmer colored pink ones. By getting to know the flowering times of your plants, you can control the associations as they wax and wane through the season.

Remember, too, that the colors of the hard landscape of your garden – walls, paths, even the paintwork on doors and garden structures – will affect the balance of harmonizing plantings. In the example *opposite, near right*, a door has been painted blue to echo the cool harmonies of the border in front. Another idea, especially suited to smaller gardens, is to group a collection of potted cool colored plants to achieve a concentration of color that is harder to obtain in a border, *opposite, far right*.

RIGHT The colors of the white fireweed (*Epilobium angustifolium album*) and its accompanying blue catmint (*Nepeta* 'Six Hills Giant') still stand out even though it is well after sunset. This fireweed goes on to produce fluffy white seeds, but because the seeds do not germinate, it will not invade your garden in the same way as the more common pink form. The catmint will flower again later in the season if the flowering stems are cut back to ground level as soon as they begin to fade.

ABOVE A coat of blue paint has transformed a garden door from what might have been an eyesore into an intrinsic element of a cool planting that includes blue-violet pansies, the green foliage of a daphne in the center and of spider flowers (*Cleome hassleriana*) to the left of the door, very pale pink Japanese anemones (*Anemone* x *hybrida*), and the tall, flowering tobacco with white flowers (*Nicotiana sylvestris*).

ABOVE Tender and exotic plants that would struggle to survive in the more competitive situation of a border have been planted in a group of containers to make a cool harmony that is in sympathy with the border behind. (For a diagram of this planting, see page 175.)

Blues, Mauves, and Violets

You can safely put blues with mauves, purples, and violets to make a resonant jumble of cool summer color. Summer-flowering bulbs such as ornamental onions are useful ingredients in plantings like this. Ornamental onions come in a range of suitable colors, from deepest purple through lilac and pink, to blue and white, and in heights from a few inches to several feet. Plant them among perennials that will provide them with the support they need, and you will not need to stake them, *right above*. The perennial wallflower 'Bowles' Mauve' is also a good plant to choose because it has blue-green leaves as well as a prolific out put of mauve flowers from spring to fall. Even ornamental cabbages, *opposite, right*, can be incorporated in a planting of these colors. Their purple ribs echo the purple of adjacent flowers. Bronze fennel makes a harmonizing background. Its feathery foliage sets into relief the brighter spots of color of the flowers and emphasizes their sharper outlines, *right below*.

RIGHT ABOVE Seen in early summer, the globes of drumstick chives (*Allium sphaerocephalon*) are supported by sea holly (*E.* x *tripartitum*) which has flowers of the same shape, but these are blue rather than red-purple. Pink opium poppies (*Papaver somniferum*), garden phlox (*P. paniculata* 'Eventide' and 'Franz Schubert'), and catmint (*Nepeta racemosa*) complete this rich planting.

RIGHT Shaped like purple shuttlecocks, the flowers of Spanish lavender (*Lavandula stoechas* subsp. *pedunculata*) pick up the color of the flowerheads of the Persian onion (*Allium aflatunense* 'Purple Sensation'). There are also suggestions of purple in the bronze fennel (*Foeniculum vulgare* 'Purpureum') beyond.

LEFT In a border that has been specially created for a flower show, two onion flowers of different heights – tall white *Allium nigrum* and the Turkestan onion (*A. karataviense*) with gray flowers and broad blue-green leaves – are combined with perennial wallflower (*Erysimum* 'Bowles' Mauve'), dame's rocket (*Hesperis matronalis*), and some sun-loving plants – Spanish lavender (*Lavendula stoechas* subsp. *pedunculata*), purple sage and rosemary. These last plants do not really thrive in such cramped quarters, but need well drained soil, and full sunlight.

BELOW Pots can be used as small raised beds. Take advantage of their height by planting trailing plants like verbenas around their edges. Here, a deep purple-pink verbena and the smaller flowered *Verbena tenuisecta* accompany the freeway daisy with flowers shaped like a watersplash (*Osteospermum* 'Pink Whirls'), and the kale 'Red Peacock'. At the base of the container, the silver foliage of snow-in-summer (*Cerastium tomentosum*) gives a cool context to the scheme. In containers you can break all the rules about the required distance between plants as long as you keep up the routine of watering and feeding.

LEFT When planning an ambitious border like this one, it pays to take account of the shapes and sizes of your color masses, so the result is structured but full of variety and interest. This border is masterfully controlled, from its loosely trained backdrop of climbing pink roses to the clusters of deadnettles and catmints that tumble on to the gravel at the front. Interspersed among the mounds of color are vertical accents of pink foxgloves which find their reflection, both in color and form, in the pink beard tongues in the foreground. The huge flowerheads of the downy onion – each one a mass of individual flowers – are visually balanced by complete clumps of pinks. The repeated gray foliage of the campion is a cooling influence and helps to hold the planting together. (For a diagram of this planting, see page 175.)

Harmonies with Pink

The pinks are such a diverse family of colors that you cannot apply a general rule of color association to all of them. Broadly, the pinks can be divided into two groups, the cool pinks and the warm ones. The larger proportion of pinks in the garden tend to be cool pinks like crimsons that are derived from reds and have a touch of blue in them. These pinks look good with other colors with a blue bias, such as violet, blue itself, and with neutral white. The warm pinks, on the other hand, are those that are derived from mixtures of vermilion and orange-red with white; these seem to have a trace of yellow in them, and they make harmonies with other colors with a yellow bias such as yellow-greens and apricots.

The pinkness of flowers is often underlaid with other hues that modulate the overall color, especially when they are seen at a distance. Pink peonies, roses such as 'Ballerina', and tulips such as 'Angélique' have white centers that lighten the overall effect as well as providing a link with neighboring white flowers. Other pink flowers, like sun roses, have yellow centers that tend to push the overall color toward the warmer pinks.

The cool pinks that dominate the plantings shown on these two pages associate comfortably with their blue and violet companions, while the white flowers make links with the implied white content of the pinks and also lighten the composition.

ABOVE With clusters of blue forget-me-nots at their feet, peony-flowered pink 'Angélique' tulips, tall Lily-flowered 'White Triumphator' tulips, and the pink primula are backed by variegated buckthorn. Later, pink and magenta geraniums will occupy the middle ground, and colewort (*Crambe cordifolia*) will replace the vertical white element at the back.

ABOVE Pink bleeding heart (*Dicentra*) and blue lungwort (*Pulmonaria*) and forget-me-nots make a harmonious jumble of spring foliage and flower color in the shade. The only white accents are the variegations of the honesty (*Lunaria annua* 'Alba Variegata'), and the grass at the back. Both of these will make stronger contributions when they are taller.

Pinks and Whites

Pink and white associations always work well. The palest pinks of some roses and peonies are light enough to combine in harmonies with white, which enhances their brilliance so that from a distance they appear as a unity. However, you need to beware of planting pale pink and white on a large scale: the effect can be overly sweet.

For a sharper, crisper effect, use dark pink with white; the contrast of tone prevents the colors from merging together. Although the white flowers are inert in color terms, they act as tonal highlights, lightening and brightening the overall effect.

Pink and white is a color combination that you can use all the year round, start-ing in early spring with snowdrops and deep pink cyclamen, and moving on with clouds of cherry blossom and ribbons of tulips. The peak seasons for this color pairing are late spring and early summer, when festoons of roses, spires of foxgloves, and banks of peonies, all in pinks and whites, come into glorious bloom.

ABOVE A ribbon of tulips – a mix of pink 'Peerless Pink', white 'Pax', and purple 'Negrita' – is threaded with bicolored flowers of the perennial bleeding heart (*Dicentra spectabilis*).

ABOVE Perennial white horned violets (*Viola cornuta* Alba Group) underplant a pink rose (*Rosa* 'Yesterday'). The color of the yellow throated flowers of the tender perennial Chinese foxglove (*Rehmannia elata*) is reflected in the smaller yellow-pink flowers of the twinspur (*Diascia* 'Ruby Field') growing beside them.

BELOW This early spring planting that includes snowdrops (*Galanthus nivalis* 'Flore Pleno') will increase every year. You can help the snowdrop bulbs to spread by splitting the clumps – complete with leaves – after flowering and replanting immediately. You can assist the deep pink cyclamen (*C. coum*) to spread by splitting the ripe seedheads in early summer and sprinkling the seeds around. The Tommasini's crocuses (*C. tommasinianus*), seen here in bud, naturalize well without help.

ABOVE White foxgloves add a vertical accent to the horizontal sprawl of heavy-headed double pink peonies.

ABOVE At the height of summer, old fashioned pink roses (here *Rosa* 'Mary Rose' with paler pink *Rosa* 'Gruss an Aachen'), are surmounted by foxgloves (*Digitalis purpurea*), and underplanted with sweet Williams (*Dianthus barbatus*) in colors from cerise extending to white with a pink "eye." Together they make a harmonious combination, with all three plants displaying a range of pinks. Foxgloves are biennials and will self-seed freely.

113

Pinks, Blues, and Violets

Midsummer offers the gardener the widest possible choice of flowering plants. It is also the season when scented plants come into their own, since most need warmth to release their fragrance. A cool planting of harmonizing muted pinks, blues, and violets is the perfect antidote to the heat of summer, and by repeating the colors along a lengthy garden feature, a calming color rhythm is established. Beneath the pergola, *right*, clumps of blue catmint, with aromatic foliage, have been planted at regular intervals, interspersed with low mounds of violet-blue and white horned violets. The tall delphiniums and the clematis pick up the violet-blue theme, and the various roses contribute their scent as well as their color to this sensuous summer harmony.

LEFT TOP Annual cosmos in deep pink through pale pink to white, with self-seeding violet-blue perennial bellflowers and long-flowering horned violets (*Viola cornuta*) make a harmonious drift of summer color.

LEFT CENTER The pink climbing rose 'Blairii Number Two' provides a cool root run for the violet-blue clematis (*C.* 'Lasurstern') and shade for dark pink foxgloves, which self-seed profusely.

LEFT BOTTOM This subtle harmony is fortuitous since the colors of the mixed biennial sweet Williams cannot be predicted, and the opium poppy (*Papaver somniferum*) has seeded itself among the pinkish-blue perennial beard tongues (*Penstemon*) and the silver foliage of an artemisia (*A.* 'Powis Castle').

RIGHT Catmint and horned violets, good edging plants, will bloom again if clipped back after the first display is over. The delphiniums, planted in the sun outside the pergola, will sometimes flower a second time, if cut back. The roses need regular deadheading to encourage repeat flowering.
(For a diagram of this planting, see page 176.)

Strong Pinks and Blues

Clear, strong pink is an exuberant color, bold and uncompromising, and almost as strong as magenta. It is at its best in the company of blue where its essential blueness is underscored.

If this rich harmony is to your taste, you can enjoy it in your garden from spring through to fall. Begin the season with naturalized corms and bulbs of dark pink cyclamen, partnered with the cool blue of Siberian squill. A little later, you can enjoy vivid pink anemones and rhododendrons, introduced on the edge of woodland to coincide with bluebells, either the wild hyacinths or Spanish bluebells, *below*, and *opposite, top left*. The examples *opposite, bottom left* and *opposite, bottom center* show how, as summer unfolds in your borders, you can partner deep pink roses and geraniums with blue perennials – delphiniums, Italian bugloss, and bellflowers. For growing over walls and trellises, try combining a large flowered deep pink clematis with a violet-blue one. For fall color in the same vein, partner a vivid mauve Michaelmas daisy, such as *Aster novae-angliae* 'Andenken an Alma Pötschke', with late-flowering dark blue monkshood (*Aconitum carmichaelii*).

FACING PAGE: Color relationships are strongest when companion hues are close in tone. The deep pinks are almost as dark as the blues. Vivid pinks like these are often regarded as "hot," but they contain a strong ingredient of blue, which places them among the cool pinks.

TOP LEFT In late spring, bluebells mingle with the lower branches of a dark pink rhododendron.
TOP CENTER The perennial wallflower (*Erysimum* 'Bowles' Mauve') will still be flowering long after its blue late spring companions, the forget-me-nots, fade in early summer. To continue the harmony, plant blue annuals such as California bluebell (*Phacelia campanularia*).
TOP RIGHT Coming to their peak in late summer, the wand flower (*Dierama pulcherrimum*) waves in the slightest breeze, setting up a shimmering association with the blue lily-of-the-Nile (*Agapanthus campanulatus*) nearby.

BOTTOM LEFT Exploit the blueness in the pink of the apothecary's rose (*Rosa gallica* var. *officinalis*) by partnering it with annual summer flowering Italian bugloss (*Anchusa* 'Loddon Royalist').
BOTTOM CENTER Interplant hummocks of bloody cranesbill (*Geranium sanguineum*) with the creeping bellflower (*Campanula portenschlagiana*) so that their colors blend together like a piece of rich embroidery.
BOTTOM RIGHT The pink of a pink and blue summer-flowering bicolored lupine perfectly matches the color of an accompanying thistle.

ABOVE It is worth the trouble finding named dark pink varieties of the spring-flowering *Anemone coronaria* for a woodland setting where you can plants drifts of the tubers among naturalized bluebells and wild white wood anemones. Many spring bulbs and perennials originate in woodland, drawing their energy from the sunlight that reaches them before the leaves appear on the trees. In summer, when they are dormant, the trees' canopy protects them from being dried out by the sun.

ABOVE Bluebells and rhododendron BELOW Roses and bugloss

ABOVE Wallflowers and forget-me-nots BELOW Cranesbill and bellflowers

ABOVE Wandflowers and lily-of-the-Nile BELOW Lupine and thistle

Magenta, Purples, and Maroons

These are some of the darkest colors available to the gardener. They all derive from the crimson-reds, although the blue component may range from the merest nuance, as in the knautia, to become the dominating element, as in the catmint, *left*. The basil foliage, *right top*, and the leaves of the sweet Williams, *right below*, contain red pigments too, but the redness is tempered by the waxy shine on the leaves that reflects back the blueness of the sky. The result is a deep purple color with ink-black shadows. Avoid using deep colored flowers with near-black foliage on a large scale; it may be too heavy. However, a containerful, as illustrated here, can make a powerful and profound effect.

LEFT Drifts of *Salvia nemorosa* 'East Friesland' – violet in the shade and magenta where the sunlight reaches it – are densely planted with other perennials including dusky red *Knautia macedonica,* beard tongues (*Penstemon* 'Stapleford Gem' and 'Hidcote Pink'), and catmint (*Nepeta* x *faassenii*).

RIGHT ABOVE A terracotta pot of dark magenta petunias and purple leaved basil (*Ocimum basilicum purpurascens*) creates a link with the paler magenta flowers of *Geranium* x *riversleaianum* 'Russell Prichard' and the bloody cranesbill (*Geranium sanguineum*) beyond.

RIGHT In a sunny border, a maroon 'William Lobb' rose is accompanied by ribbons of darkest red sweet Williams (*Dianthus barbatus* Nigrescens Group), a dark magenta lupine, and a clump of *Salvia nemorosa* 'Lubecca'. To make color matches that are this subtle, you may need to move plants when they are in flower – a procedure not generally recommended but possible if you follow up with regular watering.

119

Silver-Grays and Pastels

Combinations of silver and variegated foliage with pastel flowers are doubly harmonious. First, the combination of mainly pale colors makes a harmony of tone. Second, the component colors are muted in hue – also giving a harmony of saturation. One harmony reinforces the other, making them especially peaceable together.

Because these harmonies are so subtle, it requires a good eye to create them. As far as possible, use light toned variegated plants or, best of all, silver leaved plants together with pastel flowers. Some pink flowers – especially those with a metallic sheen – are particularly suitable, a fact that is acknowledged in the name of the pale pink ver-

bena 'Silver Anne', *opposite, far right*. You need a strong vertical element to give backbone to such subdued compositions as these. The planting *below* has repeated spires of pinky white mullein, while the border *opposite, near right*, includes a stand of apricot-pink foxgloves, and a tall, bold, gray leaved thistle.

ABOVE Silver leaved rose campion is accompanied by a red-leaf rose and spires of white mullein in a sunny border in midsummer. In the foreground a smaller pink rose mingles with two silver leaved artemisias. Deadheading the mullein and roses will encourage repeat flowering, and selectively trimming the artemisias will galvanize new growth. (For a diagram of this planting, see page 176.)

ABOVE An early autumn flowering bulb, the Belladonna lily (*Amaryllis belladonna*), flowers in a border. In front, *Verbena* 'Silver Anne' and the darker variety *V.* 'Sissinghurst' trail from containers with silver leaved licorice plant (*Helichrysum petiolare*). White flowered tobacco (*Nicotiana affinis*) and argyranthemum (chrysanthemum) daisies lighten the tone. At the back, in an interval between flowering, the rose 'Ballerina' will contribute its distinctive bicolored pink to the scheme.

LEFT Foxgloves and the gray leaved cotton thistle provide the vertical element in this border. Obelisks supporting white sweet peas or clematis would make a more permanent arrangement. The variegated plants – gardener's garters and mock orange – reinforce the lightening effect of the artemisias and lavender cotton in the foreground. Roses are limited to white and pale pink. The strongest colors are the lilac-pink Persian onions that echo the low growing hump of thrift to their right. (For a diagram of this planting, see page 176.)

Harmonies with Red

Red provides the basis for "hot" color harmonies when it is accompanied by other warm colors such as orange and yellow. Adjacent to each other on the color wheel, these three colors harmonize well together, but unlike most other cooler, harmonies, they are not restful. Instead, by putting together three of the brightest, most intense colors, you increase their vitality and encourage each to "sing out" at full strength. Concentrate these colors together in the garden and sparks seem to fly.

Hot plantings can be so powerful that they eclipse more subdued ones, so it is best to keep them quite separate from the rest of the garden. For maximum impact, surround a pair of hot borders by a hedge or walled enclosure. The effect will be all the more startling to your visitors when they unexpectedly come upon it. For slightly less drama, you can tone down your hot planting a little, by mixing hot colors with some dark foliage, *right*.

Foliage has an important part to play in hot plantings. Back your borders with foliage shrubs such as the red leaved varieties of barberry, smokebush, or hazel, and include castor oil plants and golden ray for their dusky foliage interest. With such dark toned foliage, you can lighten the overall effect by mixing in some yellow-green foliage too, such as golden grasses and bamboos.

Hot colors look best soon after dawn or before sunset in the flattering warm light of low sun. By coincidence, plants that lend themselves to hot plantings are predominantly late summer flowerers, when the sun is relatively low in the sky all day.

RIGHT In an inspirational planting, large drifts of bright yellow prevent the dark-toned flowers and foliage from dominating and making the scene gloomy. The graduated heights of the plants in these double borders are partly the result of careful planning, but also depend on meticulous staking. To achieve a successful late season border like this, you need to make preparations early in the summer by setting metal or twig supports in the ground, so that the perennials grow into them naturally and, ultimately, cover them completely. This has been so well done here that the plant supports have become invisible. (For a diagram of this planting, see page 177.)

LEFT Montbretia (*Crocosmia* 'Lucifer' and, further back, *C. masoniorum*) adds scarlet and vermilion flames to a hot planting in which a pale orange daylily separates two other lilies – the apricot-orange *Lilium* African Queen Group, and the bright yellow *Lilium* Citronella Group. In the foreground are the broad velvety leaves of a fuchsia whose red flowers will follow later, carrying the color theme farther into the season; behind the lilies is the yellow foliage of a dogwood (*Cornus alba* 'Aurea').

Russet Reds and Yellows

BELOW Evening sunlight burnishes a planting on the edge of a stream that leads toward russet maples. Clumps of pale yellow Tibetan primroses, spires of deeper yellow Shavalski's ligularia, hostas, and ferns are backed by rhododendrons and bamboo. These plants, and the white plumed astilbe on the other side of the path, are a good choice for the damp conditions of an area that is shaded for much of the day. (For a diagram of this planting, see page 178.)

In late spring, many perennials have new foliage with a yellow-bronze cast. At the same time, the strengthening light picks out the bare cinnamon- colored stems of shrubs and trees. Later in the year, evening sunlight bathes the garden in a warm yellow glow. You can build on these natural color effects by choosing plants within the limited range of yellows, rust-browns, and reds to make warm color harmonies. "Red" shrubs look especially good in the early summer light, when red leaved maples, plums, barberries, and smokebushes have the translucence and color of malt or dark toffee. In the planting *below*, russet maples make an effective backdrop to clumps of yellow Tibetan primroses and ligularia. Gold-brown irises can be matched with the rust color of a spurge or with a mullein, *opposite, above left*. Yellow-green foliage will lighten the effect and make a link with the yellow flowers.

FAR LEFT A bearded iris makes a clever color association with its neighbor, the mullein (*Verbascum* 'Cotswold Queen').

LEFT The rusty brown stems of the spurge (*Euphorbia griffithii* 'Fireglow') have infiltrated bulbs of the yellow trout lily (*Erythronium* 'Pagoda'). In a close planting like this, the stronger partner – here the spurge – will need occasional judicious dividing to prevent it from crowding out the trout lily.

BELOW Early morning sunlight casts a unifying mellow glow over a harmonious spring scene of russet reds and yellows. This includes spurge with fox-red foliage and orange flowers, rusty orange wallflowers and tulips, golden feverfew and, in the distance, yellow azaleas. (For a diagram of this planting, see page 178.)

CONTRASTS

Contrasts in the garden are stimulating. You can achieve contrasts in several ways, depending on how dramatic an effect you want. To create bright, strong schemes, combine intense colors or juxtapose very dark and very light colors. To make a quieter, less demanding scheme, use subtle colors and subdued tonal contrasts.

The strongest color contrasts are created by associations of complementary colors – that is, those colors opposite each other on the color wheel (see page 15): red with green, blue with orange, and yellow with violet. Variations on these three combinations can produce a range of less obvious contrasts such as deep plum-red with silver-gray – which is seen here in the garden, *right* – or pale blue with apricot, creamy yellow with lilac. In general, it is better to keep color contrasts simple, sticking to a single pair of contrasting colors throughout a particular area of the garden. Several color contrasts together can be too much.

Contrasts of light and dark tone can be used in much the same way. The backdrop provided by a dark yew hedge, for example, will make contrasting white and silver plants seem even lighter and brighter. In the garden shown *right*, the strongest tonal contrasts are made by the dark purple-red plum hedge setting off the pale pink roses planted in front of it. More subtly, the mounds of light silver-gray lavender cotton are juxtaposed with dark red barberry.

Color temperature also plays a role in color associations. It can have a major effect when two closely related colors, one warm and one relatively cool, are planted together. Hot orange and cool pink, for example, are said to "clash." Shocking contrasts like this can be deliberately used as isolated and arresting incidents within a larger, more soothing framework. Gentler effects occur when differences in color temperature are used simply to heighten the difference between two colors. In the garden pictured here, the warm colors derived from red – the pinks and deep purple-reds – make the silver-grays appear relatively cool.

RIGHT This subtle scheme uses three forms of contrast: of color, tone, and temperature. The mounds of dark barberry and hedge of red leaved plum are muted reds, and contrast with the pale gray foliage of the artemisias, lavender cotton, and lamb's ears, which are less saturated versions of green. The reds are so dark in tone, and so warm, that they make the silver-grays seem both lighter and cooler by comparison.
(For a diagram of this planting, see page 178.)

Reds and Greens

Red and green make one of the strongest color contrasts, not only because the two are complementary colors but also because they are very close in tone, and this emphasizes their color difference. In the garden, red flowers are usually seen against a backdrop of green foliage, so part of the drama of an all-red planting comes from the red and green contrast. Exploit this contrast by using red flowers, such as the flame creeper, *below left*, to brighten dark evergreens, or green foliage to intensify the color of a clump of red poppies.

With a prominent background such as a red brick wall, it is difficult to find plants that can hold their own. The bold red-green planting, *below right*, offers a solution, using plants with strong green foliage and flowers of an even more intense red than the brick.

In nature, fall is when the red and green contrast comes into its own. Red berries ripen against the foliage of evergreen hollies, firethorns, and cotoneasters. Deciduous foliage reddens in the company of evergreens. You can take a cue from nature by growing evergreens alongside plants with foliage that turns red in fall. Dark green ivy, for example, would be almost invisible for much of the year among Virginia creeper, until the creeper turns red, when it makes an intense red-green contrast.

ABOVE The perennial flame creeper (*Tropaeolum speciosum*) climbs well through yew (*Taxus baccata*) because the yew has so many small stems and leaves for its tendrils to hold onto. The flame creeper will overwinter underground as a swollen rhizome.

ABOVE A multiple planting of a scarlet pelargonium, perennial *Verbena peruviana* of matching flower color, and the annual petunia 'Red Joy', gives a concentrated color effect which is stronger than the patterns of the brickwork behind. Plants can be crammed together closely like this in pots for the few weeks of summer provided that you keep them watered and fed.

ABOVE For the longest lasting fall effects, plant climbers so they change color at slightly different times. Here, crimson glory vine (*Vitis coignetiae*) is turning color early. Its redness is made more pronounced by the contrast with the green of its companion Virginia creeper (*Parthenocissus quinquefolia*) which is yet to turn.

RIGHT You can boost the dramatic color of maples (here two varieties of *Acer palmatum*) by interplanting them with evergreen pines or spruces (here *Pinus parviflora*).

Muted Reds and Gray-Greens

Combining plants with flowers or foliage that are muted, unsaturated versions of red and green creates subtle contrasts. If you choose reds that are either very dark or so pale that they become pink, the intensity of the red is reduced and will make a less startling contrast than, for example, a bright vermilion when seen against adjacent green foliage. The border *opposite, below* consists of two distinct groups of muted reds – dark red barberry, snapdragons, sweet Williams and red mountain spinach, and pink twinspurs, foxgloves, roses, and valerian. The planting in the container *opposite, above* is dominated by two begonias with muted, metallic red leaves. The greens, with their touches of red and purple, are muted too, so the effect is still more subtle.

By using deep muted reds with gray-green foliage, you can achieve definite yet still subtle contrasts in which tonal differences also come into play. The plum colored leaves of some barberries, smokebushes, and plums are so dark in tone that they look almost black against silver foliage. Here, *below left*, the feathery gray leaves of white sagebush make a dramatic contrast with the rounded, plum-red leaves of a smokebush.

BELOW One of the best small trees with plum foliage is the Eastern redbud tree (*Cercis canadensis* 'Forest Pansy') seen here against a gray-green background of the white sagebush (*Artemisia ludoviciana* 'Silver Queen') and a pampas grass (*Cortaderia selloana* 'Pumila'). You could grow this relative of the Judas tree as a specimen in a lawn, underplanted with a carpet of silvery lamb's-ears (*Stachys byzantina*).

ABOVE Cut the purple leaved smokebush (*Cotinus coggygria* 'Royal Purple') right back in early spring. Its fresh growth will have larger leaves, closer to the ground, making better partners for the silver leaved white sagebush (*Artemisia ludoviciana*).

ABOVE Stems of the lightly variegated Roseglow Japanese barberry (*Berberis thunbergii* 'Rose Glow') reach up into the branches of the willow leaf pear tree (*Pyrus salicifolia* 'Pendula'). Both plants enjoy a sunny site.

RIGHT Rex begonias with purple or pink tinged leaves take center stage in a stone container. They are accompanied by two clovers – the dark, four-leaved *Trifolium repens* 'Purpurascens Quadrifolium' and a lighter-colored, three-leaved form – a spiderwort (*Tradescantia* 'Zebrina'), a variety of betony, and hare's tail grass (*Lagurus ovatus*) with fluffy flower heads. The begonias can be propagated from leaf cuttings, while the clovers and grass self-seed readily.

BELOW The permanent framework of this border of muted reds and greens is formed by shrubs such as the purple leaved barberry at the top right and the rose ('Pink Perpétué') toward the top left, together with perennials such as the figwort (*Filipendula rubra*) on the left, and the pink twinspur (*Diascia rigescens*) and variegated water figwort (*Scrophularia auriculata* 'Variegata') on the right. The pink valerian on the left and biennial strawberry foxgloves in the center are self-seeding. The spaces between them are filled each summer with annuals, biennials and tender perennials such as the black cherry colored sweet Williams (*Dianthus barbatus* Nigrescens Group), the snapdragons (*Antirrhinum* 'Black Prince'), and a type of beet.

131

Oranges and Blues

Orange is one of the most vibrant colors in the gardener's palette. Seen alongside blue, which is its complementary color, it is all the more intense. Orange and blue combinations are not for the faint-hearted. If you feel that a massed planting of orange and blue is too strong for you, you could try a more restrained approach by using spot plantings of orange to animate an expanse of blue. Here, *right,* the dramatic planting is dominated by the blue backdrop of the Californian lilac echoed by the blue-gray of the path, but the flashes of bright orange wallflowers in the wings make the scene spectacular. For spring, you could enjoy the sight of orange tulips and wallflowers pushing through a mass of purple leaved bugle, *opposite, below right,* while in summer, orange lilies look stunning nodding as splashes of contrast above a bed of blue clary, *below.* The reverse effect can be dramatic too. An orange flowered sun rose dominates when grown with an accompaniment of lilac-blue Serbian bellflower, *opposite, above right.*

ABOVE Unlike many lilies, this orange *Lilium henryi* prefers alkaline soil. Here it grows with the annual blue clary (*Salvia viridis* 'Blue Beard') whose color comes from long lasting bracts or modified leaves around the tiny flowers.

ABOVE Ribbons of biennial orange wallflowers lead the eye to a large container planted with a standard grass palm (*Cordyline australis*), freeway daisy (*Osteospermum caulescens*), and perennial wallflower (*Erysimum* 'Bowles' Mauve'), with London pride (*Saxifraga* x *urbium*) planted round its base, seen against a background of blue Californian lilac (*Ceanothus*). Californian lilac is somewhat tender; training it against a wall assures it of some protection during the winter. Prune it immediately after flowering, taking all the green side shoots back to within an inch or two of the old wood. They will sprout again to give next year's flowers; but avoid cutting into old wood.

ABOVE This summer-flowering collection of mainly perennial plants includes violets (*Viola cornuta* and *V.* 'Maggie Mott'), strong blue Hungarian speedwell (*Veronica austriaca* 'Crater Lake Blue'), bright yellow St. John's chamomile, rich yellow inula (*I. orientalis*), dark orange hawkweed (*Pilosella aurantiaca*), and avens (*Geum* 'Fire Opal'), as well as a biennial, the double orange form of the Welsh poppy (*Meconopsis cambrica* var. *flore-pleno*). The chamomile flowers intermittently all summer, but the other plants have a relatively short flowering season. To extend the effect until fall, supplement the perennials with annuals. For orange, try Californian poppies, marigolds, and nasturtiums. For blue, try *Echium* 'Blue Bedder', love-in-a-mist (*Nigella* 'Miss Jekyll'), or mealy-cup sage (*Salvia farinacea* 'Victoria').

ABOVE In spring, elegant orange species tulips and orange wallflowers grow through the purple leaved bugle (*Ajuga reptans* 'Atropurpurea').

TOP An orange sun rose (*Helianthemum*) provides a shrubby mound of color for the creeping lilac-blue Serbian bellflower (*Campanula poscharskyana*) to thread its way through. Both plants like sunny, well drained soil, and will thrive in the cracks between the stones in a terrace garden.

133

Oranges and Blue-Green

You can moderate the contrast between the complementary colors orange and blue by using muted versions of one or both. There are many plants, like the irises and yarrows, *right*, whose foliage has just a hint of blue – enough to provide a gentle contrast with neighboring orange flowers. In a planting like this, take care with the shapes and sizes of the blocks of color. The brilliant orange wallflowers need a large expanse of blue-green iris foliage to balance them. The more diffused orange of the spurges looks most effective in a large drift, whereas the sharp stab of color of the tulips works best in compact clumps.

Likewise, muted orange enhances blue flowers as in the planting *below* where the orange of the American marigolds and of the spines of the *Solanum pyracanthum* bring the blue-greens to life.

RIGHT This spring color scheme suits a garden in full sun, not only because wallflowers, tulips, irises, and yarrow thrive in this situation, but also because the hot colors, orange, red, and yellow, look brightest in sunshine. In a few weeks' time the scene will change completely: the vivid blue-green of the iris and yarrow foliage will be eclipsed by their own flowers, and by orange, red, and yellow lilies, daylilies, and dahlias. (For a diagram of this planting, see page 179.)

BELOW The "red" cabbage (*Brassica* 'Scarlett O'Hara') In this planting of vegetables among flowers is actually distinctly blue with purple veining. More blue comes from the violet-blue petunias and sea lavender (*Limonium latifolium*). The upright *Solanum pyracanthum* has orange spines that echo the color of the American marigold (*Tagetes* 'Tangerine Gem'). For a planting like this of annuals and biennials, you need to grow your plants from seed, starting afresh each year.

Yellows and Violets

Yellow and violet plant associations create intense contrasts both of color and of tone. Nature herself exploits these in bicolored flowers, particularly irises and violets. Yellow and violet are complementary colors (see the color wheel on page 15) and also, since violets tend to be darker than yellows, violet flowers make yellow companions appear lighter. This means that in associations such as the primroses and violets, *below right*, the primroses will seem to dominate the violets because their color is much paler in tone. The yellow color is also warmer and so catches the eye more than the recessive, cooler color of the violets. To make the colors balance, you would need many more violets than primroses.

Schemes based on yellows and violets are particularly appealing, and can be carried through the garden for most of the year. They are especially successful in spring when yellow prevails both in flowers and in the yellowish tinge of the fresh new foliage of trees and shrubs. Early spring brings primroses and miniature narcissi; these could be combined with violets and anemones, and with crocuses and dwarf irises of either color. Winter hazel or spurge would add another layer of yellow above them. In late spring, the choice of plants widens and includes cowslips, jonquils, yellow tulips, and brooms that could be teamed with violet columbines and planted beneath violet alpine clematis. In the natural looking garden *right*, tall bearded irises create an intense color contrast with yellow corydalis and Welsh poppies. In a sunnier situation, yellow primulas could be combined with aubrieta or, for a softer effect, with the pale violet of the Pasque flower.

ABOVE The pale yellow stripes of variegated sweet iris (*I. pallida* 'Variegata') draw the eye to the violet flowers of the Grecian windflower (*Anemone blanda*), both allowed to spread in an area of dappled shade. This early spring partnership between horizontal and vertical accents of color is a risk that has paid off, because the iris would prefer full sunlight in summer, and the anemone full shade. Although this iris, which has pale blue flowers in the summer, may not flower out of the sun, it has been grown here primarily for its foliage effect.

ABOVE Primroses and violets are natural early spring partners since they frequently appear growing together in the wild. Although they are easily cultivated, they are – like many spring-flowering bulbs – best left to naturalize on banks and hillsides, or on the edges of woodland.

RIGHT Yellow corydalis (*Corydalis lutea*) and Welsh poppies (*Meconopsis cambrica*) have seeded themselves around a stand of violet irises. The paler blue forget-me-nots beyond are also self-seeding. The sparse branches of the Maidenhair tree (*Ginkgo biloba*) allow the irises to get the sun they need. The silvery buds of *Nectaroscordum siculum* are opening into rusty green flowers, and the pale pink anemone clematis (*C. montana*) has just come into bloom.

Yellows and Warm Violets

Warm violets – those with a tinge of red – come in all tints and shades from palest pink-lilac to strong purple-violet. All combine well with yellows, but the gentlest associations occur when cream or pale yellow flowers are teamed with the soft violet colors of plants such as wisteria, lavender, lilac, or the butterfly bush. These colors come into their own in the summer. Hanging yellow clusters of laburnum and lilac ornamental onions would make a stunning start to the season, which might finish with pale yellow dahlias and lilac Michaelmas daisies.

The sun of late evening can change the appearance of pale yellows and soft violets, making the yellows more yellow and the violets more pink. Under the laburnum, *left*, the creamy fringecups are yellow in the setting sun, while the true lilac color of the Persian onions is only seen in the shade. The slanting rays of the sun have given the boxwood globes yellow rims that harmonize with the laburnum flowers.

LEFT A tunnel of trained laburnum (*Laburnum* x *watereri* 'Vossii') is underplanted with the Persian onion (*Allium aflatunense*) whose flower heads echo the shape of the clipped boxwood globes. The hosta (*H. sieboldiana* var. *elegans*) thrives in dappled shade, as does evergreen Alaska fringecups (*Tellima grandiflora*).

RIGHT ABOVE The frothy flowerheads of solidaster (x *S. luteus* 'Lemore') create a haze of pale yellow beneath the more sharply defined flowers of the butterfly bush (*Buddleja davidii* 'Glasnevin').

RIGHT In a formal planting of long lasting annuals, warm violet rigid verbena (*Verbena rigida*) contrasts with pale yellow snapdragons. The topiary bird of golden English yew (*Taxus baccata* 'Aurea') makes a sharper yellow contrast, but its curves and right angles are reflected in the shapes of the boxwood-edged beds.

Yellows and Blues

Yellows and blues make potent and popular color contrasts. Although not exactly opposite each other on the color wheel, they behave as if they were true complementaries, each enhancing the other. Given the wide range of blues and yellows in flowers and foliage, it is possible to use the blue-yellow contrast through the seasons and across all plant groups. All the plantings shown *opposite* demonstrate this color theme, starting in spring, *opposite, below right*, with narcissi and tulips, accompanied by forget-me-nots; following in early summer, *opposite, below left*, with veronica and leopard's bane; and in high summer, *opposite, above*, with roses, lupines, and mullein, accompanied by delphiniums, catmint, and salvias. In fall, you might pair coneflowers and yellow waxbells with monkshood and Michaelmas daisies. Even in winter you can keep the blue-yellow theme alive with the foliage of "blue" cedars and spruces combined with yellow leaved evergreens.

Planting for sustained color through the seasons generally means that effects will be less concentrated at any one moment. If you are prepared to sacrifice some earlier and later color, a border like this one, *right,* will reward you with a sumptuous summer show. It requires much preparation and planning, since it relies chiefly upon generous clumps of perennials such as catmint, sneezeweed, mullein, and delphiniums, with tender annuals like American marigolds and flowering tobacco to fill the gaps.

RIGHT Here is a yellow and blue border pictured at the height of summer. The whole border can either be cut back to ground level in the fall or left until spring. The dead material looks decorative in winter and affords some protection to the dormant roots of the perennials. (For a diagram of this planting, see page 180.)

RIGHT A creamy yellow lupine (*Lupinus* 'Chandelier', with oriental iris (*I.orientalis*), the mullein (*Verbascum* 'Gainsborough'), and the 'Graham Thomas' rose of similar hues, accompany dark blue delphiniums and monkshood, and the paler violet-blue catmint (*Nepeta* 'Six Hills Giant'). All these plants do best in a sunny, well drained site.

BELOW RIGHT The elegant *Narcissus* 'Hawera' surrounded by a haze of blue forget-me-nots accompanies yellow double tulips. This blue and yellow spring display anticipates the color theme of a summer-flowering herbaceous border.

BELOW Pale blue Gentian speedwell (*Veronica gentianoides*) accompanies bright yellow leopard's bane (*Doronicum*) in early summer. At about 18in (45cm), this speedwell is usually grown at the front of a border. It is daring to plant it behind the taller leopard's bane, which creates a frame through which the shorter flowers can be seen.

Lime-Green and Blues

The yellow that you see in some foliage and in the bracts surrounding spurge flowers is sharp and acidic, like the color of limes. It is a color that is seen in abundance in spring and early summer, when the newly emerged leaves of many shrubs and trees are tinged with yellow; late in the year foliage yellows tend to lose their sparkle and become drab. Use blue spring bulbs like hyacinths, squills, and grape hyacinths to enhance the sharp yellow of spring foliage and spurge flowerheads. Later, blue summer-flowering plants, such as Italian bugloss, bellflowers, delphiniums and love-in-a-mist, make good companions for the yellow leaves of maples and golden hop, *right* and *far right*. The "golden" forms of mock orange, honeysuckle, nine bark, privet, or yew would also make good yellow backdrops of foliage.

If you have the courage, an audacious variation on the blue with lime-yellow planting scheme involves introducing blue in the form of a piece of garden furniture. In the garden pictured *left*, a brilliant blue bench looks superb alongside the lime-yellow flowerheads of spurge in spring. This bold splash of blue contrasts in tone as well as in color with the yellow and the two balance each other well.

LEFT It is usually advisable to be more restrained with the color of garden furniture, but this combination of a bright blue-painted bench with the lime-yellow flowerheads of spurge (*Euphorbia characias* subsp.*wulfenii*) is a risk that has paid off. The combination of yellow with blue – the blue of the bench harmonizing with the forget-me-nots alongside – will be continued later in the summer when the felty gray leaves of the mullein send up spikes of creamy yellow flowers.

ABOVE A clump of dark blue Black Knight Group delphiniums is effective against a backdrop of the Japanese maple (*Acer shirasawanum* 'Aureum'). This sharp yellow foliage holds its color well, but the maple is very slow growing. For quicker growing yellow trees, consider the golden leaved black locust (*Robinia pseudoacacia* 'Frisia'), or the Sunburst honey locust (*Gleditsia triacanthos* 'Sunburst'). Grown in a border with perennials, these two will need to be kept within bounds by careful pruning.

ABOVE Self-seeded love-in-the-mist (*Nigella damascena* 'Miss Jekyll') grows through the vines of the golden leaved hop (*Humulus lupulus* 'Aureus') accompanied by the New Zealand flax (*Phormium cookianum* 'Cream Delight') and the variegated Silver Queen winter creeper euonymus (*E. fortunei* 'Silver Queen'). This hop has foliage of a beautiful color early in the season, but needs to be kept in check as it is something of a horticultural thug that can overwhelm its neighbors. Restricted to its own section of wall or fence, it will make a yellow-green curtain during the course of one summer.

Scarlet, Pink, and Orange Shocks

You often see startling combinations of color in paintings, textile design, and fashion, but rarely in gardens and then often as accidents. Blue-pink with vermilion, magenta with orange – these colors react together so shockingly that their effect is often described as a "clash." This slightly pejorative term can obscure the fact that color shocks do sometimes have a place in the garden. They are the equivalent of the clash of cymbals in a symphony — a vital element of the music but one that makes the audience jump with astonishment.

Color shocks occur between colors that are quite close together both in hue and tone, such as pink and red, or pink and orange.

They share a common ingredient – red, and so might be expected to harmonize. The reaction between them has to do with the cooling blue content of the pink, and the warming yellow content of the red or orange. When you look at the two colors together, the conflicting messages of harmony and contrast can be disturbing to the eye. This is exacerbated when there is little or no foliage to dilute or neutralize the flower color.

The pleasure (or pain) that color shocks can give depends very much upon the context and the light conditions in which they are seen. Shocking schemes might be appropriate in a public park that is the setting for games and entertainment, but would be out of place in a private garden intended for repose. Shocking contrasts look wonderful in the intense light of the tropics, but can seem too strong in the pallid light of temperate regions. Generally, they are best used as isolated incidents that enliven a planting and prevent it from becoming predictable.

Some of the most effective color shocks can be created among single-color plantings. Try pink or magenta in a red border to make you jump, or shocking scarlet in a pink border to shake off any feelings of calm and sweetness that the pinks may induce. Adding cool pink to a hot orange planting will have a similar effect.

LEFT Plant rhizomes of the flame creeper (*Tropaeolum speciosum*) between the roots of a deep pink climbing rose (here, *Rosa* 'Dorothy Perkins') if you want a cascade of intense and shocking color in summer.

FACING PAGE: Each picture contains its own color shock: seen together the four have a cumulatively disturbing effect.
TOP LEFT The dark pink spires of so-called purple loosestrife (*Lythrum salicaria* 'Morden's Pink') are seen against a drift of yellow and orange sneezeweed (*Helenium autumnale*). The loosestrife grows in boggy soil while the sneezeweed favors the well drained conditions of its higher patch of ground.
TOP RIGHT The strength of the color shocks that deciduous azaleas can produce in combination with other flowering plants – here wild bluebells – is even greater due to their almost complete lack of neutral green foliage at flowering time in late spring.
BOTTOM LEFT Scarlet and pink annual verbenas provide long lasting color in summer bedding schemes. For similar effects using perennial verbenas, choose red 'Taylor Town Red' and pink 'Sissinghurst'.
BOTTOM RIGHT For a spring scheme of bold color shocks, plant double orange tulips with mixed pink and scarlet English daisies (*Bellis perennis*).

ABOVE Loosestrife and sneezeweed   **BELOW** Two verbenas

ABOVE Azaleas and bluebells   **BELOW** Tulips and daisies

Fall Color Shocks

When leaves turn and berries ripen in late summer and fall, carefully planned color schemes may be taken over by nature. Bright scarlet berries and vivid orange and yellow leaves can dominate parts of the garden that were previously devoted to totally different colors. This can result in some surprising juxtapositions and happy accidents, like the unplanned combination of rich pink autumn-flowering cyclamen with the fallen orange and red leaves of the Persian parrotia tree, *opposite, left*.

These color partnerships can be mildly shocking, but are somehow acceptable, even to those who normally prefer more muted effects. Maybe it is because we take delight in seeing the same natural color changes in our gardens that we enjoy in the parks and woods outside. Maybe too it is because the sun is low in the sky in fall, and bathes everything in a uniform warm yellow light, touching each color and having a softening influence on even the strongest contrasts.

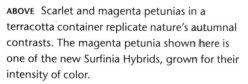

ABOVE Scarlet and magenta petunias in a terracotta container replicate nature's autumnal contrasts. The magenta petunia shown here is one of the new Surfinia Hybrids, grown for their intensity of color.

RIGHT ABOVE The scarlet berries of Italian arum (*Arum italicum* subsp. *italicum* 'Marmoratum') look especially good combined with the deep pink autumn-flowering crocus (*Colchicum speciosum*).

RIGHT A rich color combination for fall consists of pink stonecrop (*Sedum* 'Autumn Joy') with violet-flowered rigid verbena (*V. rigida*).

ABOVE Autumn-flowering *Cyclamen hederifolium* combines with the fallen leaves of Persian parrotia (*Parrotia persica*) to make an unexpected bold color marriage. For a similar effect plant the cyclamen under maples or fothergillas which also have red and yellow fall foliage.

RIGHT Shrubs in a mixed border, like this cut leaved maple (*Acer palmatum* var. *dissectum*), evergreen "yellow" privet (*Ligustrum ovalifolium* 'Aureum'), spurge (*Euphorbia griffithii*), and dark leaved smokebush (*Cotinus coggygria* 'Royal Purple'), give a backbone of foliage that contributes dazzling color changes through late summer and fall. They also set up vivid new color partnerships with the dark pinks of Michaelmas daisies (*Aster amellus* 'Violet Queen'), the lingering flowers of a purple heliotrope (*Heliotropium* 'Marine'), and the purple sage (*Salvia officinalis* Purpurascens Group). The gentle autumnal light softens what might otherwise be a harsh color contrast.

Blacks and Whites

Putting light and dark plants together in the garden creates contrasts of tone. The greatest possible tonal contrast would be between the two extremes, black and white, but you rarely see these pure colors in nature. "Black" flowers or foliage have a hint of red or purple in them that makes them lighter in tone than pure black. White flowers often have colored centers, and a hint of green: the effect of this is to make them seem darker in tone than pure white.

Tonal contrasts that are nearly black and white are pleasing to the eye because the limitation of color makes their relationship relatively ordered and formal. Black and white combinations in the garden are striking and smart, just as they are in formal dress.

As with pairs of complementary colors on the color wheel, black and white enhance each other, the black bringing out the "whiteness" of the white, and vice versa. The black tulips in front of the cardoon, *opposite, below,* emphasize the cardoon's silvery foliage, making it appear almost white. Similarly, the inky black barberry, *opposite, above left,* seems darker with a white climber through it.

You can easily incorporate the architecture of your garden and its furniture into a black and white scheme. Use a white wall as a backdrop for black hollyhocks, or train a white clematis through a black-painted wrought iron fence or gate. The risers of the steps *below* have been stained black to echo the tree trunks, and to make horizontal black features that balance the vertical ones.

BELOW In early summer, the white flowers of an Eastern dogwood (*Cornus florida*) make an intense tonal contrast with the black tree trunks, the wooden risers of the steps, and the dark foliage of the purple leaved Japanese barberry (*Berberis thunbergii* f. *atropurpurea*).

RIGHT The perennial sweet pea (*Lathyrus latifolius* 'Albus') enhances the dark foliage of a barberry. Deadhead the pea regularly for a continuous display of flowers.

BELOW Purple sage (*Salvia officinalis* Purpurascens Group) makes an excellent two-toned underplanting for 'Queen of the Night' tulips and the light-toned young foliage of the cardoon (*Cynara cardunculus*). A sunny, well drained spot in the vegetable garden is normally home to the cardoon and sage, but they can make an attractive foliage contribution to the flower garden.

LEFT The variegated grass (*Holcus mollis* 'Albovariegatus') together with purple clover (*Trifolium repens* 'Purpurascens Quadrifolium'), one of the stonecrops (*Sedum sieboldii* 'Mediovariegatum'), and the oval seedheads of *Tulipa tarda*, make an eye catching black and white combination in early summer. At different times of year, the effect will be different. In early spring, the *Tulipa tarda* will bear several yellow-white flowers to each stem, while the variegated stonecrop will carry open star shaped pink flowers in late summer.

Violets, Blues, and White

White flowers give the lightest and brightest color in the garden, violets some of the darkest. Planted together, the white flowers will make the colored ones seem even darker than they really are. Thise is because the white stimulates the eye to see a contrasting dark tone beside it that reinforces any dark color that really is there. So when you look at any color relationship involving white, the first thing that strikes you, subliminally, is the strong tonal contrast, and any subtle relationships within a scheme can simply be overpowered.

At the same time it exaggerates tonal differences, white has an invigorating effect on dark colors. The best way to see this effect is to imagine the plantings on these pages without the white flowers. Take them away, and the violets and blues would sink into gloom, the dark flowers merging with the dark foliage. The overall effect would be much more somber. Restore the whites, and the color schemes are instantly lighter and more cheerful, with highlights that draw the eye. You could create a lighter scheme without whites by using lighter colors overall, such as pale lilac clematis and light blue petunias, but the result would be totally different. Such a scheme would be harmonious and restful on the eye, but would lack the energy that the contrast with white creates. Besides, you would be passing up the chance to use the rich and velvety hues of pure blues and violets.

LEFT At the height of summer, the violet Italian clematis (*C. viticella*) makes a tonal contrast with the white painted door. This contrast is taken up in a stronger form by the violet and white petunias. Prune the clematis in early spring before the new growth begins, as this clematis produces flowers on its new shoots.

LEFT In spring, dark blue common bugle (*Ajuga reptans*) is brightened with white lily-of-the-valley (*Convallaria majalis*). Both moisture-loving plants are invasive, but are equally matched, so one will not overwhelm the other.

RIGHT The blue 'Prince Charles' clematis flowers at the same time as the mock orange (*Philadelphus* 'Belle Étoile'). Growing clematis through shrubs is a way to introduce color after the shrubs have finished flowering.

RIGHT This richly planted midsummer scheme of violets, blues, and white consists of hardy perennials – 'Johnson's Blue' geranium, sea lavender (*Limonium latifolium*), and paler violet, self-seeding horned violets (*Viola cornuta*), with the tender white marguerite (*Argyranthemum foeniculaceum*); annuals – bright violet-blue clary (*Salvia viridis*), and the deep blue delphinium (*D. grandiflorum*); and the gray leaved shrub, lavender cotton (*Santolina chamaecyparissus*). It takes great gardening skill to make such a complicated planting look so natural and effortless. Each spring you need to grow annuals from seed and bring them on to a size at which they can hold their own with the tender perennials that you plant at the same time. Throughout the summer you need to make sure that the plants do not swamp their neighbors, and stake them discreetly to prevent the whole assembly from collapsing in summer storms.

MIXED COLORS

Gardens filled with myriad colors are the result either of highly sophisticated planning or no planning at all. You can orchestrate mixed color plantings to achieve a complex symphony of color. For instance, you could lay out a border across the full spectrum of colors to make a rainbow effect. Another ambitious approach would be to combine two separate harmonizing plantings that together create a contrast: a harmony of yellows, creams and lime-greens, for example, could be intermixed with an opposing harmony of blues, blue-violets and even blue-pinks. Associations like these look colorful but remain controlled. The color palette is broad but it still excludes certain colors, in this case reds and oranges. Alternatively, a judicious sprinkling of the "wrong" colors in an otherwise harmonious planting – a few bright red or yellow flowers, for example, among soft violets and pinks – will add zest and a welcome element of surprise. But even this needs control and a sure eye.

At the other extreme is the *laissez-faire* approach of the cottage gardener. Here, all color is welcome, the more the merrier. The effect can be exhilarating, but it is worth analyzing the reasons why random color works so well in this context. First, the area is small. The exuberance of color in a cottage garden is thrilling on a small scale, whereas over a large area it could become tiresome and even disturbing. Second, by virtue of its rural location and its vernacular style, the traditional cottage garden merges with its natural surroundings, and its colorful plantings are contiguous with the random colors of the natural vegetation around them. In an urban or suburban context the cottage garden color is less convincing.

RIGHT At first glance, this cottage garden looks like an explosion of random color, in which all the color conventions have been ignored. But although a wide range of colors has been used, the liberal use of white, the cooling green surroundings and, most especially, the repetition of colors and shapes transforms what might have been a haphazard arrangement into a rhythmical pattern. This quality makes the eye accept the broken conventions, such as the partnering of a salmon-pink poppy with a blue-pink geranium. (For a diagram of this planting, see page 180.)

Blues and Pinks with Yellow

LEFT A mastery of propagation techniques will help you achieve the overflowing exuberance of this long established double border without the need for buying large quantities of plants. You can increase your stock of delphiniums by dividing their crowns every two or three years, and retaining only the outer roots. Propagate the geraniums and pale yellow giant scabious by division too, and grow marguerites from seed. (For a diagram of this planting, see page 181.)

Mixing a harmonious planting with a contrasting one is an ambitious undertaking, but can be very successful, especially in a large garden. The overall energy of such a combination can override the occasional unhappy juxtaposition of color.

Start with the color blue, achieved by repeated plantings of, for example, delphiniums or African lilies. Next, think of blue as part of a harmony with pinks and violets, and make repeated plantings of these colors along the border, using perhaps ornamental onions or lupines. Finally, treat the blue as part of a blue and yellow contrast and put together a series of yellow flowers or foliage – yarrow or cinquefoil are possibilities – to partner it. In the double border *below*, the yellow-green hedges provide the yellow component. The harmony and contrast combination is comfortable as long as the strongest yellows, as in the border *opposite*, are kept away from the pinks, and instead partnered with blue, violet, or even lilac.

ABOVE As in this newly planted double border, use blue flowers to make a harmony with pink and lilac companions, and to contrast with the yellow-green foliage of the hedge. In a few years' time the strict, straight edges of the path will be completely concealed by the plants that are already spilling over. (For a diagram of this planting, see page 181.)

ABOVE In a mainly harmonious planting of blue-green, silver, pink, and magenta, the incidents of understated yellow – seen in the pale lime-green flowering tobacco plants and spurge – do not detract from the gentle transitions between colors. Only the deep red sweet Williams attract attention. The permanent planting includes delphiniums, roses, geraniums, sage, and bulbs, and is infilled with annuals in the summer. (For a diagram of this planting, see page 182.)

Deep Pinks, Blues, and Violets with Yellows

A harmonious theme of pinks, mauves, violets, and gray-blues – roses, delphiniums, ornamental onions, sweet peas – is the common thread linking the three plantings here. Woven through these predominantly dark, cool harmonies is a secondary contrasting theme of pale yellows. By acting as a subtle contrast, these enhance the blues and blue-pinks of the main color theme. They also lighten the plantings, making them less somber than they would be without them.

There is a danger, though, if you introduce yellow to a cool color scheme. Large drifts of strong yellow would set up a sense of conflict, and the cooler colors could easily be overpowered. To counteract this effect, use pale, unsaturated tints of yellow as in some mulleins, or choose flowers in which the color is dispersed in small dots, as in the flowerheads of the dill, *right above,* In the variegation of the iris foliage, *right below,* the yellow is a mere suggestion.

RIGHT ABOVE Sweet peas (*Lathyrus odoratus*), restricted to mixtures of mauves and violets, scramble across the corner of a border planted with yarrow (*Achillea filipendulina* 'Gold Plate'), dill (*Anethum graveolens*), creamy yellow marguerites (*Anthemis tinctoria* 'E.C.Buxton'), Shasta daisies (*Leucanthemum* x *superbum*), a yellow daylily (*Hemerocallis* 'Stella de Oro'), and archangel (*Angelica archangelica*).

RIGHT Compared with the dense deep pink dollops of the rose 'Charles de Mills' and the violet-blue of the delphiniums, the pale yellows of the catmint (*Nepeta govaniana*) on the right, mullein (*Verbascum* 'Gainsborough') on the left, and iris foliage (*Iris pallida* 'Variegata'), are understated. Blue alpine sea holly (*Eryngium alpinum*) and pink beard tongue (*Penstemon* 'Evelyn') help to diffuse the colors.

Blues and Violets with Red and Yellow

BELOW In this apparently informal garden, plants have been carefully chosen to make diaphanous pastel clouds. Dots of bright red salvias and smoky red knautia, and of clear yellow Welsh poppies and ornamental onions spice up the color without spoiling the overall harmony. (For a diagram of this planting see page 183.)

Imagine the two gardens shown here stripped of their red and yellow flowers. They would still be beautiful plantings – perfect harmonies of blues, violets, lilacs, and whites. But they would have lost an important element – the element of slight agitation supplied by the red and yellow

that prevents the eye settling on the harmonious colors and becoming too relaxed.

However, when you add contrasts to harmonics, you need to be careful. Here, the contrasting colors are used quite differently from the harmonizing ones. The harmonious plants are grown in relatively dense

drifts and patches of color, each melding into the next, or into an equally solid patch of green. The red and yellow flowers, on the other hand, are used as separate dots and splashes of color. They are present as a suggestion of contrast, not as a lead player in the overall scheme. In the border *opposite*, the yellow Welsh poppies, the red salvias, and the deep red knautia add a few touches of sharp contrast to the ethereal blocks of blue and violet.

To achieve this, you have to have a good eye and a knowledge of which plants produce scattered, less densely packed flowers. Then plant them as highlights in a border, rather than in solid blocks or drifts so they make their contribution without becoming overwhelming.

BELOW In a garden that is largely the result of self-seeding, the pastel geraniums, columbines, and ornamental onions flow through like a river. Crimson peonies and yellow Welsh poppies energize the otherwise placid effect. To maintain such a garden, weed out any colors that seed themselves in the wrong spot. (For a diagram of this planting see page 183.)

Greens and Yellows with Pink

In the plantings shown here, the greens and yellows provide a framework for the flowers in a single hue of pink. But these borders rely for their effect chiefly upon tonal contrasts. In the informal border *below*, there is a satisfying rhythm of contrasting light and dark set up by the deep purple foliage of the red mountain spinach, the pale cream variegated leaves of the figwort, and the cream flowers of the lavender cotton. There are also more subtle tonal contrasts between the dark green and the gray-green foliage. In the formal garden *opposite*, the tonal contrasts come from the garden's foliage backbone. If you shape boxwood trees into globes and spirals, as here, and choose dome-shaped plants like stonecrop, their effect is to create patterns of highlight and shadow, even when the sun is not shining. These tonal contrasts are the equivalent to those made by the foliage contrasts in the other planting.

RIGHT The tonal contrasts created by light falling on the boxwood shapes add another dimension to the junction between two areas of color, pink and yellow-orange. (For a diagram of this planting, see page 184.)

BELOW Clumps of purple leaved red mountain spinach grow between mallows and a lupine with matching pink flowers. An artichoke bud, a lily, a cranesbill, drumstick chives, and a butterfly bush pick up the prevailing note of pink. (For a diagram of this planting, see page 184.)

Pinks and Yellows with White

Pink and yellow can make an uncomfortable partnership because they set up a warm/cool tension. They are two of the most common flower colors, so it is often difficult to avoid using them together. But there are ways you can minimize the discord between the two, and even turn it to your advantage.

If you are using flowers of a saturated yellow, use them in small quantities relative to the amount of pink; otherwise the yellow, being a stronger color, will overpower the pink. In the border *below*, the pink roses outnumber the strong yellow flowers of the Jerusalem sage so that the colors of the two balance out.

It is also important to create a buffer of white or green between the colors. In the same planting *below*, the white foxgloves and the white stripes of the Rosa mundi fulfill this role. In the combination *opposite, above*, the white rays of the daisies reduce the impact of their egg-yolk yellow centers on the strong pink of the everlasting peas, making the relationship a peaceable one. Even in the multicolored cottage garden-style planting *opposite, below*, in which pink cosmos and coneflowers and yellow montbretia are crammed in with orange nasturtiums and red beard tongue, there is a sprinkling of white flowers and enough green to stop the resulting exuberance from becoming overwhelming.

RIGHT The everlasting climbing pea (*Lathyrus grandiflorus*) scrambles horizontally through pink *Geranium* x *oxonianum* and white daisy-flowered marguerites (*Anthemis tinctoria* 'Alba').

OPPOSITE BELOW A sunny summer border is dominated by roses – the deep cerise English rose 'Chianti', vivid pink 'De Rescht' at its foot, pink and white striped Rosa mundi, and white 'Yvonne Rabier'. White foxgloves stand erect between the roses and the massed rich yellow flowers of Jerusalem sage (*Phlomis fruticosa*).

BELOW Between espaliered apples and a low boxwood hedge, a cottage garden-style planting offers a cornucopia of color in late summer. In the foreground are spears of yellow montbretia in front of pink, red, and white annual cosmos. Farther back, perennial red beard tongue and annual orange nasturtium grow with white flowering tobacco, white bellflowers, and white dahlias (*D.* 'My Love'). Beyond, pink coneflowers (*Rudbeckia* 'Brilliant Star') mix with pink and white flowering tobacco, and taller white tobaccco (*Nicotiana sylvestris*) stands behind.

Lime-Green with Blues, Violets, and Deep Red

The complementary colors of violet and yellow form the basis of one of the main contrasting schemes available to the gardener. Elaborate on this pair of colors – or on other complementary pairs – by thinking of each color as the center of a harmonizing planting. You could use the violet as the starting point for harmonizing pockets of blues, violets, and crimsons, and use yellows based on foliage plants. Put the two plantings together and where they meet they will make a strong contrast.

This is a color scheme that can work throughout the spring and summer. The pictures here show the same border in early and late summer. Start in spring with contrasting yellow and purple tulips and blue-pink forget-me-nots. In early summer, *below*, the border is dominated by ornamental onions and Italian bugloss, contrasting with the young lime-green foliage of a mock orange and flowerheads of spurge. A magenta geranium at left is poised to come into full flower, to be followed, as at *right*, by blue cornflowers and deep smoky red knautia against a background of violet-blue clematis, yellow leaved mock orange, and golden leaved black locust.

ABOVE To achieve this early summer effect, plant the bulbs of the ornamental onions in the fall at the same time as the tulips. The onions will flower a month after the tulips fade. Prune the mock orange back to the ground in winter, to encourage its bright new foliage. (For a diagram of this planting, see page 184.)

RIGHT Later in summer, a clematis (C. 'Perle d'Azur') partners the perennial knautia (*Knautia macedonica*) and annual blue cornflowers (*Centaurea cyanus*) to continue the border's blue and violet harmony. Once the danger of frost has passed, you can safely plant young cornflower plants grown indoors from seed.

Red and Yellow with Cream and Purple

Bright red flowers always stand out in the garden. One way to make them less dominant is to partner them with strong yellows and oranges so that they become equal partners in "hot" plantings. But a more subtle and sophisticated approach, as in these pictures, is to use the red as a basis for color harmonies with pale yellows, creams, and even lime-greens, and then to lower the color temperature with the addition of gently contrasting muted blue-reds and purples. The light and dark elements of such plantings also provide tonal contrasts that help to draw the eye away from the intensity of the reds.

In the examples shown *left* and *right*, the yellow harmonies are provided by cream and lime-green flowers and yellow foliage. The color contrasts come from crimson and almost black flowers, dark purple-red foliage, and seedheads.

LEFT A deep scarlet rose (*Rosa* 'Frensham') draws the eye into a summer border. Without it, this planting would be dominated by the tonal contrast between white clematis (*C. recta*), pale cream blue-eyed grass (*Sisyrinchium striatum*), lime-green lady's mantle (*Alchemilla mollis*), and fluffy white goat's beard (*Aruncus dioicus* 'Kneiffii'), and the dark foliage of fringed loosestrife (*Lysimachia ciliata* 'Firecracker') and the almost black sweet Williams (*Dianthus barbatus* Nigrescens Group). You might expect the rose to make this border a "hot" one, but it is cooled down by the creamy yellow flowers and the silver foliage of artemisia (*A.* 'Powis Castle'). White and deep orange lilies (*Lilium regale* and *L. henryi*) and phygelius (*P. aequalis* 'Yellow Trumpet' and *P.* x *rectus* 'African Queen'), and the lime-green foliage of Indian currant (*Symphoricarpos orbiculatus* 'Foliis Variegatis') will carry the color theme through into early fall.

RIGHT Deep red oriental poppies (*Papaver orientale* 'Beauty of Livermere') peer through a thicket of honesty (*Lunaria annua*), whose ripening seedheads have a touch of purple in them, echoed in the purple sage (*Salvia officinalis* Purpurascens Group) toward the bottom. These three plants make a muted harmony of blue-red and purple, which contrasts with the other plants in this scheme, all of which are variants on a theme of yellow. The muted yellow leaves of boxwood honeysuckle (*Lonicera nitida* 'Baggesen's Gold') at the back, meadow foam (*Limnanthes douglasii*), the wispy Bowles' golden grass (*Milium effusum* 'Aureum'), and the wallflower, all bring lightness into the scheme as well as a contrast with the purple.

Yellows and Creams with Muted Reds

When you combine muted, unsaturated colors, be they dark or light variations of the parent color, the end results – whether harmonies or contrasts – are also muted. If you use muted colors almost exclusively with occasional strong hues for emphasis, then even when mixing contrasts with harmonies, you are very likely to have success.

The plantings shown on these pages all employ red that is so unsaturated that it is difficult to recognize that it is red at all. The 'Queen of the Night' tulips, *opposite, right*, certainly have a hint of red in them, but they are so deep that they are usually described as purple, or even black. Similarly, the irises, *left*, are such a subtle mixture of hues, from dark pink, through lilac, to pale yellow, that their relationship to red is tenuous. By contrast, the unsaturated yellows – the creamy yellow of the lupine, *left*, the wallflowers, *opposite, right*, and the green-yellow foliage of the golden leaved black locust, *opposite, above* – are still recognizably yellow.

When you use unsaturated yellow or red foliage, remember that the yellow is always light in tone and will always have a lightening effect in the garden, while the red – even if it has patterns of pink variegation, like the barberry, *opposite, above* – is almost always dark in tone, and will make the garden darker. If you use a lot of trees and shrubs with red foliage, you might find that you need to "lift" the tone with some light yellow-green or gray foliage.

ABOVE In early summer, the pale yellow flowers of a tree lupine (*Lupinus arboreus*) radiate light and harmonize with the hint of yellow of the iris, whose cool lilac-pink color also harmonizes with the *Geranium* 'Johnson's Blue'. These perennials all flourish in the sun, but the tree lupine is fast growing and may need to be kept in check by judicious pruning after flowering to prevent it from overpowering the subtle color association.

ABOVE The color balance between the yellow of the fast-growing deciduous golden leaved black locust tree (*Robinia pseudoacacia* 'Frisia') and the muted red of the deciduous variegated Roseglow Japanese barberry (*Berberis thunbergii* 'Rose Glow'), seen here in early fall, is upset in summer by the yellow flowers of the adjacent Jerusalem sage (*Phlomis fruticosa*).

RIGHT These late spring flowering tulips – the yellow Lily-flowered 'West Point', and the near black 'Queen of the Night' – together with primrose-yellow wallflowers, have been planted in a heavily shaded spot. The shade makes them grow taller and lean toward the light. You can treat bulbs and annuals this way since they can be dug up after flowering and the bulbs planted somewhere more favorable next year. But always plant perennials and shrubs in locations where they will receive the correct amount of light or they will not thrive.

Winter Plantings

Many gardeners are content to leave winter color for nature to resolve, and you will have no choice if your climate serves up constant snow and ice. In milder regions, though, you can plan for winter color. As well as useful evergreens, you can exploit the little incidents of color that winter brings – vividly colored tree bark, for example, the sparse but sweetly scented flowers of a winter flowering shrub, or a clump of early crocus. You can also create striking effects by massed plantings of evergreen grass with repeated sprays of red stemmed dogwoods or white stemmed brambles, *opposite, left.* If you do not have the space or the inclination to make a special winter planting, then garden for color in a more passive way. Resist the urge to tidy up in fall and when frost and snow settle on the shapes of brown and gray and dark green (which are all that remain of your colorful summer borders), they will be transformed into subtle confections of silvers, cold whites and blue-greens, *opposite, right.*

LEFT ABOVE The broad, floppy leaves of heart-leaf bergenia (*B. cordifolia*) turn crimson in cold weather, making a color connection with the pink heather (*Erica* x *darleyensis* 'Furzey'). The bare stems of the Tatarian dogwood (*Cornus alba* 'Sibirica') give vivid flashes of red against the predominantly yellow foliage of the large leaved Colchis ivy (*Hedera colchica* 'Sulphur Heart'). This in turn makes an effective groundcover as it clambers among plants, filling the spaces between them.

LEFT The evergreen shrub laurustinus (*Viburnum tinus* 'Eve Price') begins flowering in late fall and produces flowers through any mild interludes of winter. If it is underplanted with heart-leaf bergenia (*B. cordifolia*), its pink buds will pick up the color of the bergenia's spring flowers.

ABOVE The bare white stems of *Rubus biflorus* make a shapely network that catches the low winter light. The whiteness comes from a thin layer of "bloom" on the stems. Behind it is a viburnum (*V.* x *bodnantense* 'Dawn') which produces pink flowers on bare stems through the late winter and early spring in zones 7–9. Grasses are a great asset in the winter garden; even the dead foliage of deciduous grasses can look striking. Here, the evergreen pheasant grass, (*Stipa arundinacea*), turns a russet color in cold weather, giving off a warming glow in sunlight.

RIGHT The pepperpot seedheads of Jerusalem sage (*Phlomis russeliana*) collect a layer of frost that transmutes them into out-of-season flowers unknown to science. The same dusting of frost adds pallor to the dark pink flowerheads of a stonecrop (*Sedum* 'Autumn Joy'). Even the browns and yellows of decaying stems and leaves contribute their color. If you wait until spring before tidying your borders, the dead perennial material acts like a blanket to protect the living roots below ground.

Keyline Diagrams of Major Plantings

ABOVE PAGE 28–29

1 Gold moss stonecrop (*Sedum acre*)
2 Boxleaf honeysuckle (*Lonicera nitida* 'Baggesen's Gold')
3 Tradescant's aster (*A.* spp.)
4 Golden feverfew (*Tanacetum parthenium* 'Aureum')
5 Giant sea holly (*Eryngium giganteum*)
6 Green fennel (*Foeniculum vulgare*)
7 Lady's mantle (*Alchemilla mollis*)
8 Cinquefoil (*Potentilla recta*)
9 Argyranthemum (*A.* cv.)
10 Lupine (*Lupinus* 'Chandelier')
11 Rose (*Rosa* 'Graham Thomas')

12 Yarrow (*Achillea chrysocoma* 'Grandiflora')
13 *Brachyglottis* 'Sunshine'
14 Woad (*Isatis tinctoria*)
15 *Phlomis longifolia*
16 Golden marguerite (*Anthemis tinctoria* 'E.C. Buxton')
17 Wormwood (*Artemisia absinthium*)
18 Catmint (*Nepeta sibirica* 'Souvenir d'André Chaudron')
19 Spurge (*Euphorbia characias* subsp. *wulfenii*)

LEFT PAGE 33

1 Monkey flower (*Mimulus guttatus*)
2 Royal fern (*Osmunda regalis*)
3 Tibetan primrose (*Primula florindae*)
4 Variegated manna grass (*Glyceria maxima* var. *variegata*)
5 Bowles' golden sedge (*Carex elata* 'Aurea')
6 Gardener's garters (*Phalaris arundinacea* var. *picta* 'Picta')
7 Oriental iris (*I. orientalis*)
8 Willow (*Salix* spp.)

LEFT PAGE 46

1   Ruby chard (*Beta*)
2   Flowering tobacco (*Nicotiana* x *sanderae*)
3   Pelargonium (*P.* cv.)
4   *Aeonium* 'Zwartkop'
5   Beetroot (*Beta* cv.)
6   Verbena (*V.* cv.)
7   Tuberous begonia (*Begonia* x *tuberhybrida*)
8   Beefsteak plant (*Iresine herbstii*)
9   Beard tongue (*Penstemon* 'Schoenholzeri')
10 Bee balm (*Monarda* 'Mrs Perry')
11 Purple leaved orpine (*Sedum telephium* subsp.
    maximum 'Atropurpureum')
12 Dahlia (*D.* 'Bishop of Llandaff')
13 Dahlia (*D.* cv.)
14 Castor oil plant (*Ricinus communis* cv.)
15 Dahlia (*D.* cv.)
16 Purple leaved smokebush (*Cotinus coggygria* cv.)
17 Purple leaved barberry (*Berberis* cv.)
18 Purple giant filbert (*Corylus maxima* 'Purpurea')
19 Crimson glory vine (*Vitis coignetiae*)

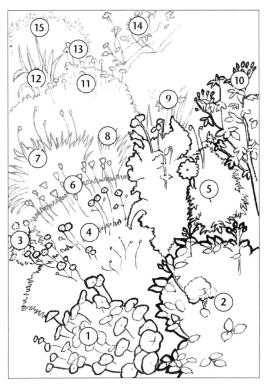

LEFT PAGE 47

1   Nasturtium (*Tropaeolum majus*)
    with avens (*Geum* 'Mrs J. Bradshaw')
2   Rose (*Rosa* 'Lilli Marlene')
3   Sweet William (*Dianthus
    barbatus* Nigrescens Group)
4   Avens (*Geum* 'Mrs J. Bradshaw')
5   Dahlia (*D.* 'Bishop of Llandaff')
6   African daisy (*Arctotis* x *hybrida*)
7   African lily (*Agapanthus*)
8   Montbretia (*Crocosmia* 'Lucifer')
9   Lily (*Lilium* cv.)
10 Rose (*Rosa* 'William Lobb')
11 Maltese cross (*Lychnis chalcedonica*)
12 New Zealand flax (*Phormium tenax*)
13 Opium poppy (*Papaver somniferum*)
14 Rose (*Rosa* 'Parkdirektor Riggers')
15 Chinese privet (*Ligustrum
    lucidum* cv.)

ABOVE PAGE 79

1   Foxglove (*Digitalis purpurea*)
2   Golden lemon thyme (*Thymus
    x citriodorus* 'Aureus')
3   Clover (*Trifolium repens* 'Purpurascens')
4   Bowles' golden grass (*Milium effusum*
    'Aureum')
5   Jacob's ladder (*Polemonium pauciflorum*)
6   Boxwood (*Buxus sempervirens*
    'Elegantissima')
7   White peach leaf bellflower (*Campanula
    persicifolia alba*)
8   Silver mound artemisia (*Artemisia
    schmidtiana*)
9   Cushion spurge (*Euphorbia polychroma*)
10 Lavender (*Lavandula angustifolia*)
11 *Artemisia pontica*
12 Bloody cranesbill (*Geranium
    sanguineum*)

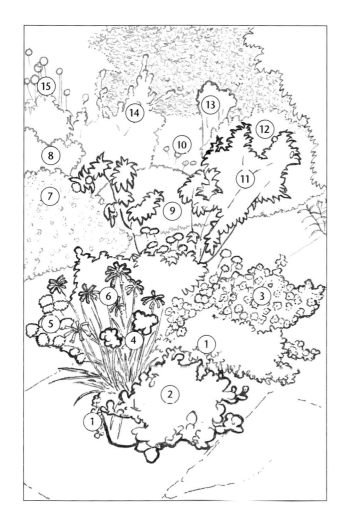

ABOVE PAGE 107

1   Licorice plant (*Helichrysum petiolare*)
2   *Mertensia* spp.
3   Mallow (*Malva sylvestris* cv.)
4   Heliotrope (*Heliotropium* cv.)
5   Verbena (*V.* cv.)
6   African lily (*Agapanthus* cv.)
7   Love-in-a-mist (*Nigella damascena* 'Miss Jekyll')
8   Meadow cranesbill (*Geranium pratense* 'Plenum Caeruleum')
9   Cranesbill (*Geranium* 'Johnson's Blue')

10   Opium poppy (*Papaver somniferum* cv.)
11   Blue potato bush (*Solanum rantonnetii*)
12   Meadow sage (*Salvia pratensis* Haematodes Group)
13   Sweet pea (*Lathyrus odoratus* 'Noel Sutton')
14   Delphinium (*D.* Pacific Hybrid)
15   Globe thistle (*Echinops bannaticus* 'Taplow Blue')

ABOVE PAGE 110

1   Deadnettle (*Lamium maculatum* cv.)
2   Faassen's catmint (*Nepeta* x *faassenii*)
3   Pink mountain knapweed (*Centaurea montana* spp.)
4   Pink (*Dianthus* 'Rainbow Loveliness')
5   Beard tongue (*Penstemon* cv.)
6   Rose campion (*Lychnis coronaria* Alba Group)
7   Opium poppy (*Papaver somniferum* cv.)
8   Beard tongue (*Penstemon* 'Stapleford Gem')
9   Deadnettle (*Lamium maculatum* cv.)
10   Beard tongue (*Penstemon* 'Garnet')
11   Double flowered feverfew (*Tanacetum parthenium* 'Plenum')

12   White foxglove (*Digitalis purpurea* f. *albiflora*)
13   Foxglove (*Digitalis purpurea*)
14   Foxglove hybrids (*Digitalis purpurea* 'Sutton's Apricot')
15   Rose (*Rosa* 'Magenta')
16   Downy onion (*Allium christophii*)
17   Rose (*Rosa* 'Pink Prosperity')
18   Rose (*Rosa* 'Felicia')
19   Lady Banks' rose (*Rosa banksiae* 'Lutea') with Russian vine (*Fallopia baldschuanica*)
20   Rose (*Rosa* 'François Juranville')
21   California lilac (*Ceanothus impressus*)

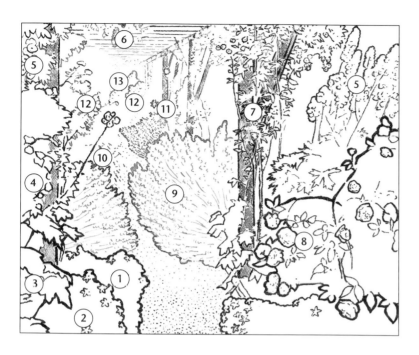

1 Horned violet (*Viola cornuta*)
2 White horned violet (*Viola cornuta* Alba Group)
3 Japanese anemone (*Anemone* x *hybrida*)
4 Rose (*Rosa* 'Commandant Beaurepaire')
5 Delphinium (*D.* Pacific Hybrids)
6 Rose (*Rosa* 'Violette')
7 Rose (*Rosa* 'Veilchenblau')
8 Rose (*Rosa* 'Comte de Chambord')
9 Catmint (*Nepeta* 'Six Hills Giant')
10 Dwarf chamomile (*Anthemis punctata* subsp. *cupaniana*)
11 Clematis (*C.* 'Bees' Jubilee')
12 Rose (*Rosa* 'Ballerina')
13 Rose (*Rosa* 'Penelope')

1 Rose (*Rosa* 'White Meidiland')
2 Lavender cotton (*Santolina pinnata* subsp. *neapolitana*)
3 *Artemisia arborescens*
4 Ornamental onion (*Allium nigrum*)
5 Rose (*Rosa* 'Boule de Neige')
6 Hosta (*H.* 'Francee')
7 Boxwood (*Buxus*)
8 Cotton thistle (*Onopordum nervosum*)
9 Thrift (*Armeria maritima*)
10 Bear's breeches (*Acanthus mollis*)
11 Variegated eulalia grass (*Miscanthus sinensis* 'Variegatus')
12 Foxglove hybrids (*Digitalis purpurea*)
13 Lady's mantle (*Alchemilla mollis*)
14 Curry plant (*Helichrysum italicum*)
15 Wormwood (*Artemisia* 'Powis Castle')
16 Persian onion (*Allium aflatunense* 'Purple Sensation')
17 Delphinium (*D.* x *belladonna* 'Casa Blanca')
18 Rose (*Rosa* 'Iceberg')
19 Columbine meadow rue (*Thalictrum aquilegiifolium*)
20 Bowles' golden grass (*Milium effusum* 'Aureum')
21 White dame's rocket (*Hesperis matronalis* var. *albiflora*)
22 Variegated weigela (*W.* cv.)
23 Black leaved elder (*Sambucus nigra*)
24 Rose (*Rosa* 'New Dawn')
25 Variegated Portugal laurel (*Prunus lusitanica* cv.)
26 Pittosporum (*P.* cv)

1 Rose (*Rosa* 'The Fairy')
2 Beard tongue (*Penstemon* 'Apple Blossom')
3 White sagebush (*Artemisia ludoviciana*)
4 Oregano (*Origanum laevigatum* 'Hopleys')
5 Southern wormwood (*Artemisia abrotanum*)
6 Rose (*Rosa* 'Mevrouw Nathalie Nypels')
7 Opium poppy (*Papaver somniferum*)
8 Musk mallow (*Malva moschata alba*)
9 Mullein (*Verbascum chaixii* 'Album')
10 Red leaf rose (*Rosa glauca*)
11 Rose campion (*Lychnis coronaria* Oculata Group)
12 Tree mallow (*Lavatera* 'Barnsley')
13 Billiard spirea (*Spiraea* x *billiardii*)

ABOVE PAGE 123

1 Tiger lily (*Lilium lancifolium*)
2 Orange coneflower (*Rudbeckia fulgida* var. *sullivantii* 'Goldsturm')
3 *Hypericum x inodorum*
4 *Plantago major* 'Rubrifolia'
5 Nasturtium (*Tropaeolum majus* cv.)
6 *Cuphea ignea*
7 Daylily (*Hemerocallis* 'Golden Chimes')
8 Sedge (*Carex comans*)
9 Montbretia (*Crocosmia* cv.)
10 African daisy (*Arctotis* x *hybrida* cv.)
11 Lobelia (*L.* 'Queen Victoria')
12 Dahlia (*D.* cv.)

13 Nasturtium (*Trapaeolum majus* cv.)
14 Small flowered alumroot (*Heuchera micrantha* var. *diversifolia* 'Palace Purple')
15 Fern leaved beggar tick (*Bidens ferulifolia*)
16 Hosta (*H. fortunei* var. *aureomarginata*)
17 Montbretia (Crocosmia masoniorum)
18 Striped bamboo (*Pleioblastus auricomus*)
19 Bee balm (*Monarda* 'Cambridge Scarlet')
20 Pineapple sage (*Salvia elegans* 'Scarlet Pineapple')
21 Big leaf ligularia (*Ligularia dentata* 'Desdemona')
22 *Inula hookeri*

23 Ornamental rhubarb (*Rheum palmatum*)
24 Dark crusader lobelia (*L.* cv.)
25 Red mountain spinach (*Atriplex hortensis* var. *rubra*)
26 Sneezeweed (*Helenium* cv.)
27 Castor oil plant (*Ricinus communis*)
28 Hybrid lobelia (*Lobelia* x *speciosa*)
29 Dahlia (*D.* 'Arabian Night')
30 Montbretia (*Crocosmia* cv.)
31 European copper beech (*Fagus sylvatica* 'Dawyck Purple')
32 Golden ray (*Ligularia* 'The Rocket')
33 Sunflower (*Helianthus* cv.)

34 *Sinacalia tangutica*
35 Purple leaved Japanese barberry (*Berberis thunbergii* f. *atropurpurea*)
36 Sunflower (*Helianthus decapetalus* cv.)
37 Dahlia (*D.* 'Bishop of Llandaff)
38 Bladder senna (*Colutea* spp.)
39 Norway maple (*Acer platanoides* 'Crimson King')

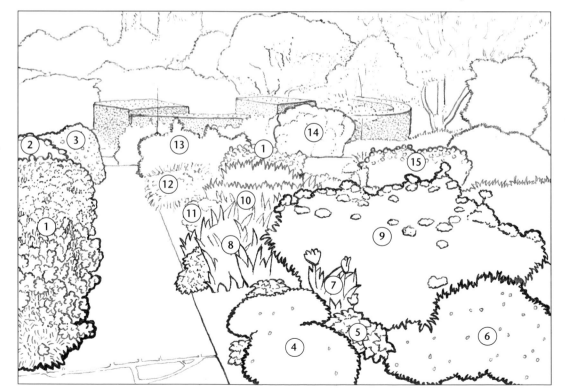

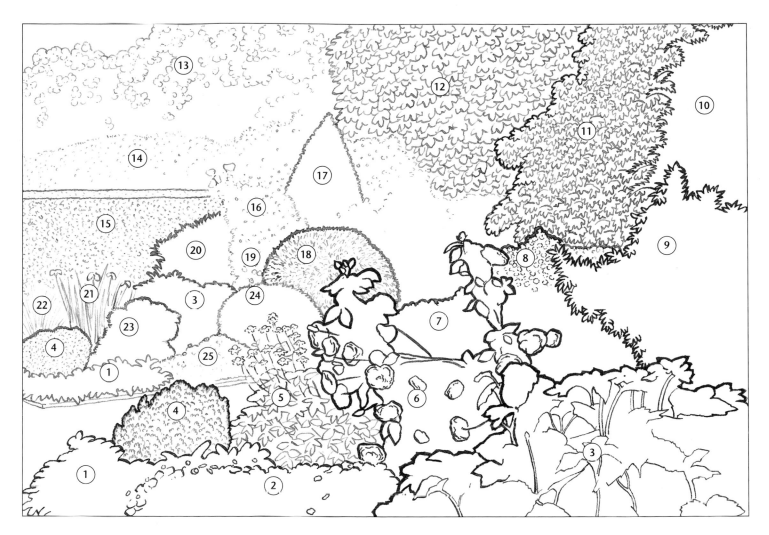

RIGHT **PAGE 135**

1 Wallflower (*Erysimum cheiri* 'Fire King')
2 Iris (*I.* cv.)
3 *Othonna* spp.
4 Siberian wallflower (*Erysimum* x *allionii*)
5 Tulip (*Tulipa* 'Aladdin')
6 Spurge (*Euphorbia griffithii*)
7 Rose (*Rosa foetida*)
8 Peony (*Paeonia* cv.)
9 Tulip (*Tulipa* cv.)
10 Yarrow (*Achillea* 'Moonshine')
11 Daylily (*Hemerocallis lilioasphodelus*)
12 Warminster broom (*Cytisus* x *praecox* 'Warminster')
13 Panicled golden rain tree (*Koelreuteria paniculata* spp.)
14 Lily (*Lilium* cv.)
15 Butterfly iris (*I. spuria*)
16 Wallflower (*Erysimum cheiri* 'Blood Red')
17 Meadow foam (*Limnanthes douglasii*)
18 Iris (*I.* cv.)
19 Golden feverfew (*Tanacetum parthenium* 'Aureum')

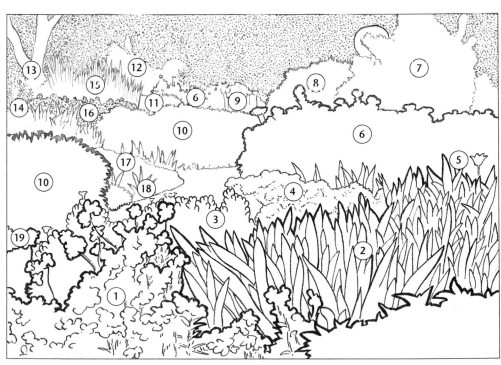

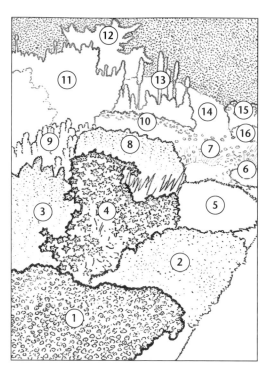

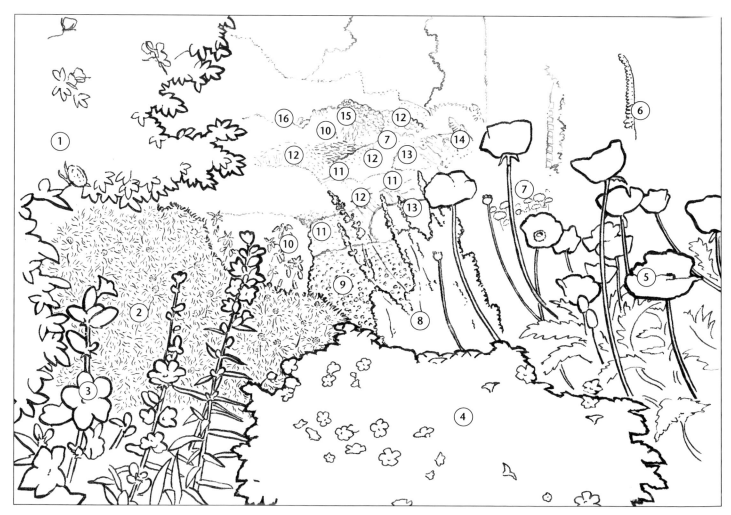

RIGHT PAGE 154

1 Lamb's ears (*Stachys byzantina*)
2 Golden marguerite (*Anthemis tinctoria*)
3 Gardener's garters (*Phalaris arundinacea* var. *picta*)
4 Big root geranium (*G. macrorrhizum*)
5 Double German catchfly (*Lychnis viscaria* 'Splendens Plena')
6 Gentian speedwell (*Veronica gentianoides*)
7 Daylily (*Hemerocallis* 'Marion Vaughn')
8 Armenian geranium (*G. psilostemon*)
9 Monkshood (*Aconitum* 'Ivorine')
10 Delphinium (*D.* cv.)
11 Meadow rue (*Thalictrum flavum*)
12 Giant scabious (*Cephalaria gigantea*)
13 Cherry plum (*Prunus cerasifera* 'Pissardii')
14 Orange Peruvian lily (*Alstroemeria aurea*)
15 Alpine sea holly (*Eryngium alpinum* cv.)
16 Meadow cranesbill (*G. pratense* 'Plenum Violaceum')
17 Lesser meadow rue (*Thalictrum minus adiantifolium*)
18 Siberian flag iris (*I. sibirica*)
19 Pearl everlasting (*Anaphalis triplinervis*)
20 False mallow (*Sidalcea* cv.)

BELOW PAGE 155

1 Cardoon (*Cynara cardunculus*)
2 Beard tongue (*Penstemon* 'Evelyn')
3 Milky belllflower (*Campanula lactiflora* 'Loddon Anna')
4 African lily (*Agapanthus* Headbourne Hybrid)
5 Moss verbena (*Verbena tenuisecta*)
6 Beard tongue (*Penstemon* 'Stapleford Gem')
7 Common monkshood (*Aconitum napellus*)
8 Butterfly bush (*Buddleja* 'Lochinch')
9 Goat's rue (*Galega orientalis*)
10 Drumstick chives (*Allium sphaerocephalon*)
11 Stonecrop (*Sedum* 'Autumn Joy')
12 Clary sage (*Salvia sclarea* var. *turkestanica*)
13 English holly (*Ilex aquifolium* 'Aurea Marginata')
14 Golden English yew (*Taxus baccata* 'Aurea')
15 Beard tongue (*Penstemon* 'Burgundy')
16 Phlox (*P.* cv.)
17 Nemesia (*N. lilacina*)
18 Purple leaved bugle (*Ajuga reptans* 'Atropurpurea')
19 Rue (*Ruta graveolens*)
20 Hybrid sage (*Salvia* spp.)

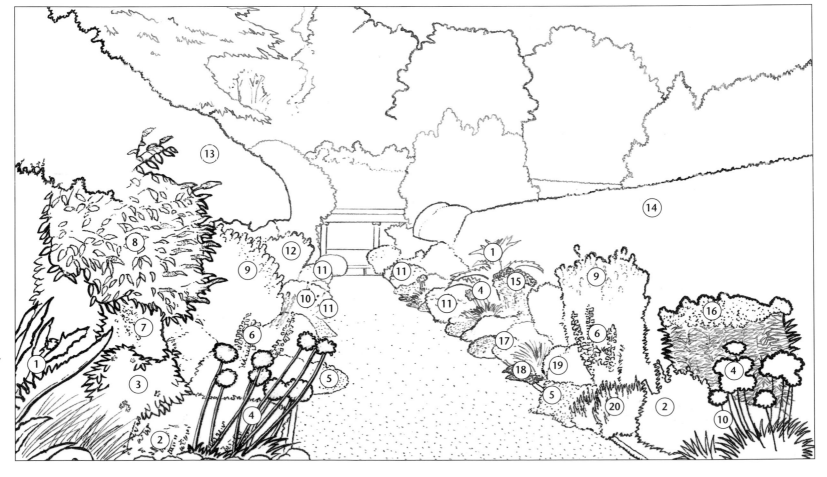

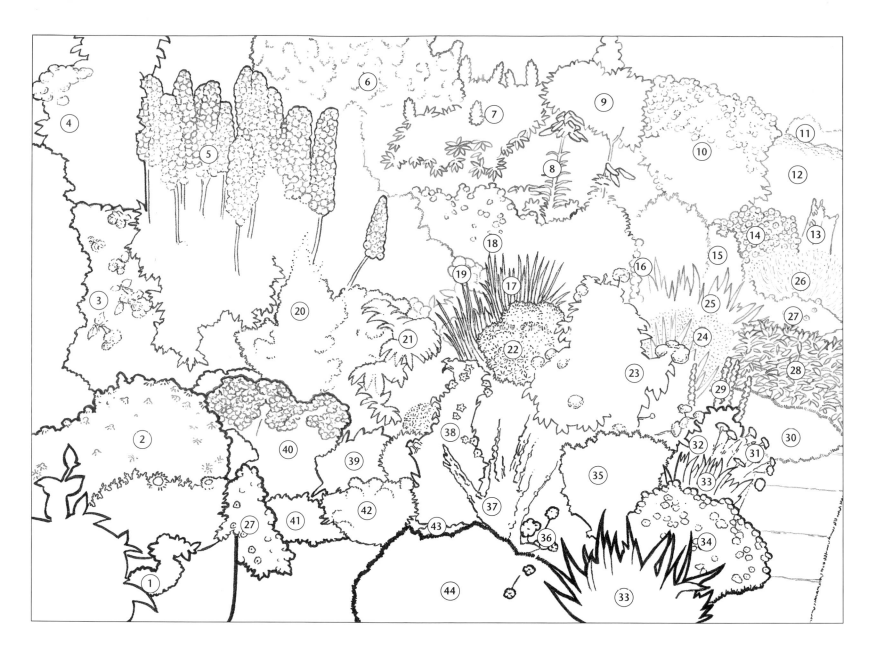

1   Rose (*Rosa* 'Francis E. Lester')
2   Bowman's root (*Gillenia trifoliata*)
3   Boxwood (*Buxus sempervirens*)
4   Hybrid sage (*Salvia* x *superba*)
5   Meadow cranesbill (*Salvia pratensis* Haematodes Group)
6   Southern wormwood (*Artemisia abrotanum*)
7   Lamb's ears (*Stachys byzantina*)
8   Feverfew (*Tanacetum parthenium*)
9   Gladiolus (*G.* 'The Bride')
10 Cinquefoil (*Potentilla* 'Yellow Queen')
11 Baby sage (*Salvia microphylla* spp.)
12 *Knautia macedonica*
13 Regal lily (*Lilium regale*)
14 Lily leek (*Allium moly*) with Welsh poppy (*Meconopsis cambrica*)
15 Beard tongue (*Penstemon* spp.)
16 Foxglove (*Digitalis purpurea*)
17 Purple toadflax (*Linaria purpurea*)
18 Columbine meadow rue (*Thalictrum aquilegiifolium*)
19 Clematis (*C.* 'Étoile Violette')
20 Plum (*Prunus* 'Taihaku')
21 Rose (*Rosa* 'Goldfinch')
22 Delphinium (*D.* Pacific Hybrids)
23 Cardoon (*Cynara cardunculus*)
24 Meadow cranesbill (*Geranium pratense* cv.)
25 *Argyranthemum* cv.

1   Bloody cranesbill (*Geranium sanguineum*)
2   Columbine (*Aquilegia vulgaris*)
3   Catmint (*Nepeta sibirica* 'Souvenir d'André Chaudron')
4   Wood cranesbill (*Geranium sylvaticum* 'Mayflower')
5   Welsh poppy (*Meconopsis cambrica*)
6   Columbine (*Aquilegia* 'Hensol Harebell')
7   Peony (*Paeonia officinalis* 'Rubra Plena')
8   Turkestan onion (*Allium karataviense*)
9   White variegated honesty (*Lunaria annua* 'Alba Variegata')
10 Hybrid sage (*Salvia nemorosa* 'East Friesland')
11 Forget-me-not (*Myosotis*)
12 Jacob's ladder (*Polemonium caeruleum*)
13 Mourning widow's cranesbill (*Geranium phaeum* 'Lily Lovell')
14 Persian onion (*Allium aflatunense*)
15 Rose (*Rosa* 'William Lobb')
16 Omei rose (*Rosa sericea* subsp. *omeiensis* f. *pteracantha*)

DIAGRAMS

ABOVE PAGE 160

1   Lavender cotton (*Santolina pinnata* subsp. *neapolitana* 'Edward Bowles')
2   Rose (*Rosa* 'Wife of Bath')
3   Lupine (*Lupinus* 'The Chatelaine')
4   Red mountain spinach (*Atriplex hortensis* var. *rubra*)
5   Tree mallow (*Lavatera* 'Rosea')
6   False mallow (*Sidalcea* cv.)
7   Cardoon (*Cynara cardunculus*)
8   Variegated obedient plant (*Physostegia virginiana* 'Variegata')
9   Lily (*Lilium* Pink Perfection Group)
10 Pink cow parsley (*Chaerophyllum hirsutum* 'Roseum')
11 Garden phlox (*Phlox paniculata* 'Norah Leigh')
12 Mourning widow's cranesbill (*Geranium phaeum*)
13 Drumstick chives (*Allium sphaerocephalon*)
14 Butterfly bush (*Buddleja davidii* 'Nanho Purple')
15 White mugwort (*Artemisia lactiflora*)

ABOVE PAGE 161

1   Campion (*Silene compacta*)
2   Orpine (*Sedum telephium*)
3   Campion (*Lychnis yunnanensis*)
4   Gooseneck loosestrife (*Lysimachia clethroides*)
5   Pyrethrum (*P.* spp.)
6   Forget-me-not (*Myosotis*)
7   Pink catmint (*Nepeta* cv.)
8   Chives (*Allium schoenoprasum*)
9   Prairie mallow (*Sidalcea* 'Loveliness')
10 Double columbine (*Aquilegia vulgaris* var. *stellata*)
11 Boxwood (*Buxus sempervirens* 'Notata')
12 Yellow leaved nine bark (*Physocarpus opulifolius* 'Luteus')
13 Thrift (*Armeria alliacea* Formosa Hybrids)
14 Yellow poppies (*Papaver* spp.)
15 Sun rose (*Helianthemum* 'Amy Baring')
16 Stonecrop (*Sedum kamtschaticum* 'Variegatum')
17 Single columbine (*Aquilegia vulgaris* var. *stellata*)
18 Columbine (*Aquilegia formosa*)
19 Golden filbert (*Corylus avellana* cv.)

LEFT PAGE 164

1   English yew (*Taxus baccata*)
2   Clematis (*C.* 'Etoile Violette')
3   English ivy (*Hedera helix* 'Buttercup')
4   Yellow leaf Tatarian dogwood (*Cornus alba* 'Aurea')
5   Golden leaved black locust (*Robinia pseudoacacia* 'Frisia')
6   Golden leaved hop (*Humulus lupulus* 'Aureus')
7   Ornamental onion (*Allium rosenbachianum*)
8   Persian onion (*Allium aflatunense* 'Purple Sensation')
9   Yellow leaved mock orange (*Philadephus coronarius* 'Aureus')
10 Italian bugloss (*Anchusa azurea* 'Loddon Royalist')
11 Armenian geranium (*Geranium psilostemon*)
12 Cranesbill (*Geranium* 'Johnson's Blue')
13 White variegated honesty (*Lunaria annua* 'Alba Variegata')
14 Wallflower (*Erysimum cheiri* cv.)
15 Beard tongue (*Penstemon* cv.)
16 Forget-me-not (*Myosotis*)
17 Horned violet (*Viola cornuta*)
18 Cushion spurge (*Euphorbia polychroma*)
19 Siberian flag iris (*I. sibirica*)
20 Altaclara holly (*Ilex* x *altaclerensis* cv.)
21 Giant dogwood (*Cornus controversa*)
22 Spurge (*Euphorbia characias* subsp. *wulfenii*)
23 Cranesbill (*Geranium* x *magnificum*)
24 Bowles's golden grass (*Milium effussum* 'Aureum')

BIBLIOGRAPHY

Garden Color

Hobhouse, Penelope. *Color in Your Garden*. Boston: Little, Brown & Company, 1985.

Jekyll, Gertrude. *Color Schemes for the Flower Garden*. Boston: Little, Brown & Company, 1988.

Jekyll, Gertrude. *Wood and Garden. Notes and thoughts, practical and critical, of a working amateur*. London: Longmans, reprinted 1981.

Keen, Mary. *Gardening with Color. A Portfolio of Inventive Planting Schemes*. New York: Random House, 1991.

Lacey, Stephen. *The Startling Jungle. Color and Scent in the Romantic Garden*. Boston: David Godine, 1990.

Verey, Rosemary. *The Art of Planting*. Boston: Little, Brown & Company, 1990.

Color for Artists

de Sausmarez, Maurice. *Basic Design: The Dynamics of Visual Form*. London: The Herbert Press, 1992.

Gage, John. *Color and Culture. Practice and Meaning from Antiquity to Abstraction*. Boston: Bullfinch, 1993.

Homer, William Innes. *Seurat and the Science of Painting*. Boston: The MIT Press, 1964.

Itten, Johannes. *The Art of Color*. New York: Van Nostrand Reinhold, Reprinted 1973.

Nicholson, Winifred. *Unknown Colour. Paintings, Letters, Writings*. London: Faber & Faber, 1987.

Wilcox, Michael. *Colour Theory. For Artists working in Oil colours or Acrylics*. London: Colour Mixing Ltd., 1981.

Information on Plants

Hillier's Manual of Trees & Shrubs. Newton Abbott, England: David & Charles Publishing, 1984.

Hobhouse, Penelope. *Flower Gardens*. New York: Viking Penguin, 1989.

Lawson, Andrew. *Performance Plants*. New York: Viking Penguin, 1993.

Phillips, Roger & Martyn Rix. *The Random House Book of Bulbs* 1989; *Perennials*, 2 vols. 1991; *Roses* 1988. New York: Random House

RHS Gardeners' Encyclopedia of Plants and Flowers. New York: Dorling Kindersley Inc., 1989.

RHS Plant Finder 1995/6 Edition. Ashbourne, England: Moorland Publishing Co. Ltd., 1995.

Thomas, Graham Stuart. *Perennial Garden Plants or The Modern Florilegium*. London: Dent, 1976, reprinted, 1993.

Miscellaneous

Birren, Faber. *Color Psychology and Color Therapy*. New York: University Books, 1961.

Gregory, R.L. *Eye and Brain. The Psychology of Seeing*. Princeton: Princeton University Press, 1990.

Jackson, Carole. *Color Me Beautiful*. New York: Ballantine Books, 1981.

INDEX OF PLANTS

NOTE Page numbers in **_bold italic type_** refer to illustrations and their captions. Page numbers in **bold type** refer to descriptions in the plant lists, and adjacent code letters indicate the "single color" chapter in which the plants occur: **B** = Blues, **G** = Greens, **O** = Oranges, **P** = Pinks, **R** = Reds, **S** = Silvers and grays, **V** = Violets, **W** = Whites, **Y** = Yellows.

PHOTOGRAPHER'S ACKNOWLEDGMENTS

I am most grateful to garden owners and gardeners who have permitted me to take pictures. Many of them have also taken great pains to help with the identification of plants. My special thanks to the following, whose plantings appear in the more general views (*a* = above, *b* = below, *c* = center, *l* = left, *r* = right): Lesley and John Jenkins, Wollerton Old Hall, Shropshire 1; The National Trust, Sissinghurst Castle, Kent 6,57*l*,125*b*,134-35; Fiona and John Owen, The Old Chapel, Gloucestershire 7,106,141*t*; Mr and Mrs H. Wakefield, Bramdean House, Hampshire 8; Laura Fisher, White Meadows Farm, Katonah, New York 9*t*; Winterthur Gardens, Delaware 9*b*; Gothic House, Oxfordshire 10-11,5*l*,62,73*l*,109*r*,111*l* and *r*,119*l*,121*r*,164-65,169*r*; Wendy and Michael Perry, Bosvigo House, Cornwall 18,122-23,126-27; The National Trust, Powis Castle, Powys 19*t*,52*br*,117*tr*; Clare College, Cambridge 19*b*,140; Sir Roy Strong and Dr Julia Trevelyan Oman, The Laskett, Hereford and Worcester 20; The National Trust, Tintinhull House, Somerset 21,166; Lord and Lady Saye and Sele, Broughton Castle, Oxfordshire 22*l*,110,151*b*; Randal Anderson, private garden, Oxfordshire 22*r*,118; Pam and Peter Lewis, Sticky Wicket, Dorset 2,23,108*t*,117*br*,120,131*b*,160; Nori and Sandra Pope, Hadspen Gardens, Somerset 28-9, 39*br*,45*l*,47,48*bl*,57*tr*,81*tl*,96,107*l* and *r*,119*b*,149*b*; The late Nancy Lancaster, The Coach House, Oxfordshire 30*l*; Susan Strange, Holywell Manor, Oxford 31*l*,79*r*; RHS Gardens, Wisley, Surrey 32*l*,116; Mr and Mrs Thomas Gibson, Westwell Manor, Oxfordshire 33; Keith and Ros Wiley, The Garden House, Devon 38,128*l*; Het Loo, Apeldoorn, Holland 39*t*; Frank and Marjorie Lawley, Herterton House, Northumberland 39*bl*,133*l*,161; Stavordale Priory, Somerset 41*t*; Dr James Smart, Marwood Hill, Devon 41*b*; Planting by Sue Dickinson, private garden, Buckinghamshire 44; The National Trust, Hidcote Gardens, Gloucestershire 45*r*,83,95*l*; The Hon Mrs P. Healing, The Priory, Kemerton, Hereford and Worcester 46; Longwood Gardens, Pennsylvania 53*b*; Caroline Eckersley, Woodside Farm, Oxfordshire 65; Stobshiel House, East Lothian 72; Ralph Merton, Old Rectory, Burghfield, Berkshire 24*t*,64*r*,73*r*; Rosemary Verey, Barnsley House, Gloucestershire 78*l*,114*t*,138-9,149*tl*,168,171*r*; Mr and Mrs R. Paice, Bourton House, Gloucestershire 35*bl*,31*r*,82,122*l*,131*t*; Anthony Noel, 17 Fulham Park Gardens, London 90*l*; Wendy and Len Lauderdale, Ashtree Cottage, Wiltshire 90*r*,104-05,114-15; John Brookes, Denmans, Sussex 94*r*,142; Planting by Bill Frederick, Delaware 53*t*,97,148; Andy and Polly Garnett, Cannwood Farm, Somerset 98; Lynden Miller, Bryant Park, New York 112*l*; John and Caryl Hubbard, Chilcombe, Dorset 112*r*,158; Ian Kirby, The Menagerie, Northamptonshire 113*r*; Arabella Lennox-Boyd, planting at RHS Flower Show, Chelsea 121*l*; Anthony and Lynn Archer-Wills, West Chiltington, Sussex 124; Rupert Golby, Adderbury, Oxfordshire 52*l*,128*r*; Westonbirt Arboretum, Gloucestershire 129*r*; RHS Gardens, Rosemoor, Devon 130*r*; Mr and Mrs Peter Aldington, Turn End, Buckinghamshire 132*r*,136*l*; Waterperry Gardens, Oxfordshire 133*br*; Mrs Gwen Beaumont, Stoke-sub-Hamdon, Somerset 137; Levens Hall, Cumbria 139*b*; Mr and Mrs John Chambers, Kiftsgate Court, Gloucestershire 143*l*; Mrs Gerda Barlow, Stancombe Park, Gloucestershire 143*r*; Carol and Malcolm Skinner, Eastgrove Cottage, Hereford and Worcester 147*r*; Private garden, Chedworth, Gloucestershire 150; Mrs M.J. Coombe, Yew Tree Cottage, Hampshire 152-53; Mrs Margaret Farquar Ogilvie, House of Pitmuies, Tayside 114*b*,154; The National Trust, Ascott, Buckinghamshire 155; Planting by Pam Schwert and Sibylle Kreutzberger, private garden, Gloucestershire 156,157*b*; Ethne and Donald Clarke, Yaxham, Norfolk 157*t*; Nell Maydew, Daglingworth, Gloucestershire 159; Sir Hardy Amies, Langford, Oxfordshire 162; Myles Hildyard, Flintham Hall, Nottinghamshire 163*b*; Mr and Mrs John Sales, Cirencester, Gloucestershire 167; University Botanic Garden, Cambridge 170*t*, 171*tl*; Mr and Mrs J. Wallinger, The Manor House, Upton Grey, Hampshire 170*b*.

My thanks too to gardeners and garden owners whose plantings appear only as details. They include: Putsborough Manor, Devon; Rousham House, Oxfordshire; Thuja Garden, Maine; Charlie and Amanda Hornby, Hodges Barn, Gloucestershire; Caroline Burgess, Stonecrop, Cold Spring, New York; University Botanic Garden, Oxford; Robert Cooper, Ablington, Gloucestershire; Veronica and Giles Cross, Stoke Lacy, Hereford; John and Eve Meares, Norton-sub-Hamdon, Somerset; Gwladys Tonge, Winslow, Buckinghamshire; Annie Huntingdon, Sudborough, Northamptonshire; Lucy Gent, London; Sir Peter and Lady Parker, Manor Farm, Oxfordshire; Peggy Jeffery, Mount Pleasant, Devon; Dan Pearson, London.

AUTHOR'S ACKNOWLEDGMENTS

Frances Lincoln's team has included the most inspiring and thorough of editors who has coached me over the jumps and hurdles with the lightest of touches, and a designer with a very sensitive feel for the material. Judy Dod and Gillian Naish have done an immaculate job of word-processing my scruffy typescript, produced on a broken-down manual typewriter (vintage 1961), crunching it into a miniscule computer disk.

The plant directories are the equivalent of a complete book in themselves and I have had great help with the research from Carolyn McNab, Judy Dod, Jane Douglas, Sue Smith and Hetty Sookias, and I am especially grateful for the expertise of Antonia Johnson. Pennie Cullen came up with some bright ideas over lunch at Claridges. John Elsley and Tony Lord have very kindly checked the nomenclature of plants. Joanna Logan drew the diagrams, and Penny David compiled the index. To them all, my warmest thanks.